FUNDAMENTALS OF UNDERGRADUATE EDUCATION & LEARNING

Second Edition

D1531526

JAMES M. LIPUMA, Ph.D.
New Jersey Institute of Technology

Kendall Hunt
publishing company

Kendall Hunt
publishing company

www.kendallhunt.com
Send all inquiries to:
4050 Westmark Drive
Dubuque, IA 52004-1840

Printed in the United States of America
10 9 8 7 6 5 4 3 2 1

To Sandy, the one who makes all my life possible
and all my work worth doing.

Brief Contents

Contents

Introduction

Chapter 1: Self-Directed Learning

The book begins with a discussion of self-learning, self-awareness, and the need to know some things about one's personal desires, abilities, and capacities before even beginning to try to learn. The ideas of capacity building, self-directed learning, autodidactic attitude, and an understanding of how to balance one's use of time, effort, and resources are presented.

Chapter 2: Basic Tools of Thinking

Chapter 2 discusses the basic techniques necessary to learn the skills and processes presented in the remainder of the text. First is the idea of making valid and good definitions. One of the most important uses of this relates to the identification of categories and examples along with the distinction between these types of delineations.

Chapter 3: Decision Making and Related Skills

Chapter 3 covers decision making and other related skills that underpin it, such as critical thinking and research. The techniques presented serve as a launching point for the reader to identify methods to clarify and improve the decision-making process. The different types of research—literature searches, surveying, and experimentation—are discussed.

Chapter 4: Focus on Questioning

Chapter 4 examines the various types and levels of good questions and relates this to Bloom's Taxonomy. The movement in education towards outcomes based upon clear questions will be discussed with an emphasis on the concept of essential and leading questions. This will be connected to ideas of different forms of literacy and how this is tested with objective and subjective questions in various types of assessment methods.

Chapter 5: Basics of Effective Communication—Reading, Writing, Speaking, Thinking

Chapter 5 covers the processes and concepts related to communication. It opens with a description of different aspects of the process of communication. It then details four areas of concern that each person should be aware of when engaging in any form of communication.

Chapter 6: Written Communication

Chapter 6 covers written communication with a discussion of specific rhetorical styles such as summaries, essays, and research papers. The need for the use of quality sources and the need for citing are presented. Samples are provided to assist the reader to improve written communication.

Chapter 7: Presentations

Chapter 7 covers public speaking and the skills related to professional presentations. Different levels of formality and the roles presenters can assume are identified and explained.

Chapter 8: General Problem-Solving Process

Chapter 8 presents the general problem-solving process. The process presented might be used in any discipline to clearly frame and evaluate problems as well as generate solutions. The process presented asks the problem solver to first research and understand the situation along with past knowledge related to it and then make an argument for a course of action to be taken based on the decisions that are made. The following is a brief overview of the entire process being discussed.

1. 1.Become aware of the context and initial conditions of the problem being examined.

2. Understand the situation by researching and defining its elements.

3. Select a particular aspect of the problem to be addressed.

4. Generate potential solutions.

5. Evaluate valid potential solutions to select the best solution for the specific situation.

6. Develop an action plan to implement that best solution and highlight challenges that may be encountered during the implementation process.

As attention is focused upon a future problem to select a course of action, he or she will work through these steps either deliberately or unconsciously. Often It is necessary to iterate these steps or even return to earlier steps to rework the results with some steps being dealt with more arduously than others.

Chapter 9: Leadership

Chapter 9 presents the topic of leadership and its many subcomponents. The chapter begins with a definition and discussion of the concept of leadership. It moves to the different aspects of leadership along with the skills and abilities that comprise these more general categories. Finally, an explanation of how these areas interact and can be developed by individuals so that each person can improve his or her own leadership ability is covered.

Acknowledgments

I wish to acknowledge the many people I have worked with and learned from over the years as well as all those I have taught. All have helped to shape this text and inform its content.

I wish to give special acknowledgment and thanks to my parents, who gave me an excellent start on the path to this text, and my mother for the years of chit-chat and proofreading.

I would also be remiss if I did not acknowledge Dr. Norbert Elliot of the New Jersey Institute of Technology, who has given me invaluable advice and guidance for all my time there.

Introduction

Introduction

Throughout the years of education that have brought each reader to this text, many topics and areas of study have been examined. Some of these seem simple and elementary now, but at the time might have seemed daunting and even impossible depending on the subject. In the same way, the material presented here may seem difficult to grasp at first. However, by the end of the text, it will be clear why all of this is needed to hone the skills that assist everyone to solve problems and succeed in higher education.

This text presents a wide range of skills that have been identified as fundamental to learning and which are intended to prepare students to succeed in college as well as be prepared for jobs and a career after graduation. Though technical expertise is vital for students to master, many other abilities are necessary to achieve success as well. Studies have shown that problem-solving, decision-making, critical thinking, written and oral communication skills, the ability to work in groups and teams, as well as utilize leadership skills are all as important in today's academic and working environment. Too often in the past, these skills have been taught along with content without specific attention designed to make students aware of how to improve these areas as content knowledge was taught.

In order to teach this diverse set of topics it is necessary to first prepare the intellectual conceptual framework and raise the awareness of the students. Then the more intricate and interdisciplinary areas can be added on top of that fundamental basis. The numerous basic skills deal with enhancing thinking skills and self-awareness. The upper-level, complex skills deal with problem solving, research, and communication. Beyond this is the largest category of overarching skills, which have been specified under the topic of leadership. This text makes the reader aware of each area as well as provides exercises and examples to help the reader hone his or her skills.

The main focus of the work is to prepare the reader to understand himself or herself better and give insight into the rules that underlie the abilities and skills discussed in the text. By reviewing these basics, it is hoped that each student will be able to be a more effective learner and better identify those aspects of his or her personal skill set that need improvement. Having a good understanding of one's own thinking abilities and good communication skills are vital to becoming better at all aspects of education. The text opens with skills necessary to assist in self-improvement and ends with skills that should assist with the interface between each person and the others that become involved in the process of communication and problem solving.

The Two Voices

Wow, that's way too much to absorb all at once. This might be what you're thinking, or at least something along those lines, and we've just gotten started. Throughout the book, there are two distinct ways material is presented. There is a formal, logical, and straightforward presentation of topics and concepts. Ideas are told directly and often are too large to be swallowed in one bite. Each reader will need to go over them more than once. If the entire book were like this it would be dense and dry and difficult to digest. So there is another part. To help lessen the burden of the material, other more conversational sections are included. As you read through the work (and feel confused or that your head is starting to hurt), you will find sections that try to break the text into easier-to-follow language with less abstract or theoretical examples. Hopefully, when you hear yourself asking, "What's that mean?" or "Why do I need to know that?" or saying "I don't understand?" or even, "That makes no sense," these other sections will communicate the abstract ideas in ways that are easier to comprehend. Each section speaks to the reader in a much more informal way and gives examples or an alternate description of the material.

A word of explanation at the outset is necessary to set the stage for the rest of the text. It is my belief that each person must choose to learn and improve him or herself through thoughtful effort. I cannot know what makes sense and what examples will make the concepts put forth in the book easier to understand and use. There are no guarantees that anything I have put into this work will definitely succeed. Also, I am sure that there is much more to be said that has not been given in this book and that what is given could have been presented in hundreds of different ways depending on the background, interests, and motivation of the readers. No one way is best. The two voices used are intended to accommodate those who like more formal academic writing and those who need a less formal, more conversational way of reading material. In either case, the most important thing is that the reader is able to internalize the concepts and see how they fit with his or her own ways of thinking so a change can be made.

The text is written with these two voices in the hopes of both telling things and showing things so that all the concepts can be internalized in the easiest way. The material written in the more formal style tries to be straightforward in the telling of the basic facts and knowledge to be remembered and concepts to be understood and used. The less formal writing seeks to explain things through examples that are more easily related to by the reader and show what is meant by the ideas in a more general fashion. The balance of the two styles is sought so that the reader can be both told things and shown things so that if the ideas are internalized, each will be carried with the reader beyond the course and applied in all settings, academic or not.

I understand that many of the definitions given herein are not the only way the terms can be defined and used. A choice had to be made for the sake of clarity and to allow the topic to be discussed. Many things are set forth, and the reader is asked to agree to these definitions so that the relationship between differing ideas can be shown. Though the words selected are only one way of presenting the material, the relationships identified and the way they are built into a complex web of ideas is what is sought. Taken out of context, any one idea may seem arbitrary, abstract, overly specific, or even absurd. It is when the whole is looked upon and all the ideas viewed together that the whole is intended to make sense.

Chapter Review

The book begins in Chapter 1 with a discussion of self-learning, self-awareness, and the need to know some things about one's personal desires, abilities, and capacities before even beginning to try to learn—ideas of capacity building, self-directed learning, autodidactic attitude, and an understanding of how to balance one's use of time, effort, and resources.

Chapter 2 discusses the basic techniques necessary to learn the skills and processes presented in the remainder of the text. First is the idea of making valid and good definitions. One of the most important uses of this relates to the identification of categories and examples along with the distinction between these types of delineations. After that, exercises are presented to assist the readers in becoming aware of their own thinking and the assumptions that underlie everyday life. To assist with the skills listed, the idea of asking questions and being skeptical of simple answers to complex questions is then discussed to help with individual critical thinking skills. Finally, the distinction between the terms *goals*, *objectives*, *outcomes*, and *purpose* (GOOP) are presented as they relate to the accomplishment of tasks.

Chapter 3 covers decision making and the many other related skills that underpin it, such as critical thinking and research. This topic is particularly difficult to discuss out of context, as decisions are often dependent upon the situation that surrounds them. Nonetheless, the techniques presented serve as a launching point for the reader to identify methods to clarify and improve the decision-making process. The different types of research—literature searches, surveying, and experimentation—are discussed. In particular, the scientific method is detailed along with its applications and modern form. Numerous exercises and examples are used to help the reader better understand and explore these abilities and highlight ways to increase creativity and improve decision making.

Chapter 4 examines the various types and levels of good questions and relates this to Bloom's Taxonomy. In particular, the movement in education towards outcomes based upon clear questions will be discussed with an emphasis on the concept of essential and leading questions. This will be connected to ideas of different forms of literacy and how this is tested with objective and subjective questions in various types of assessment methods.

Chapter 5, 6, and 7 cover the processes and concepts related to communication. It opens with a description of different aspects of the process of communication. It then details four areas of concern that each person should be aware of when engaging in any form of communication. Then, the specifics of writing summaries, essays, and research papers along with the need for citing are presented. Finally, public speaking and the skills related to professional presentations are reviewed.

All of the topics in the first seven chapters can be drawn upon in a variety of situations to aid a student as he or she strives to be successful. Moreover, mastery of these topics prepares the student to become a better, more adaptable learner and so assist in the achievement of goals. Beyond these skills lies a topic that draws on all of the earlier learning to prepare the student to compete in the uncertain future that will be his or her life. Since there is no set answer that can be given for what might happen or what skill must be drawn upon to solve an unforeseen problem, the last chapters of the text are devoted to a discussion of problem solving and leadership both for oneself and of others. This, above all, is essential in the ever-changing environment that current students will face in a time of unprecedented technological development, global social interactions, and fast-paced interconnected world.

Chapter 8 presents the general problem-solving process. First, it is important to expand on the term *problem* before going any further. Throughout the text, this term will serve as a catchall phrase that could refer to an issue, concern, enigma, question, or some other term expressing the idea of a gap in knowledge that needs to be bridged. The process presented is used in any discipline to clearly frame and evaluate problems as well as generate solutions. Although it is used mainly to examine current problems, the process works equally well for problems in the near or distant future. However, because predicting the future situation requires guesses and assumptions, the solutions found are far more speculative. In addition, the process can be used to examine past decisions that have been implemented to better understand how and why a particular solution was selected. What is important to note is that many solutions are found through research based upon trial-and-error methods of refining observations and assumptions. The process presented asks the problem solver to first research and understand the situation along with past knowledge related to it and then make an argument for a course of action to be taken based on the decisions that are made. The following is a brief overview of the entire process being discussed. Later on in the text, a more detailed set of steps for the process for thinking and general problem solving will be given.

1. **Become aware of the context and initial conditions of the problem being examined.**
2. **Understand the situation by researching and defining its elements.**
3. **Select a particular aspect of the problem to be addressed.**
4. **Generate potential solutions.**
5. **Evaluate valid potential solutions to select the best solution for the specific situation.**
6. **Develop an action plan to implement that best solution and highlight challenges that may be encountered during the implementation process.**

As any person focuses attention upon a future problem to select a course of action, he or she will work through these steps either deliberately or unconsciously. Although the steps are presented here in a linear fashion, problems in the real world are not so easily tackled. It is necessary to iterate these steps or even return to earlier steps to rework the results. Often, some steps need to be dealt with more arduously than others. Many times, others have completed some of the steps. In these cases, only the results may have been passed to the current problem solver. In all cases, it is vital that an individual is aware of the various aspects of the problem-solving process as he or she works to solve a problem so that the individual can be informed about exactly what the he or she is attempting to accomplish. Also, as each person moves through the process of solving a problem, the rationale for his or her underlying assumptions as well as the proof supporting the decisions being made must be understood by the problem solver. Last, it is important to discuss the other tools and methods that are used to solve problems. The general problem-solving process presented here does not try to compete with these other processes. Rather, the tools of other disciplines can be easily incorporated throughout the various steps. This process is interdisciplinary and simply clarifies the intellectual steps any person at any time might go through when addressing a problem and coming to a conclusion about the type of action to take. Moreover, the description given here provides clear terminology and a distinction between the ideas that each individual brings to working groups as well as assists individuals to better understand their own thought processes. Each discipline has methods for conducting research and making decisions. Each person utilizes these tools when working through the overall problem-solving process and can integrate the knowledge from each discipline during each step of the process.

Chapter 9 presents the topic of leadership and its many subcomponents. The chapter begins with a definition and discussion of the concept of leadership. It moves to the different aspects of leadership along with the skills and abilities that comprise these more general categories. Finally, an explanation of how these areas interact and can be developed by individuals so that each person can improve his or her own leadership ability is covered. This last section is tied to current technologies that impact leadership in today's world.

Examples, sample papers, exercises, and other materials are given throughout the text to assist the reader. Though throughout the text there are exercises and examples, this set is not nearly complete. Other examples and cases can always be found to aid in the development of better thinking and to provide practice for all the skills and abilities discussed. As can be seen by the progression of topics, the basic skills given in the beginning of the text are revisited throughout as more complex and difficult tasks are introduced and added to the knowledge base of the reader. The text, as it should be with the experience of higher education, is a culmination of the work not just a review of items to be memorized and discarded. Knowledge and understanding is to be provided so that the reader is able to internalize the skills either through acquisition of the new tools presented or personal development of the skills from within through the process of working through examples. These two processes are slow and can only be accomplished over time and with the effort of the reader.

Moving Forward

Before moving forward with the text, it is important to note that the information presented herein is an introduction to many topics. In many cases, there are entire classes taught that explain each of these topics in much greater depth. This work is not intended to be a complete exploration of any of these areas. If the reader is just entering or planning to enter higher education, this work will help identify topics that will be addressed in classes they will take. On the other hand, if the reader is closer to the end of their academic career, this work will provide a review of those areas that should have been covered as well as help with summative courses such as capstones or senior seminars. In either case, many other classes should have presented the topics in greater detail and allowed students to hone their skills through practice. The main intent of this text is to make the reader aware of the many areas that should be mastered in the process of education and give a vocabulary for more clearly understanding what will benefit students in the society after graduation.

To assist the reader, web page URLs have been included throughout as an aid and suggestion of places to look for greater detail or additional examples. These are resources and in no way are they recommended as experts or given as anything more than easily accessible resources. Every attempt has been made to check these pages before listing them, but there is no way to be sure that they will work at the time you read this text. These happen to be the most easily found or most comprehensive pages that the author found during his research. It is important to acknowledge that any other page found using some other search engine might have been as good or better. Certain key words that were used to find these pages are given to allow the reader to choose for him- or herself if desired. The author has no vested interest in any page nor has received any input or compensation from any of these sources.

Additional examples and explanations are provided at *http://njit.mrooms.net/course/view.php?id=14403*

CHAPTER I

Self-Directed Learning

Key Concepts of this Chapter

- What is self-directed learning?
- What are multiple intelligences?
- How can you take control of learning?
- What is capacity building?
- What are the different learning styles?
- What are your resources—Brains, Interest, Time, Effort, and Spendables?
- Why is it necessary to be self-aware of one's own educational situation?

Introduction

As I put forth in the opening, the mindset of the student is a vital part of this text and education in general. One problem with this is that many students may have been trained to listen quietly, obey instructions, follow directions, and not thoughtfully explore for themselves the topics being presented during their educational career. In order to move to a higher level of learning, it is important to encourage individuals to think and reason for themselves about ideas. In addition, each student should consider his or her own desires and goals in the educational process. The sections of this chapter discuss this idea in more detail. By the end, the reader should feel more able to take control of what is happening in the educational setting and work to teach him- or herself more effectively and more completely.

Though not perfect, I want to put forth an analogy about the educational process and the student as product. There are many views of students in the system of education. Some look at students as the client to be served and others as the product being constructed or manufactured, and still others as an organism consciously grown for a particular end. All of these can be valid in proper context. I want to view the student as a complex individual in a complex learning environment called life. Learning can happen everywhere, at all times, from an infinite number of sources. It is organized in the school setting to try and maximize efficiency and allow an expert teacher to assist the learner in mastering ideas and concepts as well as practice their application in a safe and nurturing place where failure can lead to greater and more expert practice and finally mastery of the desired skills. In other words, school is the place to mess up and have someone who knows what is going on help you figure out why things were messed up and how you can fix them.

So what is my analogy then? I want to think of students as infinitely upgradeable computers, but more than just calculating boxes. If you think of the world of computers today, you can see that there are different companies producing similar but distinct models and others creating computers that operate in a similar way but the processing and interfaces are totally unique—such as the distinction between Windows, Mac, and Linux computers. Nonetheless, it is the applications that the computers are used for that matter more than the initial hardware and system configurations. Moreover, the same computers can be loaded with different software, memory, and operating systems for different situations. Each person customizes the computer by storing things, creating new things, and adding components. In the end, the additions are what make the computer useful and unique not the initial conditions. Furthermore, an improved computer is one that has the ability to work faster, do more at the same time, store more in memory, and work more efficiently. When a person finally chooses to invest in one of the newer, better computers, the important pieces of data, software, and tools are brought forward to the new computer along with the knowledge gained about how to use these things. In this way, the student who advances through the educational system is taking the knowledge learned with them as they upgrade themselves. But students are not just computers to be loaded with software, specialized hardware, and data and then assigned a specific task. I wanted to put forth this analogy to highlight that many times a greater emphasis is placed on memory and skills rather than improvement of the learner's ability to think and process things. As learners, humans have the ability to improve thinking and not just increase memory or add programs and tools. This entire text attempts to help students to improve thinking processes. This begins with awareness and so must start by discussing the learner's role in the educational process.

The main reason the computer model of learning does not work well is that there are complex social forces at work, and computers do not have internal motivation. A computer might malfunction, hang, or even crash, but that is not due to personal problems or psychological pressures. The first step to better thinking is the engagement of the student in the learning process. A learner must come to the learning process openly and choose to learn. Forcing learning leads to difficulties when trying to improve the thinking process. The other side of the intellectual choice to learn for oneself is the motivation behind the decision to participate in learning. The intention of this book is not to motivate the reader to read on, force my ideas on others, or convince people to learn. Procrastination, laziness, distraction, and many other terms are given to the obstacles to learning and task completion related to the idea of motivation. The choice to learn and put forth effort is something that must be done by the student. The next sections will help the reader identify more clearly what needs to be done, but it does not make him or her actually want to do it. The decision to learn and what to learn is a personal choice.

So what am I saying? It all comes down to you—the person doing the learning. Good or bad, the teacher or the school can only do so much to help or hinder the learner. Brilliant people have learned from books isolated in the wilderness while others have failed out of school despite the best attempts of people to help. What you want and why you are doing what you are doing matters more than having a great teacher or great book. There are no guarantees, but if you are motivated to succeed and can advocate for yourself, you stand a better chance of succeeding than if you do not care or are actively doing things that thwart the learning process. Of course, overburdened, uninspired, or even incompetent teachers in a bad environment can do much to hinder you. Nonetheless, you are the one thing that you can control and know better than any challenge you might face from outside sources. An old adage in sports says when a loser faces defeat he or she points to everyone else while a winner facing defeat looks to themselves for the reasons for the loss and the ways to improve. That is why this chapter starts with getting to know yourself and how you learn before getting into how to become a better learner and a winner.

Multiple Intelligences and Knowing Yourself

So if each person is an individual and education teaches generally, what is the next thing to be done? Each person must become aware of his or her own strengths and weaknesses, goals and ambitions, as well as desires and resources to determine what will work best for them.

Everyone is not the same and so, even though education can provide something for everyone, the education process must be seen as a resource to provide what each person needs rather than the blanket answer to every question. Many people are thought of as intelligent or "smart" if they can remember a great deal or can access information quickly. Knowing a great deal of things does not make someone intelligent, though it can help. This is only one aspect of intelligence.

Dr. Howard Gardner, professor of education at Harvard University, developed categories of intelligences that went beyond memory and quick logical thinking and that might be considered a grouping of thinking strengths. These are not mutually exclusive or the only way to organize these ideas, but they are a good start for you as you identify personal strengths and weaknesses. To assist with this, the first step is to identify a general type of intelligence that one possesses. Many books, articles, and Web pages present and discuss the topic of multiple intelligences. Part of the material given on the Humanities 2000 Web page is presented in Figure 1.1, to provide a general overview of each type of intelligence listed and elaborated by Gardner.

Other sources have identified additional intelligences to be considered as well. For example, Natural Intelligence is one in which the person understands and can work with the natural world, such as a farmer or zoologist. Others have suggested that some people have Multicultural, Spiritual, or Inter/multidisciplinary Intelligences, among many other types of intelligence. It does not matter what name is used, only that the concept of strength in different, equally valuable areas can be identified. Rarely is one type of intelligence or one skill utilized solely and exclusively when completing a task. Whether simple or complex, most applications of knowledge and skill require a series of interconnected intelligences to be accessed and applied. Having said that, it is now necessary to discuss the role of the student in the process of education. Each person must take control of the process and utilize it to attain his or her own goals.

So now what do you do? Finding yourself in one of these or other groups doesn't do much for you if that's all there is. The key is to recognize that different people start out with different strengths or tendencies. You need to see what you want and work to acquire and refine a set of skills that helps you get there. Don't just take what's given to you or react to the

---

FIGURE 1.1
Multiple Intelligences

Following is a list of some of the multiple intelligences identified by research conducted by Howard Gardner. If you access the URL below, you can read a full description of each.

- Linguistic Intelligence
- Logical-Mathematical Intelligence
- Spatial Intelligence
- Bodily-Kinesthetic Intelligence
- Musical Intelligence
- Interpersonal Intelligence
- Intrapersonal Intelligence

---

http://www.learner.org/courses/learningclassroom/support/04_mult_intel.pdf
http://www.infed.org/thinkers/gardner.htm

world by rolling along with the waves of life. Being proactive and actively working to improve is what education should be about. Later in this text we'll talk about decision making and other skills needed to "get ahead." For now, it is important to recognize that what you are is not always the best for what you want to be. Most things take hard work to achieve. I'm not saying you need to work hard for everything, but don't be surprised when things don't come easy. The first step is honestly seeing where you are, where you want to be, and what lies along the path from here to there. Then you can decide what to do about starting to head in the right direction.

Learning takes many forms and there are many things that a student learns to do as he or she moves through the educational process. Generally, the purpose of education should be to prepare students to know what to expect as well as deal with the unexpected. At first, a child imitates the models that are shown and learns to memorize and repeat things. Directions are given and learning to understand and follow these instructions is an essential part of education. As time passes and experience is gained, learning moves to the knowledge that is internalized and thus known. This body of knowledge is added to as learning progresses so that skills are developed in the learner. Modeling continues as more complex processes are attempted and a depth and breadth of knowledge is attempted. These two types of learning go hand in hand to help the student develop.

Eventually, the student needs to develop the ability to handle problems that have not been experienced. Education prepares students to figure out what to do when facing an unknown situation. Adaptability and the ability to solve problems are key to the future success of any student. This leads to the highest levels of education in which a student seeks his or her own ends. By leading oneself to goals set for one's own desires, learning allows students to seek his or her own path and lead others along the way.

All of this can be summarized by the following four things:

- You are told what to do
- You know what to do
- You can figure out what to do
- You can lead yourself and others to what you want to do

As you work through these steps, one thing to mention is a major problem many students have that comes from earlier years of the educational process and life in general. This is the idea of preconceptions about things and the conflict that exists between common sense and accepted knowledge. Preexisting knowledge can be misunderstood or wrong. If these types of misconceptions are not highlighted and addressed, the student may compound these as new knowledge is associated with these incorrect ideas. Furthermore, some observations and common sense understandings of the world do not agree with what is generally accepted as correct by scholarly experts. As a result, it is necessary to be willing to question what you know and examine new knowledge. Knowing you might not always be correct allows for the potential to change what you know in light of new ideas.

Self-Directed Learning

The first step for all students is to become aware of what is happening when learning is occurring. Once this has happened, the next step is to become better at the process of learning. Finally, the learner can take control and direct the learning process for him or herself. There are many things that must happen to accomplish this, and it continues throughout a person's life. Nonetheless, being aware is the first step, so it is important to define the aspects of self-directed learning (SDL).

FIGURE 1.2
Profile of Self-Directed Learners

The literature on self-direction speaks to the skills that students must have in three phases of the learning process: planning and goal setting, performance, and evaluation and reflection. During these phases, self-directed learners work to teach themselves, take the lead in their own education, and can self-assess so that they are able to make adjustments and accurately measure their own progress so that areas that need work can be identified and addressed. For a more detailed discussion of self-directed learning, please see:

---

http://www.eiconsortium.org/reprints/self-directed_learning.html

---

Self-directed learning is the process of taking control of the learning process—from envisioning what needs to be learned, to motivating oneself to do the work, to assessing the results. The self-directed learners will cultivate the ability to set and work to achieve goals; plan, investigate, and assess achievement of those goals; independently manage time, effort, and resources; as well as accurately and honestly assess the results and products of the learning process and experiences. Figure 1.2 gives a list of the skills that are exhibited by self-directed learners.

All this may seem like too much to do, but much of it is already in place at most universities and in many high schools as well. Students are not always made aware of its aspects and moreover, are not shown how to deliberately foster these skills to improve the learning ability associated with each aspect. Accreditation boards have begun moving toward the measurement and assessment of some of these skills under the heading of information literacy rather than SDL. According to the Middle States Commission on Higher Education:

Information literacy is an intellectual framework for identifying, finding, understanding, evaluating, and using information. It includes determining the nature and extent of needed information; accessing information effectively and efficiently; evaluating critically information and its sources; incorporating selected information in the learner's knowledge base and value system; using information effectively to accomplish a specific purpose. (Middle States Commission on Higher Education, 2002, p. 32)

As you can see, many of the ideas that the board says should be and currently are present in education match up with what is listed as the skills needed for a self-directed learner. There are other skills as well, but students should not feel that they have to start from scratch. Much of what is being discussed here is already in place. What is needed is for it to be identified, brought together, and then honed so that the skills work well and can be used together to greater advantage. In order to do this, the learner must take control and not be a bystander in the educational process. Each person must lead their own learning and, therefore, know where he or she is going in order to direct him or herself effectively. Being in control with a course to steer or the knowledge of how to steer is not helpful. All three must come together to provide the learner the proper cohort of skills needed to know where he or she is going, how to get there, and determine if that is where he or she wants to go.

Do you have to do this? Of course not; it's always up to you. No matter how much people try to force you in a direction, as an adult, you can always choose something else. The point here is that knowing about this and choosing to do all, some, or none of these things is up to you. But, be ready for the consequences when you do not get what you want. These ideas are designed to help you learn but are not prerequisites. The higher one goes in education, the more the burden rests upon you to choose and make your own way. You can always blame someone else, but by the time you are an adult, learning is your own responsibility. That does not mean others don't share that responsibility, but in the end, the consequences for decisions rest with you, and you must be prepared to overcome the obstacles that are confronted. You are in control whether you know it or not.

Memory and Theories of Learning

Though becoming a self-directed learner is a powerful thing, much of learning happens in classrooms led by teachers and surrounded by other learners. Within this context, a self-directed learner can exist but must see the limits on freedom of exploration and understand that the teacher might see the learning process in a different way. Before going further, a brief overview of memory, learning theory, and educational philosophy can help give you a picture of what others may think about what is happening when you are learning. Having a glimpse of this can help you as you seek out your own path to gaining knowledge.

First is memory. Many people rely on memorizing things so that it is known and can be accessed when needed. There are many descriptions of memory identified by research and many theories of how memory works. That is beyond our discussion. Knowing that short-term memory holds information for a few seconds and long-term memory holds it potentially forever is the key. If information does not pass from short- to long-term memory, it is lost. Once in long-term memory, it is remembered. Every person has different memory capacity and speed of recall. You most likely have a good feel for your own memory capacity and ability to recall facts. Through work and exercises, memory can be improved and expanded, but learning is something beyond just remembering.

Learning relates to adding information and making sense of it. Jean Piaget and other psychologists have put forth theories about memory and given terms to the different activities related to learning. Generally, when a new concept is encountered a person tends to do one of three things according to these theories: assimilate, accommodate, or avoid. Assimilation associates new knowledge with what is already known and therefore is added to the existing body of thoughts and ideas held by the learner. Accommodation means that the new idea contests what is already known so it makes a change in the body of knowledge. This new information changes the person's thinking. Lastly is ignoring things, which means that the person disregards or ignores the new information. This can be due to a lack of understanding, as with complex topics or because the person simply refuses to accept things.

These two ideas, memory and learning, are important to how teachers lead the learning process in the classroom. What is being presented is a vast simplification of ideas and is only intended to highlight major differences. Each teacher has a unique style that reflects the complex situation that he or she faces. Nonetheless, the self-directed learner will be able to recognize some traits of his or her teacher from the descriptions that follow. For many years, teachers relied upon students to rehearse and repeat new knowledge until the new skill was drilled into the minds of the pupil. In college, lectures and texts delivered knowledge to the student for reflection and memorization. Over time, however, this model of education was challenged and new theories were introduced about a hundred years ago. Two of the new major theories are Behaviorism and Constructivism. The Behaviorists feel students or any learner can be trained through modeling behaviors and then following this with rewards for desired behaviors and punishments for undesired behaviors. Constructivists feel that knowledge is constructed in the minds of students and not transferred so that the student must be the center of attention in education, allowing each to experience learning in the way that best suits his or her own interests.

Beyond these general distinctions, there are many fine distinctions within these major theories that have been refined and adjusted for the last century. Today, many different names are used to describe the means that teachers use to present material to students and foster learning. Knowing the name of what the teacher does is not as important as seeing the distinctions between those things that are used to force an end goal or behavior versus those that are designed to allow the learner to grow guided by the teacher toward the end. Learning that is problem-based, inquiry-based, active, experiential, holistic, or emergent is more constructivist and student centered. Learning that is goal oriented, standards-based, outcome assessed, or has behavioral objectives is more of a behavioral learning environment. Other environments exist, such as an apprenticing or mentoring system that allows pupils to work with experts or home schooling that delivers knowledge to students from parents through prepared materials and individual desires. The self-directed learner should be aware that there is not one way to learn and not one way that teachers teach. As a result, you as learner must be prepared to recognize what works best for you and adapt the situation to fit your learning better. In some cases this may pose a problem as the student and teacher struggle to negotiate a common ground of style. In the end, no matter how much someone outside you tries to force you to learn, you are in control, and if you decided to avoid or ignore learning, you will not learn.

For more on this, you can view the following site:

http://www.learningandteaching.info/learning/memory.htm

Locus of Control and Capacity Building

It is one thing to say that all these aspects of thinking and self-direction are being taught or exist, and it is another to actually find and highlight them. Two of the most vital parts of this concept for students deal with locus of control and capacity building. Locus of control concerns who is in charge of the learning experience, sets goals, and measures success. Capacity building deals with adding more ability to the learner so that greater things can be achieved. Both work together to allow students to move toward SDL.

First is the cultivation of an awareness of what is happening when learning occurs. Too often, students are passive during classroom learning—waiting for learning to be given to them and happy to accept whatever is given them. Students may strive to keep the learning process and the teacher at a distance without engaging in thoughtful reflection. In this way, little is invested and it is easier to just move along without truly learning things. Each class being completed and eventually the entire degree being conferred lacks value due to this lack of true learning. The student never assumes control of the learning process to achieve a goal other than attendance and eventual completion of requirements. At some point, it is vital that the student sees the value of the process of gaining knowledge and the knowledge itself so that he or she can assume more control for his or her own education. This is difficult because many students do not have the maturity or vision to do this. Many educators do not trust students to direct learning or are not comfortable relinquishing control. As the transition from dutiful follower to self-directed leader of one's own learning occurs, many obstacles, problems, and trials can daunt and derail a student. During this difficult process of maturation and self-discovery, using the classroom as a safe, experimental laboratory of learning is key to allow students to grow through trial-and-error, in which a failure is accompanied with direction and encouragement so that each may try again.

Another part of this discussion is capacity building. A vital part of all education and especially SDL deals with providing a student the knowledge, skills, and abilities to actually take control. If one thinks of capacity as the amount of something that can be held, a limited picture of what is being discussed is created. Capacity should not only be seen as a larger container, but also as more and different containers as well as the tools needed to obtain and use the material that fills them. Returning to the computer analogy from earlier, capacity building is vital because without it, the computer is never equipped with more software or hardware to meet new challenges. Capacity building for self-directed learners allows for students to improve on the current things they can do as well as learn to identify, tackle, and solve new problems. A more complete student learner can be created at the end of a degree program by shifting the locus of control to the student and preparing them through capacity building to recognize and overcome new challenges. If SDL is instilled in a student, he or she will be aware that learning never stops and that the process of education assists him or her to be the one who decides the details of his or her own education. The key is that teachers must help students gain the capacity to accomplish SDL, and learners must work to teach themselves the capacities needed for SDL.

Learning Styles

One important aspect of self-directed learning and knowledge acquisition relates to a person's learning style. Learning styles are descriptions of the tendencies you show with regard to how information is best gathered and remembered by a student and therefore how learning is best accomplished. There are many models and theories of learning styles but most identify three major distinctions—visual, auditory, and kinesthetic/tactile. Though you may not fall into one of these exclusively and each can be broken into subsets, the three major divisions are useful at this point to help you become more aware of how you approach information and approach learning.

Visual learners prefer to have things shown or written out. This type of learner usually prefers pictures, written text, or both. Writing items down and reviewing material visually reinforces learning for these types of learners. The auditory learner prefers to have things presented orally or through discussion. This type of learner often learns better by repeating aloud and discussing concepts or even by using audiotapes and e-books. Finally, the kinesthetic/tactile learner prefers to be involved in the learning process through active learning, demonstrations, and hands-on activity in the class. Many times asking questions and engaging in laboratory or multimedia learning tools assists students to comprehend learning. Often, visits to locations related to the topic being studied, such as parks, historical sites, museums, learning centers, etc., or having actual examples of the subject is useful for this type of learner.

Other researchers discuss other terms related to learning, such as active versus passive or top-down/global versus bottom-up/detail learning, to describe the ways in which people build understanding based upon knowledge. Some people are even multimodal or can change styles depending on subject, environment, age, or many other aspects. It is not important to know the name but rather, it is useful to understand how learning styles affect you and fit better with how people teach. Simply realizing that you may be more comfortable learning in one style rather than another or that one style works better for certain material can assist you in taking more control over your own learning process.

So why is this important? Most teachers do not cater to all learning styles and often teach in one predominant style. Knowing how you learn best and how you are being taught can prepare you to adjust the flow of information to fit your learning style best. Also, if your teacher is

---

FIGURE 1.3
Learning Styles

It is useful to find a learning style survey on the Internet and assess yourself. The pages listed here are links to surveys, tests, and explanations that can assist you in knowing your own learning style.

Discover Your Learning Styles–Graphically! *http://www.learning-styles-online.com/*
This page has a good overview of the learning styles surveys with tests that you can take:
http://www.howtolearn.com/learning-styles-quiz

Figure 1.3 gives links to different tools designed to help determine your learning style.

---

open to it, you can give him or her a set of things that help you learn better that he or she might be able to do in class. In any event, knowing what works for you can make your learning easier and promote success by saving resources and reducing frustration and other obstacles.

Resources—Brains, Interest, Time, Effort, and Spendables (BITES)

It is now time to look at the tasks needed to learn and what has to be invested to accomplish these tasks. The problem, of course, is that this is often dictated by the interactions of the particular situation. A teacher can empower a student or a student can independently become a self-directed learner, but everything has limits. Preparation is only part of it. Every student should realize that all tasks require an investment of his or her resources—**Brains, Interest, Time, Effort,** and something I call **Spendables,** or BITES, for short. Though investing these things ahead of time to make oneself a more efficient learner and more effective at task completion can reduce the cost of investing more resources later, there is always some cost.

Resources can be anything that a person needs to use or rely upon when doing a task. The concept of BITES tries to highlight major categories of resources that are used by most people. Of course, there are many others that might not fall into these areas. Anything that is invested when a project is undertaken is a resource. Resources can be physical abilities one possesses, learned skills, connections with people and organizations, free time, persistent effort, or even just extra cash in your pocket. Whatever the resource, the way it is spent is vital to getting a job done. In education, especially in college, resources are vital to success so it is important to examine them and know the BITES you use as you face challenges.

The first category to discuss is **Brains** or one's mental power and learned abilities. As mentioned earlier, each person possesses some aspects of the multiple intelligences that make him or her better suited to deal with the specifics of a problem. Knowing personal strengths and limitations helps determine the amount of other resources that might be needed to achieve success. If you do not have the skills and abilities to solve a problem, you might need to spend more time, effort, and money to solve the problem.

Along with brains, comes Interest. Interest is connected with brains since many times a person's level of interest is as important to getting something done as whether or not they could actually intellectually face the challenge. One's level of ability and level of interest often determine if a task is even engaged much less completed. Interest can exist without you working at generating it, so it is easy to put forth other resources, such as time and effort, even if you do not have the brains when the task is started. Conversely, even if you know you could accomplish the task because you are smart enough to figure it out, without the interest to engage, you may not even bother. The interface between brains and interest is an important one in education because not all lessons are immediately interesting and do not always present a clear pay-off in the short term. Learning is difficult so knowing how to generate interest as well as recognize the mental power needed for a task is useful.

Next we need to discuss Time since it is something that is often seen as beyond your control. Time marches on with or without you and when it runs out, you cannot go back and get more. In an educational setting especially, time is often used as a way to measure student ability. Timed tests, hours of studying, time-management skills, and other such time-limited measures are looked at in order to judge good students. As a result, being aware of how you invest and use your time is a valuable resource management tool. Too often there is insufficient time to do everything, but if you can plan ahead and invest time when there is not a "time crunch" you can become more efficient at completing necessary tasks in the process and have more time to work on more difficult and time-consuming tasks when they arise.

Along with time spent on a task, Effort is used to judge how hard you are working as a student. Working hard to complete a task successfully is one measure that some people use to judge your work. Completing things successfully or getting the right answer in a given time is important, however; even if you fail, how hard you worked is seen as important to whether or not you are a good student and are trying to learn the material. Effort, like time, is a difficult resource to judge since it is different for each person in each situation. Moreover, one's effort is dependent on many different factors you might face at the specific moment related to your physical, mental, social, or emotional state. Many of us have been prepared for a test or task only to fail due to illness or having missed a meal. No matter how hard you tried, things can happen to interfere. Nonetheless, knowing that putting in effort ahead of time to prepare so that when the time comes to act you are ready is important. Effort is too often viewed as the work done at the specific time of the task or test. What is needed is a more global view in which all of the effort put in during preparation is seen as part of the entire picture. A team needs to practice and prepare for the game in order to do well. Even so, effort is rarely seen as enough when winning the game is the goal. As a result, effort is rarely looked at separately from the other things mentioned previously.

Time and effort are often considered together because they are usually linked and often are seen as the most commonly accessed resources for most people who do things themselves. Both are limited but are often viewed as without cost or free. How long you spend on a task and how hard you work will often equate to how successful you are. However, this is not always true. Many people have "banged their heads against the wall" for hours or days and still not found a solution while other just lucked into an answer on the first try. I am not suggesting you always know how much to invest, but being aware of your personal limits and desires is important. Many people do not like to work at problems for a long period of time, while others will spend hours as long as there is no physical exertion required. Knowing what you tend to do is important to being more efficient and more successful when using resources. Others often judge use of time and expended effort when you are being assessed. If you have been labeled as a procrastinator, lazy, good time manager, or a hard worker, you have had aspects of your use of resources judged. Ironically, none of these labels reflect your ability to get the job done, but rather just reflect how or when you spend the resources. Being aware of this is important, as others often look at this as a means of classifying and separating people in teams, jobs, and in school.

Lastly is the idea of **S**pendables. Very simply, this is all those things that are used up or spent during a task. Once you pay someone for a job, that money is gone. Imagine using a match to start a fire. After you have lit the match, it is spent, and it is gone whether or not you have been successful. Though time is fleeting, it is not as permanently spendable as many other things. Effort can be spent but it is replenished with time and rest. All of these resources work together as you learn. Rarely is it a clear-cut decision that trades one thing for another; you cannot say "If I spend ten hours sitting in a room, I will be sure to solve the problem or if I pay someone to do the job it is guaranteed to be done right."

Much of the remainder of this text attempts to improve your efficient use of time by improving your ability to recognize and use your brain, which will help you to expend less effort and other resources to accomplish your task. Each person, in each situation, has limits that affect the ability to know and accomplish the goals set forth for that task. Therefore, everyone must decide how to allocate his or her resources at different times in differing amounts. The BITES used and expended on any task to reach the goals vary. It is important to be aware of this because even the most well-prepared learner can fail if he or she refuses to invest the necessary resources, especially those listed in the BITES. On the other hand, sometimes goal attainment is stressed so much that far too much is invested in order to accomplish a relatively unimportant goal. Part of being expert at SDL is knowing what level is to be invested to gain a desired return.

This, however, leads to a word of caution. Today many times a conscious or unconscious cost-benefit analysis is done to see the amount to invest. A self-directed learner has a good grasp of what is or is not valuable to their overall interests and has sufficient vision and ability to decide for themselves. Some people feel that there is a constant struggle between the amount of work assigned and the need to finish the course. As was mentioned earlier, if a student is not engaged in the learning process as more than attendance and completion, the idea of investment in education does not ever mean more than the lowest amount of BITES for the highest return—do as little as possible for the best grade. It is important at times like this that a teacher and learner understand one another. If the goals of the two are not in agreement, problems can arise and the entire education process can devolve into little more than an agreement to coexist quietly and meet external requirements rather than work together to reach commonly agreed upon and mutually beneficial goals.

The remainder of the text discusses the aspects necessary to assist learners to become more accomplished in learning as well as move toward SDL. It begins with awareness and provides examples and skill-building exercises in order to help students become better masters of the basics as well as more able to honestly and accurately assess things so that better decisions can be made. In the end, each student will be assisted to become a better leader for themselves and so a better follower and leader of others.

So now what should you do? That's up to you as the reader. All of this may seem obvious or just not important, but I hope it sounds interesting and makes you ask yourself questions. Hopefully, you are open to the idea that this is the beginning of making you more aware of what you need to be successful as a learner. The next step is to learn some basic skills used to become better at doing the things needed to learn more effectively. The next chapter starts getting into greater detail on the fundamental skills needed in college. If you work on the questions that follow and try your best to read and understand the ideas in the rest of the book, you are well on your way to being a better learner and more successful in whatever you choose to do.

SUMMARY

This chapter discussed self-directed learning, personal learning styles, as well as the goals and motivations of the learner. The types of multiple intelligences—Linguistic, Logical-Mathematical, Spatial, Bodily-Kinesthetic, Musical, Interpersonal, and Intrapersonal—were described and explained. Next, the characteristics of a good self-directed learner were presented. This was followed by a description of three major theories of learning styles—visual, auditory, and kinesthetic/tactile. The remainder of the chapter was devoted to a discussion of resources and how each person uses them to accomplish things; in particular, Brains, Interest, Time, Effort, and Spendables.

Questions and Exercises

1. What type of multiple intelligences do you possess and why do you think this?
2. Make a list of your own self-directed learning skills. How can you improve them? What skills do you want to cultivate and why?
3. How can you take control of your own learning? What can your teacher do to help this?
4. Make a list of your resources. What are your greatest strengths and limitations? How can you overcome these?

References and Other Readings

Additional examples and explanations are provided on Dr. Lipuma's Web page at
http://njit.mrooms.net/course/view.php?id=14403

Advanogy.com. (2007). Learning-styles-online.com. Retrieved on December 25, 2008, from: http://www.learning-styles-online.com/

Atherton, J. (2005). Memory. Retrieved on January 5, 2009, from: http://www.learningandteaching.info/learning/memory.htm

Donovan, S., & Bransford, J. (2004). How Students Learn: Science In The Classroom. Washington, DC: National Academies Press.

Humanities. (2000). Teaching to Multiple Intelligences (MI) in the Classroom. Retrieved on December 25, 2008, from: http://www.learner.org/courses/learningclassroom/support/04_mult_intel.pdf

McNamara, C. (1999). Strong Value of Self-Directed Learning in the Workplace: How Supervisors and Learners Gain Leaps in Learning. Retrieved on December 25, 2008, from: http://www.managementhelp.org/trng_dev/methods/slf_drct.htm

Miller, S. (2000). Learning Styles Survey. Retrieved on January 5, 2009, from: http://www.metamath.com/lsweb/fourls.htm#vv

Smith, M. (2008). Howard Gardner—Multiple Intelligences and Education. Retrieved on January 5, 2009, from: http://www.infed.org/thinkers/gardner.htm

The Middle States Commission on Higher Education. (2002). Characteristics of Excellence in Higher Education: Eligibility Requirements and Standards for Accreditation. Retrieved on December 25, 2008, from: http://www.msache.org/publications.asp

Tomei, L. (2004). Learning Theories-A Primer Exercise. Retrieved on January 5, 2009, from: http://academics.rmu.edu/~tomei/ed711psy/cognitive.htm

EXERCISE 1.1

Managing Time

A Personal Time Survey

To begin managing your resources, such as time, it is necessary to observe or survey your use of that resource. To get a more accurate estimate, you might keep track of how you spend your time for a week. This will help you get a better idea of how much time you need to do things and how you spend time. It will also help you identify your time wasters. The following survey shows the amount of time you spend on various activities each week. When taking the survey, estimate the amount of time spent on each item per day and multiply by seven or give a general number for a week. Add these numbers together for your total time each week. You can then subtract this from 168, the total possible hours per week, to find your free time.

TASK	Time/Week
Sleeping	
Grooming	
Meals/snacks	
Jobs/ Volunteer work	
Preparation time	
Travel/commuting	
Regularly scheduled functions (clubs, church)	
Class	
Socializing/Dates/Parties	
Other demands on Time	
Total	

168 minus the total is the remaining hours you have allowed yourself to study or relax.

Now Let's Look at Effort Per Class:

To determine how many hours you need to study each week to get A's, use the following rule of thumb. Study 2 hours per hour in class for an easy class, 3 hours per hour in class for an average class, and 4 hours per hour in class for a difficult class. For example, weaving 101 is a relatively easy 3-hour course. Usually, a person would not do more than 6 hours of work outside of class per week. Advanced calculus is usually considered a difficult course, so it might be best to study the proposed 12 hours a week. If more hours are needed, take away some hours from easier courses. Figure out the time that you need to study by using the given formula for each of your classes.

Easy class credit hours   _____ × 2 = _____
Average class credit hours   _____ × 3 = _____
Difficult class credit hours   _____ × 4 = _____
Total   _____

Compare this number to your time left from the survey. Now is the time when many students might find themselves a bit stressed. Just a note to ease your anxieties—it is not only the quantity of study time but also the quality. This formula is a general guideline.

Daily Schedules

There are a variety of time schedules that can fit your personality. These include engagement books, a piece of poster board tacked to a wall, or 3 × 5 cards. Once you decide upon the style, the next step is construction. It is best to allow spaces for each hour, or half-hours for a busy schedule. First, put down all of the necessities—classes, work, meals, etc. Now block in your study time. Schedule it for a time when you are energized.

Also, it's best to review class notes soon after class. Make sure to schedule in study breaks, about 10 minutes each hour. Be realistic on how many courses to take. To succeed in your courses you need to have the time to study. If you find you don't have time to study and you're not socializing to an extreme, you might want to consider lightening your load.

Tips for Saving Time

Don't be a perfectionist: Nobody can be perfect. Difficult tasks usually result in avoidance and procrastination. You need to set achievable goals, but they should also be challenging. There will always be people both weaker and stronger than you.

Learn to say no: Politely saying no should become a habit. Saying no frees up time for the things that are most important.

Learn to prioritize: A "to do" list places items in order of importance. One method is the ABC list. This list is divided into three sections; A, B, or C. The items placed in the A section are those needed to be done that day. The items placed in the B section need completion within the week. The C-section items are those things that need to be done within the month. As the B and C items become more pertinent they are bumped up to the A or B list.

Combine several activities: Combine several activities into one time spot, such as listening to taped notes while commuting to school.

CHAPTER 2

Basic Tools of Thinking

Key Ideas of This Chapter

- How can ambiguity be avoided?
- What are the rules for making clearer definitions?
- Why are context and situation important to making good definitions?
- What are jargon, slang, and private language?
- How do you create categories, groups, and lists of examples?
- What is critical thinking?
- Why is critical thinking important?
- How can you improve critical thinking?
- What are goals, objectives, outcomes, purpose, and success (GOOPS)?

Beginning at the Beginning—Definitions

Before delving into the topic, it is necessary to say something generally about what it means to define something. For our discussion, the idea of creating a definition deals with giving characteristics of and setting boundaries for the ideas that one person has. Definitions are so important because it is a fundamental part of all the areas discussed in this text. This is why this vital process is presented first, as it will be used throughout the text and throughout one's life. Many times a person will just accept a word as something they know, or use a word expecting that everyone knows what it means. This is not necessarily true and can lead to problems when problem solving and communicating. As a result, the first thing that needs to be presented is a way to make and test definitions.

The most fundamental idea to any process that involves more than one person is the need for clearly communicating ideas and understanding. Too often, one person cannot put into words what they know. This leads to the statement "You know what I mean" (YKWIM). The YKWIM concept is difficult to overcome and leads to ambiguity and difficulties. Each individual may have terms they use, but as the terms are used to convey ideas, each person must be sure that others agree with their conception of these terms. Before anything else can be accomplished, ambiguity should be eliminated by clearly defining terms and establishing a common set of rules or language that everyone can use to function. In this way, a strong, common foundation is established and future problems and backtracking can be eliminated.

This is one of the most difficult things for a beginning student to become aware of and deal with. Too often, each person feels what they are saying is completely clear. Definitions will be extremely important when discussing the problem-solving process and communication. If you are aware of the problems others might have understanding your meaning when you choose a particular word, you can plan ahead and be prepared to more clearly explain yourself to them and thus facilitate processes.

To help eliminate YKWIM, let us review some rules to follow when creating a valid definition. Valid definitions are ones that follow these rules generally. However, this does not mean that the definition is a good one, as it may be too broad or too narrow for the purpose of being functional. These rules are just a starting point and a way to test to see if the definition created has met the first test as well as show where improvements can be made.

1. **Do not use the word you are defining in the definition or use a synonym to replace the word.**
2. **Do not give a list of examples instead of defining the word.**
3. **Do not include value judgments in the definitions.**
4. **Do not have cyclical or recursive definitions such that the words used in subsequent definitions are themselves defined by using the word initially being defined.**

The first rule is straightforward; do not include any form of the word being defined in the definition. Also, do not simply try to avoid defining things by substituting words that will then need to be defined. For example, do not say that problem solving is solving problems, finding solutions to dilemmas, or creating a remedy to a situation. This seems easy but as one works on definitions, it is often difficult to find the basic concepts that can be used to clarify what is being expressed. At some point, a decision about the vocabulary and knowledge of others must be made. Usually, some fundamental terms are chosen to be the base of the system of definitions, and all other terms are defined by building upon this basic set. Later in this chapter, more will be said about how to choose basic words and build valid and good definitions. For now, this rule is a way to highlight areas that will need to be addressed.

The second rule is somewhat more problematic because examples are very useful in helping others grasp what you mean. Often, it is difficult to find words to use and so the definition defaults to a list of things that fit the idea of the definition being sought. Though this is a good start, the process of defining words should not stop there. Often, the list that is created is incomplete or contains examples that others do not know or that can mislead. For example, if you try to define technology do not say it is cars, computers, and cellular phones. Much is left out of this definition and for some it includes things that are unfamiliar or confusing. Once a basic definition is set, however, examples can be given to help illustrate and clarify the meaning. When first trying to define something, creating a list of items that are and are not examples can be very helpful. Although this is not a definition in and of itself, this list of examples can be used once unambiguous, basic terms have been used to define the word. A list of examples added to a definition helps to clarify and assists others in grasping the concept.

The third rule warns against using words that are judged differently by different people due to assigned values. "Large" to one person is not the same to everyone else. Avoiding value judgments means avoiding words that can be misinterpreted by those who are trying to understand and use your definitions. Since each person has their own set of experiences and perspective on these experiences, avoiding value judgments is a necessary part of reducing ambiguity. At times, especially when defining words that are value judgments, it is almost unavoidable to use some type of measure in the definition. In these cases, the measure needs to be clearly stated or the fact that measuring is intrinsic to the term being defined needs to be explained as part of the process. Using some agreed upon external standard or actually including the process for determining the measure is a good way to avoid problems with value judgments and terms that contain a measure or degree.

Finally, the last rule deals with terms that are defined in relation to one another. Be sure to eliminate contingent definitions. If a definition has a word in it that is itself defined with the original word, a problem exists because neither word is clearly specified. When defining a series of related terms, it is important to choose a basic definition for one word. Then all other words can be defined in relation to that base without causing confusion or ambiguity.

In any case, by using the rules given, a rough definition of a term or list of terms can be made clearer. This, however, does not guarantee that the definition is a good one. For that, other steps must be taken so that the initial attempt at a clear understanding can be refined. With the rules in mind, the next thing to do is identify some distinctions among terms related to defining something. The three levels are naming, describing, and explaining.

To name something is to give it a label. To describe something means to give a list of characteristics that can include physical aspects, emotional content, or other such materials. Finally, to explain something means to give the connections surrounding the item and the processes related to it. These can include the processes that it is part of as well as those that lead to it. These three terms work together to describe different types and levels of definitions. YKWIM often results when one person feels that just naming a term is sufficient for everyone to understand the definition. Describing and explaining come into play when more information is needed so that a more specific view of the exact concept can be reached. This is very important when working with others that may not share common backgrounds or when ambiguity exists.

As one tries to describe and explain words, it is important to consider the difference between two other aspects of defining things: denotation and connotation. Often, the definition of the word is intended to exactly show what the thing is or how it is used. This would be denotation—the most basic, specific, or literal meaning of a word. Many times, however, the way the word is being used and explained changes the way it is interpreted by others and therefore gives it a different meaning. This would be the connotation of the word or an additional implied or perceived meaning that the word has beyond its denotation. This may relate to the situation in which the word is applied, the culture and background of the person defining the word or hearing it, as well as many other factors. When formulating a definition, it is important to be aware of the connotation that terms have so that the YKWIM problem can be avoided and everyone participating in the process can have the same interpretation of the terms being discussed and used.

The last consideration that will be addressed in this preliminary section relates to language and more specifically parts of speech. Knowing the distinctions between how parts of speech are used can assist greatly with the creation of good definitions. Though the same word can have many meanings, whether the word is a noun, verb, or adjective can change the way it is defined. When defining a noun, it is often easier to use words that describe it and provide characteristics that set the limits of the thing being defined. On the other hand, verbs might be more easily explained using a process description. As with generating a list of examples, identifying the part of speech is another way to begin the analysis of a word to arrive at a good definition. This is an iterative process, not just a linear action to be taken. As with many of the skills presented in the text, defining terms requires the act of creation followed by testing, refinement, and repeated decision making about the steps and level of accomplishment that has been achieved.

EXAMPLE 2.1

One of the first and most common resources for definitions is the dictionary. However, if one looks for the definition of words there and compares them to the rules, many times the definitions do not measure up. Does this mean that dictionaries are not useful? Not at all. A dictionary relies upon the YKWIM concept. There is not enough space nor do the editors of the dictionary intend the words defined therein to be exhaustive, unambiguously defined terms. Instead, the dictionary tries to allow the reader to know what is meant by a word.

If you actually look up the word *define*, you might find something as simple as

1. To create a definition.
2. Give the exact or specific meaning of a word to explain it precisely

As can be seen from the definitions listed here, a dictionary may not always be able to follow the rules. You may know what the writer meant, but is it clear to everyone at all times what the word *define* means? What rules are violated in these definitions?

The first definition is the easiest to identify because it actually uses the word *definition*. The second, however, at first may seem clear and valid. The question here is how strictly are the rules applied? Words such as *precisely* can be value judgments. The word *explain* can be a synonym. If each word is questioned at too great a level of detail, no word can be defined. For our needs, most of these definitions work because they are able to convey the idea that to define something is to specify a meaning and set boundaries upon a topic. More importantly, if you were the one defining this word, you would know to be prepared to further explain the terms used in the definition such as *precise, meaning*, or *basic qualities*. Absolute clarity is not what is being sought. Rather, this discussion hopes to raise awareness of problematic situations and areas of ambiguity.

So what is really being discussed here? That is what this whole section is about. When you communicate with someone, whether in writing or speaking, you have to be clear. The clearer you are, the less chance there will be confusion and mistakes. What each person should be seeking is common ground. Eventually, YKWIM can become normal among friends or work associates, but at the beginning, until a connection or common ground is established, avoid ambiguity.

So how far does this go and when do you stop? If you want, you can question everything and never get anywhere. That's not what we want. The point here is to realize that not everyone sees things the way you might and when you are speaking others might not be hearing the words in the same way you are meaning to convey them. Everyone has his or her own set of knowledge, and the intention is to forge connections between two or more people so there is common ground. The rules and the ideas here are meant to help highlight where problems might occur. If you or the people you are speaking to are not aware of these types of problems, confusion or misunderstandings can result and hinder your progress. This is especially true when first joining a group of people who have been together for a long time or share common experiences. Every group tends to create norms and specialized knowledge and language. It is important to look at this more closely.

Context and Situation

The concept of context deals with understanding the larger world in which the definition will be used and if the appropriate definition is being selected for that context. Words can have many meanings with a range of connotations and denotations. The creator needs to have some understanding of the way the definition will be applied in order to better understand if what is being presented is good, clear, and useful. Issues of context often relate to the social and cultural ties of the target or the surroundings that the target is in when attempting to interpret and use the definition. The context in which the definition will be used may dictate what terms are already understood or how the target perceives words and ideas. Knowing more about context makes the process of creating definitions much easier.

An example of this can be seen when trying to define the idea of perspective. In an art class, perspective may just be defined as point of view or as a technique used to depict three-dimensional objects on a two-dimensional surface. In a philosophy course, the idea of perspective might be a set of ideas on an issue open for debate. The context changes the definition to be used and the targets' understanding of what is meant and what is correct in that context. Another example would be something as simple as the word *charge*. As contexts shift, the understood meaning shifts. *Charge* when paying for something may mean using a credit card. In basketball, *charge* means illegally running over a defender. In physics, it can mean having an unbalanced number of particles carrying positive or negative attraction. This can continue as different contexts are thought of in which *charge* has different meanings and so needs to be defined differently for the target.

Another important consideration for making definitions deals with gaining an understanding of the situation that the target will be in when attempting to use the definition. Different situations call for differing levels of specificity or detail in what is being defined and how it is expressed. If too much detail or expert language (i.e., jargon) is used with a novice target, the meaning may be lost or misunderstood. If not enough detail is used, the definition may be too vague or lack usefulness for the target in making a distinction in meaning.

By understanding the level of detail needed by the target, you can create better definitions. Also, by understanding the target and the situation, it is possible to include examples that elucidate the term without confusing the target. Though a list of examples should not be used instead of a definition, using a list to clarify what was put forth in a definition is an excellent tool if it is tied to the existing understanding of the target.

An example of this can be seen when defining the Internet and how it works. For a low-level definition that would be appropriate for a situation involving young children, simply saying it is a set of computers connected by wires all around the world allowing people to pass around information electronically and that might look like a spider's web or big fishing net may be appropriate to accomplish the desired transfer of meaning. For college-level computer students learning about networks, this would not suffice because of the need for greater detail and the fact that future definitions may be built on this initial term being defined.

Jargon, Slang, and Stuff

When thinking of something in your own mind, you might have trouble remembering things, but you know what you know. When you speak to friends, you may use words that they know even if anyone else who is not part of your circle of friends would have no idea what you were talking about. Often this specialized language is exactly what you want. It builds a connection between those "in the know" and leaves the others outside the loop. Secrets are kept and bonds built. Often within the group you might just say "pass the stuff for the thing" and everyone knows exactly what you mean.

After time, private terms can become used by more and more people and then become slang. Any word can become part of the language and used to mean anything. The only thing that matters is that when one person uses the word others know what they mean. If not, communication cannot happen.

In academics, the idea is to remove ambiguity, include everyone, and eliminate the secrets. This does not mean that specialized language does not exist. It is that this specialized language, known as jargon, is something that needs to be learned so that students can be accepted into the groups that have specialized knowledge and skills and have developed jargon to communicate more easily with those in the know. Ironically, once you have mastered the technical terms and processes of specialized language, the interchange among the experts can become just like that amongst a group of friends. "Pass the stuff for the thing" can be as valid with the experts as it was with the group of friends because they all have the same knowledge. There is no need to explain what you mean because everyone knows.

All of this jargon and slang leads to a problem when the incorrect assumption of knowledge about what something means is made by one person about another person in the group. The entire discussion of clear definitions is intended to help each person identify his or her assumptions about what others know as well as help reduce the problems associated with YKWIM. Thus far, the rules given help avoid ambiguity. In addition, if ambiguity still exists, the rules can be used to highlight areas for improvement. In either case, nothing has yet been said about creating a good definition. A good definition is one that includes all the cases that the individual deems part of the term while excluding all those that are to be left out. Being aware of how words come to be defined and how one person's definition can vary greatly from another's definition of the same word is the first step to clear understanding. For now, this discussion will be left alone until later when categories and examples are examined.

EXAMPLE 2.2

The previous sections all spoke about how the same words can be interpreted differently by different people depending upon the context of the conversation and the background of the participants. Take a moment to think about the sentence, "He's getting stoned." What do you think of when you read this? What images are conjured in your mind?

There are many ways this can be thought of depending on your age, cultural background, and who is speaking or writing the sentence. The most literal meaning of the sentence is difficult to determine because there are many interpretations. If you are reading the Bible this phrase most likely refers to someone being hit by rocks as a punishment for some act. Children playing a fantasy adventure game such as *Dungeons and Dragons* may imagine a character being turned to stone. Both of these are valid but probably not what you thought of when you first read the sentence. A common usage for this term relates to the idea of getting high by smoking marijuana. People from my parents' generation might use the term in a similar fashion but would not think of it related to drug use. To them, "getting stoned" is a way of saying getting drunk. Either of these is very different from the Bible or the D&D connotation. Even with all of these ways of interpreting the phrase, many people may have no idea what this means. The idea of "getting stoned" may have no connection to that person's upbringing or cultural background. This simple statement has many connotations and all can be equally accurate. Realizing this is an important first step to creating and using good definitions and reducing ambiguity in communication.

With these ideas in mind, the process of defining things can now be undertaken in a more systematic way. Whenever a word is used, thought can be given to its definition. When the definition is given, the rules can be consulted to determine if it is a valid definition. Now an application of definitions can be considered.

Process Description

As you think about defining things and parts of speech, an issue may arise as you attempt to form definitions for complex ideas and concepts. Some of the more difficult terms to define are actions or processes. In science and engineering there are definitions that are classified as technical definitions, mechanical descriptions, and process descriptions or procedures. All of these are more advanced sets of definition, sets of steps, and instructions that come together to give someone else a clear understanding of something that person wants to do or use. Many of these terms seem to be similar and are often used interchangeably. To say something is a set of steps may not seem to be different than directions or instructions. However, as you become more familiar with these concepts you will see that they are distinct. Directions are usually associated with telling someone how to get somewhere, steps are incremental movements toward a goal, and instruction illustrates how to do something. What is important to see is that the goal of any of these is to allow someone else to gain a picture of what you are describing so that they can do what it is you are asking them to see or accomplish.

The key differences are that definitions are meant to give a specific set of characteristics that describe something while a process or procedure attempts to describe and explain how something is done. In either case, and especially with process descriptions, it is vital to narrow down what is being described and clearly define the terms involved. In addition, processes will contain steps that must be taken, so you need to tell the reader what is to be done and, when possible, show them how to accomplish this. These ideas will be discussed in more detail in chapters 5 and 6 as methods of describing and explaining are dealt with. For now, realizing that reducing ambiguity by clearly stating goals, defining terms, describing characteristics, and explaining connection will help to clarify whatever you are communicating about.

Categories, Groups, and Examples

One of the most important applications of making definitions, as well as fundamental to more advanced skills such as critical thinking, decision making, problem solving, and researching, is being able to find common traits of items, while at the same time distinguishing similar items from one another. Clear definitions of things are necessary to clearly identify examples, gather them together into groups, and bring groups together to make categories (groups of groups) all of which are based upon similarities of characteristics. Often, smaller groups can be summed together to form even larger categories that can lead to a new connection that was not seen before. The idea of an example is a single instance of something. By defining what you are talking about, you can begin to classify that example and to what larger sets of things it is related.

It is necessary to identify the characteristics of the group or example being examined. Each item has more characteristics than those that qualify it as part of a category and therefore can belong to many categories at once. The key for clear communication is that each person will define the groups according to the examples contained within it. In turn, each example in a category can actually specify a category itself. Also, several categories can be grouped together to form larger categories.

What is this all trying to say? Essentially, anything that is defined belongs to a large number of lists. These lists are nothing more than a collection of terms that are more or less related to what you are talking about. Either something has that characteristic or it does not. The broader the definition of the group is, the more things that will appear on the list. The more narrow the definition is, the shorter the list will usually be. An example will help demonstrate this idea. Start with any item and identify some of its characteristics and labels. Each term that is used to describe the item is itself a category to which the item belongs.

EXAMPLE 2.3

Start with an item such as a hammer. There are various types of hammers, such as carpenter hammers, war hammers, rock hammers, or jackhammers. At the same time, hammers can be put into many categories, such as tools, weapons, household items, or things found at a hardware store. Looking at broader categories, tools could be an example of something found at hardware stores. Looking at the problem a different way, the category might have been tools used by homebuilders. Since each item exists in numerous categories at once and can have more specific examples under it, being able to define things clearly and being aware of the complexity of the situation is useful. During the problem-solving process, the ability to recognize this complexity and then define situations clearly so that the complexity is understood and minimized will be invaluable.

This example brings to light the complex nature of the process of categorization. One important part of this process is making lists and identifying characteristics. Generally, people tend to have two different types of abilities when it comes to creating lists. Some see a wide variety of categories but have trouble generating a long list of examples for each. Others can create a long list of examples given the characteristics of a category but have trouble finding different general categories.

In either case, having the ability to define the characteristics of what is and is not part of the category is very useful. The combination of thinking and defining things can lead to the ability to generate more and better-delineated categories with a large number of distinct examples.

This raises the idea of parameters and assumptions. Ironically, the first thing that needs to be done is to define these two words. In simple terms, parameters are the facts that limit or bound a situation. Assumptions, on the other hand, are restrictions set down by the person engaged in the process that are not necessarily true but which are accepted as a fact to simplify the situation. Both parameters and assumptions are important because they can help simplify a process enough that a solution can be found. For the discussion of categories, it is necessary to clearly set the parameters of each category so items can be seen as within the bounds set or outside these bounds. Clear definitions set as parameters for discussion allow this to happen.

On the other hand, often things are assumed about categories without ever being stated. As one person works to place things within categories and distinguish between them, these assumptions can cause breakdowns. In order to avoid this, awareness of what is a fixed parameter, as defined by the decision maker, and what is an assumption is essential for clear thought and accurate thinking.

Thinking about Thinking

As stated, the first step in the process is becoming aware. However, before any process can be addressed, it is necessary to first discuss the thought processes and other aspects of the individuals themselves. At its heart, any endeavor rests upon the abilities of the individual. These abilities start with thinking. Moreover, to change and improve one's thinking, it is necessary to start by increasing self-awareness—to think about thinking. This can be known as metacognitive analysis. Whatever it is called, the idea is that one must examine how one processes information, understands things, and comes to find solutions.

Before going any further it is important to have each person think about the words *knowledge* and *understanding*. The denotation of "to know" could be to have information accessible in one's mind. The connotation of the word might be to have information easily accessible so it can be retrieved quickly. Perhaps even to have learned something in the past. This connotation may be correct, but it creates trouble as value judgments are introduced into the definition. It is helpful to show the relation between this word and another—understanding.

The denotation of understanding is the ability to grasp a meaning or to utilize a process. Ironically, some people feel that understanding is the same as knowledge or that one leads to the other. These feelings about the words are tied to the connotation rather than the basic definitions or denotations of each.

It takes time and effort to learn a new process so that it can be internalized and thus considered as having entered into the realms of knowledge and understanding. It is these two things that learning attempts to accomplish. It is vital to begin by thinking about how each individual learns and creates this knowledge and understanding. The first thing is to have an accurate assessment of your own abilities, habits, and preferences. There are many areas of thinking that can be discussed, but without self-awareness and accurate self-assessment, any critique by outsiders is not useful. The individual must make any changes to himself or herself in a way that can assist one's own personal development. However, this does not mean that others cannot help make this change.

Though knowledge and the accompanying understanding are often what students feel they are receiving from the educational process, there is more than just that being gained. Knowledge contains both the ideas of factual knowledge and process knowledge (understanding) working together as the body of learning that a person has acquired. Factual knowledge can be defined generally as the list of facts a person has gathered and can access through thoughtful reflection. Process knowledge or understanding refers to the set of processes related to gathering and use of facts. With the learned knowledge and understanding comes the idea of experience. Each time something new is lived through it is added to the list of experiences that a student has at their disposal. When a new situation is encountered, past exposure to that type of information or situation allows better judgments to be made and a clearer course of action to be taken. This leads to development of expertise. With knowing and experience to draw upon, a person can have a feel for the outcome of an undertaking or effect of a decision. As a result, an expert, one with expertise, can make choices that lead to success more often. Sometimes this type of expertise is termed *intuition* or a "gut feeling" because it relates to the ability of an expert to choose a path based upon something that cannot be explained but is attributed to the knowledge and experience that has been gained over time. This leads to the last part of KEES, skill. Having a skill means having mastery of a set of processes and knowledge so that they can be applied in the appropriate situation to obtain the desired result. Often skills are things that have been learned and practiced so many times that no thought is needed to access and use them. Though not always true, this internalized set of processes is one of the aims of education such that a student does not need to refer to a list of instructions to accomplish something and can be said to have mastered them. For some, natural ability and reactions lead to success and can be thought of as a skill, while for others, it takes many years of study and practice in order to attain a high skill level. Overall, all four of these aspects must be utilized together during learning to build better thinking and more complete learners, which in turn will lead to a more complete attainment of the KEES.

The ideas presented rely upon an individual asking him or herself questions, analyzing the answers, and searching through the wealth of internally and externally available information. All of this is predicated upon the individual's ability to think. The examination of thinking begins with asking questions of oneself and others. The basic types of questions to be asked are familiar and have been asked repeatedly over one's life: who, what, where, when, why, and how. It is the last two of these questions that are most important to begin with and discuss in greater detail.

Asking How and Why

To increase awareness, research into oneself must be done. Research is predicated on making observations and asking questions, so everyone must start by observing and asking questions about themselves and their habits. By examining how one's own mind works, how questions are formulated, and the assumptions that are made when undertaking a process, much can be learned. Though it is almost impossible to know what one does not know or is not grasping, by delving into ones own thinking process common pitfalls can be found and highlighted. Knowing one's areas of weakness can allow these areas to be improved or at a minimum compensated for.

One of the most vital things that a student gains as KEES are acquired is the ability to identify the quality of work that is produced and the decisions being made. The ability of an individual to properly assess the quality of their own decisions is vital to his or her success in all areas. Most times there is not enough time or energy to complete a work as fully as one might desire. Attaining perfection is rarely possible. The question then becomes how close to perfection can you attain? In other cases, a person seeks to give the minimum level of quality that will still be acceptable by those that are assessing the completed work. In either case, proper assessment of the quality of work is what needs to be discussed. If the student feels the work is perfect but the judge (usually a teacher) sees it as not nearly good enough, there is a failure that must be remedied. The first steps in being able to accurately assess quality and attain an acceptable solution to problems begin with knowing the two sides of the evaluation process—the creator of the work and the criteria for judgment. Often criteria for judgment are given; however, other times it is necessary to seek these criteria out through research. On the other hand, one's own judgments can be examined to determine how each individual judges the quality of his or her own work. In order to do this, each individual must start to ask questions.

For now, the best and most powerful first step is to ask the question "why?" By trying to understand the causality of events, the processes that underlie interactions can be revealed. More importantly, by asking "why" individuals can begin to train themselves to ask questions of their own thoughts and actions. This is important in order for an individual to become more introspective and to facilitate change. By being aware of actions taken and the processes that lead to particular outcomes, individuals can begin to plan ahead and alter actions to affect different consequences. Though it may sound strange, this is the basis of learning and can lead to powerful changes in thinking and, therefore, to problem solving and learning.

Beyond these things, asking "why" can allow individuals to be more contemplative and slow down the stimulus-habitual reaction process. In this way, bad habits can be identified and eliminated along with faulty assumptions and spurious logic. The aim in the "Thinking about Thinking" section is to build better thinkers. Though that end can be accomplished through a variety of educational processes, few courses at any level specifically target poor thinking practices or offer tools to improve these areas. Somehow thinking is to be learned along with learning. However, without better and clearer thinking, learning is hampered. Throughout the rest of the text, thinking skills will be continually stressed and, as new ideas are presented, the improvement in reasoning and thinking will be reinforced and highlighted.

In the end, it is hoped that through practice an inner voice can be awakened and trained to ask questions. If successful, one's mind will become skeptical, incisive, and curious. One should be skeptical because things should not just be accepted but rather examined and agreed upon. If one is incisive, he or she will have a sharp mind that can see how things fit together and locate the flaws in arguments and gaps in knowledge that exist. Finally, curiosity is sought because the desire to know how and why is driven by the spark of curiosity. A curious mind is a questioning mind, and those questions will help to solve problems more effectively and successfully.

All of this is used to develop the two types of critical thinking—reflective and analytical. Reflective critical thinking is the process by which a person is able to examine his or her own thoughts and understand what has been going on in his or her own mind. It is as if he or she can see the thought processes that lead to an action that was taken. If you have ever been unable to answer the question "what were you thinking when you did that" you can see the need for reflective critical thinking. Analytical critical thinking is the process of measuring and assessing these thought processes. It takes the reflective process further and compares the thoughts that were had or the plans being made with the outcomes that were observed or are expected. If you do something and do not like what happens, then analytical critical thinking can help change your thought processes in order to change the way you do things. The following exercise will help illustrate some of the problems with asking questions, ignoring assumptions, and making definitions. Take some time and work through this brief exercise to help with thinking and defining terms. Once you have finished, read through the explanation given.

EXERCISE 2.1

Self-Evaluation Questions—Part 1

Stop and answer each of the following questions.

1. What is 2 and 2?

2. F=

3. What are the colors of the rainbow?

4. What is going to happen Sunday?

Self-Evaluation Questions
Part 1—Explanation

Stop and answer each of the following questions.

1. **What is 2 and 2?**

   The initial reaction of many is to respond to this question with the answer 4. This is because from an early age people are trained to see numbers and words as part of a mathematical equation. The question becomes 2 + 2 =. However, this is not the case. What if the question was given more detail that violates the assumptions being made? If you have 2 apples and 2 oranges, how many pieces of fruit do you have? How many apples and how many bananas? Depending on the level of detail of the question being asked, the answer that is given may need to be changed. Going further, physical reality may impact the answer. What if the 2 and 2 referred to 2 gallons of water and 2 ounces of salt? If these two things are added, nothing adds to four at all.

   Others think more and work to find a trick. They might respond with 22, 2 numbers, or some other answer. In all cases, the best answer is that not enough information is given to conclude. If an answer has to be given, it should be broad and qualified. For example, you might say that if both numbers are integers and the word "and" means addition, the answer would be 4. This is the first example of what was mentioned earlier. Be aware of the situation and identify and define the question and the assumptions that you are working under.

2. **F=**

   Many engineers might respond with the formula for force (F= MA) while students might associate it with Failure. Unlike the first question, more information may not be needed to give an answer. The problem arises because the context of the question is not apparent. Depending on who is asking the question and in what context, the answer might change. In chemistry, "F" is different than the "F" in physics, computer science, and many other places. Defining the context of the question and the expectations of the person evaluating the answer is vital to arriving at a correct answer.

3. **What are the colors of the rainbow?**

   Many answers exist to this question. The most common is usually ROY G BIV. What color is ROY G BIV? Obviously it is not a color. ROY G BIV is a mnemonic device to help people remember red, orange, yellow, green, blue, indigo, and violet. If you were to say ROY G BIV and assume the other person knew what you meant, you might not be seen as correct. No matter how well you know the answer, oftentimes it is encoded in a way that others cannot read or understand it. Imagine that you write a wonderful report but when you print it out, the language of your computer changes to a foreign one. When the paper is turned in the content is correct, but it has been presented in a way that cannot be understood by the target audience. Even if the context is known and the answer is correct, not communicating clearly can lead to problems.

   Another level of answers can also be given for this question depending on how it was interpreted and the words defined by the reader. A technical definition from physics might have been given for colors of the rainbow. They are the dispersion of white light through a prism, usually a raindrop. Others can see the question as a metaphor or related to popular culture. The colors can represent the ethnicities of the world, the marshmallows in Lucky Charms, or the flavors in Skittles Candy. However the question is perceived, understanding the intent to the person asking the question is important. In addition, being sure that the way the answer is transmitted is important.

4. **What is going to happen Sunday?**
   Any number of answers might be given for this question. The point of this relates to the idea of "will." It is impossible to know what will happen in the future. Often we plan our lives based upon many assumptions that are not necessarily true. Being aware of this is important to begin to see the many assumptions that underlie our lives. Some are vitally necessary and must remain. However, when solving problems, distinguishing between the assumptions that are vital and those that are simply convenient or habitual is useful for finding new answers and thinking outside of the box.

As part of exercise 2.1, it is important to note that the idea of contemplative skepticism is being presented. Often in a discussion you might agree or disagree with an idea or put forth an answer without truly examining the question or situation being posed. A judgment is made based upon any number of factors and a final answer given. What is being asked of the reader here is for their decisions to be suspended at least momentarily so that he or she might consider what is being asked and the answer that is to be given. Rather than agree or disagree, the idea of thinking first about the situation before deciding is being put forth. Contemplative skepticism is the idea that one says "I do not know" and has an open mind willing to consider several possibilities. This is not always an easy thing to accomplish and at times is not advisable. If a bus is about to hit you, it is not suggested that you stop to consider the speed and mass of the bus before moving out of the way. However, not considering ideas before leaping to conclusions or giving an answer out of routine or habit is not advantageous to developing good thinking practices. Asking why and how can help develop the ability to reflect thoughtfully and eventually allow a person to plan ahead and see potential outcomes, thus allowing him or her to choose the best path to attain success. This leads our discussion to the idea of future outcomes and the terms that define different aspects of the process of goal attainment.

Self-Evaluation Questions—Part 2

Please read the following story and complete the task that follows.

THE STORY

Two people, Mark (M) and Linda (L), are madly in love and want desperately to be united. However, they are separated by a swollen river. Though they want to be together, neither has money nor other resources. Linda approaches a boatman, Bob (B), and asks if he can take her to the other side of the river. Bob offers to ferry her across the river for $20. She explains that she does not have any money and begs him for help. He, in turn, explains that he has to be paid for the work he does to provide himself a living. He must have $20. A traveling sales-man, Stan (S), overhears the conversation and offers to give Linda the $20 if she will have sex with him. Linda does not want to have sex with Stan but, at the same time, cannot stand to be apart from her love—Mark. After much debate, she agrees. Linda has sex with Stan and then Stan pays Bob so Linda can be with Mark. Once she is reunited with Mark, everything is wonderful.

A few weeks later, Mark's best friend, Frank (F), happens to run into Stan. Stan relates what happened to him a few weeks earlier. Frank, concerned for Mark, immediately tells his friend what happened between Stan and Linda. Mark cannot believe what he hears. He imme-diately tells Linda it is over between them. He never wants to see her again.

TASK

Now that you know all the players in the story, Mark (M), Linda (L), Bob (B), Stan (S), and Frank (F), you must rank them in order from most liked to least liked. If this is difficult, try and rank them from most correct to least correct. Either way, please use the letter to rank the five people—M, L, B, S, and F.

Most   1)   2)   3)   4)   5)   Least

This exercise is designed to assist the individual to become aware of and know more about him or herself. It is a psychological exercise that may not work for everyone but still illustrates some basic principles about choice, thinking, and asking why and how. Each person in the thought experiment represents a facet of personality, and the way they are ranked may provide insight into the personal preferences and values of the individual. Mark (M) represents morality, Linda (L) represents love, Bob (B) represents business or money issues, Frank (F) represents friendship, and Stan (S) represents sex. These are the attributes that are intended to be associated with each of these characters but others things can be seen. Some people feel it is more about issues of trust, resourcefulness, willingness to sacrifice, or some other attribute.

There are several important insights that this exercise can provide. First, think about why you decided to order the people in the way you have. Did you add things to the story from your own life? Did you identify people you know with the characters or attribute motives not mentioned in the story to these people? Do you feel that everyone will place the characters in the same order? These are critical-thinking questions and the type that should be considered as answers are sought.

Beyond this, the exercise gives some insight into the values of others that might be in a work group or team. Each person can look at the same task and still arrive at a completely different assessment of the situation. Knowing that this possibility exists is an important idea to be aware of and prepared for. This exercise has been administered to over 1,000 students and every variation of response has been seen, including one student that said he could not judge because he did not know the people personally or the factors weighed when making the decision. There is no "right" answer. This is a tool to assist with the process of growth and, as such, hopefully it serves as the first step toward asking why and how each individual thinks and acts.

Though much has been said about definitions thus far, the previous exercises bring to light an important area that still needs to be discussed. In many cases words need to be distinguished more than just defined. Some words have similar denotations and are used interchangeably by people. In other cases, two or more words describe a range for measuring something; therefore, a definition is not as important as understanding the range and how to use it to measure.

The following discussion about goal attainment will be used to discuss these two points and highlight the importance of making distinctions and understanding how to evaluate terms to improve the quality and applicability of definitions that are created. It begins with a brief review of the definitions of goal, objective, outcome, and purpose. These words sound similar and for many people are used interchangeably. However, each has a distinct meaning and can be distinguished from one another. This is at the heart of what is covered in the remainder of this chapter and is vital to making good definitions and engaging in clear communication.

Before defining the terms it is helpful to decide upon a context. For this discussion, it is useful to think of the terms with respect to completing a task. In other contexts the words may not have these same connotations or even be thought of as related. Also, some of the distinctions made will be tied to a person's experience and individual ideas about how things are done. Knowing a context will assist in defining the scope of each term and how different terms come together to create a coherent picture of a situation that is being described. This might lead to a problem. If each person can choose to define things in his or her own way and from his or her own perspective, coming to a uniform understanding of the terms is made more difficult. So if these distinctions are not essential to the words but decided upon, how can you know what is correct when defining terms?

The two major measures to be used are consensus and authority. Consensus means that a majority can agree upon the definition of the term or can be satisfied with a compromise that is reached. On the other hand, others use authority to determine the correct answer. This can be a person in a position of power, like a teacher, or an accepted source of reliable information, such as a dictionary. Authority can also be some standard that is set or determined by the group or governing body, such as standard measures like a meter. An agreed upon standard is a mix of both consensus and authority and is often the best for broad definitions. In smaller settings, using an authority is quicker, but a consensus may yield better results since everyone involved can participate in the decision process. With all of this in mind, let us examine the terms.

Goals, Objectives, Outcomes, Purpose, and Success (GOOPS)

Having read through a syllabus of any course it can be seen that certain goals are stated and desired outcomes listed. However, what do these words mean? Our discussion begins with the definition and examples of these common words: goals, objectives, outcomes, and purpose. All of these terms should be considered with regard to how they apply to a task, assignment, or undertaking. It is important to start by clearly defining each term and giving the relationship between them.

The first two terms are often thought of together and may seem identical to many people. *Goal* is the overarching destination toward which an endeavor is directed. It is where you are trying to go or the end that you hope to reach. Next is the term *objectives,* which are the smaller sub-goals that are set and worked toward in order to help attain the overall goal. In turn, if the smaller tasks become the context being examined, then the objectives become the goal of those smaller projects that are intended to help achieve the main overall mission that was set by the individual or group. It is how you are going to get to your final destination or the steps and milestones along the path you are traveling. For some people objectives are larger than goals and so goals become the steps along the path. Though either can work, for this text we will assume goals are larger aims than objectives. (I am using my authority to specify this.)

The third term is *outcome,* which is the result of an undertaking. If the goal is attained, the outcomes will be what has been produced or accomplished. The outcome is what happened when the task was attempted. The final term is *purpose,* which is the reason behind the undertaking and the motivation for undertaking the task. It is why you are working toward the goal and the objectives. Creating the outcomes is often the purpose of an endeavor and thus the focus of the goals and by examining the outcomes it is possible to gain insight into the purpose of the process being examined.

You might think of the goal as answering the questions, who is going where and when to obtain what? The objectives are how you want to reach the goal. The outcome is what happens when you try. Purpose is why you did it. Though we know the definitions, it is important to highlight the distinctions that are drawn and realize distinctions may be a matter of preference or convention. A goal may be thought of as a larger scope than an objective. Not everyone would agree but some choice must be made. Another distinction is that goals are planned actions while outcomes are actual tasks that have been undertaken.

To help better understand how these words are used and related, let us look at an example. Imagine you look at your watch and see it is nearing lunchtime. You decide to go to a local market and buy something to eat. You can set the goal as purchasing something to eat at your local market. Some objectives that help get you to the store might be getting dressed, driving to the store, deciding what to purchase, and actually buying lunch. The purpose for buying lunch could be that you are hungry or perhaps just want to pass the time by shopping. Finally, the outcome of this endeavor will be actually having some food for lunch. If the intention was to get food for lunch, no matter the reason why or how it is to be accomplished, the outcome of having food or not is how the effectiveness is going to be judged. If the goal is reached, the undertaking was successful. How successful is another matter, however.

If the goal was changed, the other terms might change as well. If your goal was to get food, you might not go to the store at all. Your objectives might be to find food, raise money, cook, or something else. Knowing these terms can assist while working through the process as it will assist the problem solver to be clearer about the various aspects of the process being undertaken.

On a more practical note, consider assignments given in class. If the measure of the goal were simply completing the task assigned, the outcome to be measured would just be if something were submitted. If something were submitted, full credit would be given. Usually, this is not how it works. Many smaller objectives are set as part of the overall process of an assignment. The larger and more important an assignment is, the larger the number of objectives that are included. A homework assignment may only require a set of problems to be completed or a short summary submitted. Larger assignments have other specifications, such as research to be cited, format to be followed, etc. In these cases, the measure of the outcome cannot be simply "yes" or "no." The outcome is graded on a scale that moves from A to F. Would it be fair for the teacher to grade everyone who was not perfect as having failed? This question is related to the purpose of the assignment. Homework, tests, and other assignments are given for varying purposes. Hopefully everything is done as a way to increase learning and the overarching aim is to educate. However, the grading is both a way for the teacher to measure how far one has come as well as inform students how the teacher sees their progress. Knowing the purpose of an assignment along with a clear understanding of the goals and objectives helps everyone involved match outcomes with the desired goals. Many times, not everyone shares the goal and this can lead to problems. If students and teachers are working with different sets of goals and objectives, or they have a different idea of the purpose of an endeavor, the entire process may not attain the desired outcome.

This brings us to the term *success*. For many, the idea of success is a measure of outcomes compared with goals. If the goal matches the outcome then the task is successful. However, this may not be true. For others, if the purposes are met partially or completely, then the task was successful. A problem might arise when the task is judged and depends on who oversees the measuring process. Many people would most likely not wish to be judged on the all-or-nothing measure of success that the first situation presents and would also dislike the highly subjective nature of the second. A third option is to measure success by how many objectives are met and how well each is accomplished.

All of this may be oversimplified, but at the heart of the idea of success is the fact that someone will be measuring a situation and judging if it meets the criteria determined to be that of a successful outcome. Thus, the ability to measure and judge is vital to defining terms and being clear about what is truly a match between what is sought and what is accomplished. To aid you in determining success and how well you are moving toward a successful outcome, it is useful to know something about Rubrics.

Rubrics

As you consider goal attainment and judge your level of success, it is important to consider how you will be judged and what aspects are being considered as you are evaluated. In educational areas especially, rubrics are used to identify those criteria that are being measured and how they are to be measured. For each assignment you are given, the teacher or judge should have a scoring sheet or other set of evaluation criteria that will be used to measure how well you have done on the assignment and how close you have come to successfully completing the goal. Rubrics can be very simple, such as a checklist, or extremely complex, as is the case when you give public speeches or debates. Though not exactly the same, most tests and surveys are like rubrics in the sense that they have a set of questions designed to assess how well you have mastered certain material in the class or how you feel about a certain subject.

On the syllabus for the class, you can look for a grading breakdown that lists each assignment and what percentage each is worth in the overall grade for the class. This will show you the rubric for the overall assignments. For each assignment, the teacher may not give you the rubric, but there will be some set of criteria used to judge each with a corresponding score for each criteria. Whenever possible it is a good idea to see the rubric for grading, as it will show you what is expected as well as how much weight is given to each criteria.

If no rubric is available, you can dissect the assignment sheet and grading information to make your own. The reason rubrics are important is they will help you know the overall goal and objectives of the assignment as well as determine how to expend your effort to accomplish the task most effectively and efficiently. This idea of criteria and evaluation will be discussed more in Chapter 4.

Knowing these aspects of the process fundamentally change the decisions made by those involved in the process. The idea of thinking and decision making are addressed in greater detail in the next chapter.

SUMMARY

This chapter provided three basic skills—defining terms, understanding questions, and examining endeavors. Each of these areas was highlighted because of its essential part of the self-awareness necessary to understand oneself and others. However, simply being aware of these areas and the methodology of using these terms is not enough. This chapter sought to make the reader aware of the distinctions between similar terms and provided sets of rules and guidelines to follow as individuals work to reduce ambiguity and lessen the tendency to say "You know what I mean." It went on to introduce critical thinking and the skills needed to create lists. It ended with a discussion of Goals, Objectives, Outcome, and Purpose as part of completing a task successfully.

Terms from This Chapter

Name: To label or provide a designation for something.

Describe: To provide a list of characteristics that can include physical aspects, emotional content, or other such materials.

Explain: Provide the connections surrounding the term and the processes related to it.

Denotation: The most basic, specific, or literal meaning of a word.

Connotation: An additional implied or perceived meaning that the word has beyond its denotation.

Goals: The overarching purpose toward which an endeavor is directed. It is where you are trying to go or the end that you hope to reach.

Objectives: The smaller sub-goals that are set and worked toward in order to help attain the overall goal. In turn, objectives can be thought of as goals of smaller projects that are intended to help achieve the largest or most overarching aim of the individual or group. It is how you are going to get to your final destination or the steps and milestones along the path you are traveling.

Outcomes: The results of an undertaking. If the goal is attained, the outcomes will be what has been produced or accomplished.

Purpose: The reason behind the undertaking. It is why you are working toward the goal and the objectives. Creating the outcomes is often the purpose of an endeavor and thus the focus of the goal.

Questions and Exercises

1. Start by writing each letter of the alphabet down the left margin of a blank sheet of paper. Then try to find the name of an animal whose name begins with each letter of the alphabet and write it next to the corresponding letter on the page. After you have made the list, think about these questions: How did you approach the problem? How did you create the list? Did you picture the letter, imagine you were walking through a zoo, or just let your mind wander? Did you ask someone for help or use outside resources such as the Web or an encyclopedia? Did you copy the list from someone else in class? Does it matter how you did the assignment?
    Critical-Thinking Exercise: How does this relate to your own SDL and asking questions of yourself?

2. Think about the terms you use when you speak. How might others misinterpret them? How can this ambiguity be avoided? Should you have to change how you speak or do things to help others understand you?

3. Make a list of personal characteristics of something you know such as classmates, family members, or favorite television shows. Create groups and categories and then name them. See if others can identify your groups and categories from the examples given.

4. Keep a journal of your thoughts about class assignments and interactions with members of the class. Do you see times you think critically about your own life and the class? Why is it important? How can you personally work to improve your own thinking?
    Critical-Thinking Exercise: How was your journal and the set of questions about it critical thinking?

Additional examples and explanations are provided on Dr. Lipuma's web page at
http://njit.mrooms.net/course/view.php?id=14403

CHAPTER 3

Decision Making and Related Skills

Key Ideas of This Chapter

- What are the basics of reasoning, argument, and thought?
- What is decision making, and how is it accomplished?
- How is critical thinking related to decision making, and how is it practiced?
- How are selection, decision, and choice defined and distinguished?
- How are things evaluated and measured?
- What are the different philosophical views of decisions?
- What is problem solving and research, and how are they interrelated?
- What are the types of research?
- What is the difference between quantitative and qualitative research?

Reasoning, Argument, and Thought

Before delving deeper into the topic of thinking and decision making, it is important to discuss the general topic of thinking dealing with the topics of reasoning and arguments. Some of these ideas have already been discussed. Reasoning is the mental process of working through a set of logical steps to find a clear explanation for a question or problem. In many cases reasoning seeks to find an explanation that makes sense of or explains an outcome based upon observed facts and circumstances. While reasoning is the mental process of one person to determine an answer, for many people the idea of an argument conjures up the picture of two people yelling at one another. Though an argument can be a quarrel or debate, argument has other meanings and can be more complex. In this context, arguments are the sets of statements based upon a person's reasoning that is intended to convince someone of an opinion about a situation. Arguments and reasoning are closely tied and rely upon thinking to persuade others of a course of action that is seen as best or most appropriate.

The ideas of arguments and reasoning have existed since the beginning of civilization. In the western world, the work of Socrates, Plato, and Aristotle are often used as the basis of discussion about thought and debate. The importance of these ideas should not be underestimated. Much of what is to be covered in college rests upon an individual's ability to reason things in their own minds and then argue his or her opinion with others. Both reasoning and argumentation begin with clear, logical thinking that rests upon the body of knowledge one possesses and the additional facts and information that is gathered through research. As a person examines concepts or ideas to formulate an argument, his or her thought processes and the situation in which this takes place is vital to the process. Many aspects of thinking have already been discussed. Two of the most important are the ideas of perspective and perception.

Perspective is the point of view of the thinker or from where the topic is viewed. Perception, on the other hand, is how the topic is viewed or what aspects affect the interpretation of the topic by the thinker. Thinking of a camera can help to make the distinction clearer. The perspective of the camera is where it is placed and how the shot is taken. Perception is more the type of camera used, the different filters and lenses placed on the camera, the film, and anything else that affects the way the image is taken in and processed. For humans, situational variables such as emotions, physical conditions, or other conditions that affect observations can influence and change perception and perspective. Things that can affect how one approaches a topic include: a person's background, the topic being discussed, who accompanies the person, where the topic is discussed, among many other things. Often it is difficult to separate out these external factors from the process of thought and evaluation leading to faulty logic or poor arguments.

In order to assist with clear thinking, it is important to be able to think critically, as this skill deals with honestly gathering and assessing information to arrive at justifiable conclusions based upon good reasoning.

Critical Thinking and Decision Making

Though some of the material in the earlier chapters may seem rather simplistic, these concepts help to illustrate some important points. Moreover, these ideas assist in the preparation for your discussion of critical thinking. Critical thinking is the ability to objectively examine a situation, understand motivations behind decisions, and rationally evaluate different facets of a problem and its solutions. As mentioned in the last chapter, critical thinking is both reflective and analytical. This means that each person should think back on his or her own thinking as an action was completed to understand what was done and the reasons why it was done—reflect on it. Also, the person should determine other options and outcomes that might have occurred to review and critique what was thought about and what actually happened as a result of the thinking so it can be improved—analyze it.

When looking at the process of buying lunch used in Chapter 2 to discuss GOOP, critical thinking was used to step back from the actual process and examine the steps used to arrive at the solution. In a similar way, critical thinking should be used in all rational problem solving and decision-making processes.

Critical thinking stresses that each person should think for himself or herself and arrive at a decision about the topic rather than just accept what is presented. In education, this is especially important because unless the student can think critically, it will be difficult for him or her to know what they do not understand and/or know. This is very time-consuming and can be difficult. Much of critical thinking rests upon reasoning and questioning. These skills will underpin the remainder of this chapter. However, before moving forward, let us examine some examples of good critical-thinking habits that were presented on the Web.

Critical thinking is important to the process of making decisions. As an individual makes a decision, it is vital to identify alternatives and assess the accuracy and importance of competing courses of action. By honing the skills of asking questions, researching, and assessing gathered information, the decision maker that can think critically can use logic, rationality, and other tools to make the best decisions with the most efficient use of resources including time, effort, and finances.

EXAMPLE 3.1
Critical Thinking

When thinking about a situation, critical thinkers should:

- Be contemplative, skeptical, and open-minded. Realizing that one person does not know everything and information may not be valid at all times in all situations is a key first step.
- Ask questions of themselves, others, and of the information being gathered. Do not trust in what is given without at least some investigation and thought about the validity and worth of the material.
- Weight things appropriately. It is often difficult to separate out more important ideas, facts, and opinions from those that carry less weight. Assessing the value of a source or the credentials for an expert is vital to making a decision based upon well-founded, good information. Bad information can lead to bad results. This is especially important in the age of the Internet where anyone can make statements and present opinions in a way that looks professional and appears to be well-supported by facts.
- Have intellectual curiosity, determination, and inner drive to find truth. Many times the first answer that works may not be the best answer. Sufficient solutions may work, but the critical thinker should recognize them as only sufficient and not optimal.
- Be able to clearly define and utilize criteria for judging information. Critical thinking must be based upon an unbiased set of measures used to assess things fairly so that the analysis of ideas, facts, and other materials produce results that are not flawed.
- Have a self-awareness that allows for a separation of personal preferences, assumptions, and biases from the facts and information being examined. This is one of the most difficult parts of critical thinking for beginners, as it is often unsettling to examine one's own judgments and thought processes to determine if they are fair and leading to valid justifiable outcomes.

Related URL: *http://www.criticalthinking.org/*

These ideas listed in Example 3.1 are not an exhaustive list. For now, they serve to highlight the areas that will be practiced in the exercises later in this and other chapters. Critical thinking is not something that can be learned once and forgotten. Critical thinking is a lifelong process that is continually challenged as information changes or new information comes to light. Self-discovery must continue as the individual learns because learning changes the individual's thinking.

This brings us to the topic of decision making. What is being discussed is the process used by an individual when he or she is facing two or more distinct ways of proceeding that will often have unknown outcomes. This process deals with a person picking one path based upon the available information and requires that person to evaluate, narrow, refine, or select among alternatives that may or may not be clearly explained or understood. It is important to clarify some terms before going further. Though often the words *option, alternative, selection, decision,* and *choice* are used interchangeably, for this text each will be defined to clearly separate their different meanings from one another. The important key to remember is that we are discussing a path and the means of picking one path to follow over another. The specific definitions given for the following words are not as important as the distinction being drawn for the terms as they apply to the decision maker.

Options are any path that might be taken by the decision maker. Often, people do not know that a path is open to them or even exists, but that does not mean that these paths are not options. Alternatives are a smaller set of paths that can be taken based upon the assumptions and parameters of the given situation or rules being followed. The selection, then, is the smaller set of paths that a person knows he or she can follow and which meet all the limits that the decision maker places on the situation for himself or herself. Selections are usually those alternatives that are identified in the decision maker's mind as possible routes to follow based upon a set of preferences in the decision maker's own mind. In this case, the selection for a person is the narrowest set of paths based upon the constraints of the decision maker while the options are any possible path based upon the parameters of the situation.

One way to think about this is to consider a decision about what to drink. The options can be anything that is possible to drink, such as powdered milk, dry instant coffee, blood, mercury, or anything that can be swallowed. This is obviously not what most people would think of when asked about something to drink. The options are too large a category. The alternatives are the smaller set of things that you will consider, such as potable liquids. However, this set of paths may still be too large. This is why the question "What would you like to drink?" is often followed by the question, "What do you have?" This gets at the idea of the selection that is being offered and what there is to choose from for the decision maker.

Having looked at the set of paths that might be taken, the last two terms deal with the choosing of the one path to be followed. The term *decision* refers to the process by which a person resolves to take an action or follow a particular path in his or her own mind. Though one decides to do something, actually putting that decision into action may not be possible. To act means to actually follow the chosen path. Thus, a choice or choosing is the execution of the decision so that it can become an action. Some decisions cannot be put into action and so the choice cannot be made. Other times, a person follows a path without really setting his or her mind to take an action; instead just reacting to a situation or letting someone else decide the path to follow. In either case, a choice is made without conscious thought or decision. If the person making the decision can see all of the options and those things used to limit the selection as well as anticipate what might keep a decision from becoming an action, the process of deciding can be made more effective and easy. Nonetheless, these are just some of the limitations placed upon the complex process of decision making.

Decisions usually depend on the quality of the information you have received as well as your own knowledge and understanding of that information. The terms *data, information,* and *knowledge* are often used interchangeably without distinction. In order to better handle these ideas, we will start with the concept of data. Data is the term used to describe those things gathered through observation, experimentation, or surveying of phenomena. Each individual unit is a data point or piece of datum that is summed to provide the raw material for forming information about something. A collection of these things is what people can use to build information and knowledge through analysis. By analyzing data, you are able to identify trends and connections that become information. These bits of information can become fact if they are agreed upon by others who share your experience or review the sets of observations and connections you have made. To move beyond data and information, it must be further processed in the minds of people so that it becomes knowledge and understanding. Depending on the complexity of the situation, the available resources, and the abilities of the decision maker, the quality of data and the derived information varies. Since the quality of the information and the knowledge derived from it weighs heavily on the decision process, the ability to research and process data is important. Many times, others generate the data and information for the decision maker, who then must trust upon the others in order to achieve desired goals.

In real-world situations, it is almost impossible to have all of the necessary knowledge since situations change and information is incomplete. As a result, the decision maker is faced with the problem of uncertainty. Uncertainty, risk, and probability are important terms necessary to the discussion of decisions. Uncertainty deals with the lack of knowledge of the future that a decision maker faces. If an outcome was perfectly known, there would be no uncertainty. Unfortunately, in our world, many decisions are made in a situation of great uncertainty without sufficient time to reduce it completely. Due to this, each person must weigh factors and judge the validity of their knowledge about the situation in order to arrive at a decision.

Since uncertainty exists, the person must risk something in order to gain. Risk is the concept that something is being invested in order to attain a new, better state that brings benefit to the individual. If the investment can be lost, that loss is the risk. Often, the cost to attain something is balanced by the benefit received from attaining that thing. If there is a chance that some or all of the investment will be lost, then there is risk.

Given that in the face of uncertainty a person may decide to risk something in order to gain, the decision maker often desires to know the likelihood that he or she will be successful. Probability is a measure of the likelihood that an attempt will result in a specific outcome. Unfortunately for the decision maker, in situations of uncertainty, it is often not possible to know every possible choice so the measure of probability is not completely accurate. Said differently, in the real world there is always some element of chance because nothing is fixed. Even the most likely outcome cannot be guaranteed. As a result, people are faced with taking chances every day. However, since we are faced with so many choices and often things seem unchanging, people assume that everything will work out perfectly. These assumptions are necessary to make modern life move smoothly without driving individuals insane. However, when making decisions and thinking critically, it is important to be aware of the fact that assumptions do exist. This will be discussed later. For now, it is important to realize that everything is more complex than it might seem at first and so thinking critically and considering many alternatives while making decisions is very important.

Each different discipline and each individual has methods for determining how to make decisions in complex situations. Unfortunately, the in-depth discussion of decision theory, game theory, and all the mathematical models related to making decisions is far beyond the scope of this text. The method for using these theories or building decision trees (flow diagrams that demonstrate options and potential outcomes of a process) can be very useful but are not part of the basics. The intention of this text is to make you aware of the terms and the fact that there is much greater depth of knowledge that exists. If this topic is of particular interest, there are many good texts, courses, web pages, and entire academic disciplines that deal with how to make particular types of decisions.

So how should I make decisions? That's not an easy question to answer, but many people have given it thought and have suggestions. There are four major areas to consider and balance when coming to a final decision and taking action: investment, payoff, likelihood of outcome, and consequences. All of these vary from person to person and situation to situation. The investment is the resources you are engaging in the process. The payoff is what you will get back from each alternative if you are successful. Likelihood of outcome is the probability associated with the successful pursuit of each option you have as well as the window of opportunity for that option. The consequences are the things that will affect you as you put the decision into action and moreover what will occur if you fail to be successful. So now, we bring these all together. Imagine you have a test and someone asks you to cheat. You might say that cheating is not an option for you and so not consider it. However, if it is an option, how do you weigh this option? Some people perform a cost-benefit analysis to see what it will take (more resources to study or cheat) and then pick the best based upon the benefit for each compared to the costs. For many, it is the cost of the likelihood of being caught that stops them. The more likely the cheater will be caught and the higher the penalty, the more costly it becomes. If you use the four factors to set up a series of balances, you begin to be able to compare options to see which provides the largest benefit with the least cost and the highest probability of success.

This is a very important idea to highlight. For some people, winning is the only option, and he or she will do whatever it takes to be successful no matter what must be invested and what consequences must be faced because victory matters above all. For others, success is not the ultimate end. Therefore, decisions are based upon a consideration of risk, probability, and reducing uncertainty. These people think it is better safe than sorry. Still others have a rule that will not be violated no matter the consequences or cost. Codes of conduct, social norms, or ways of deciding beyond relative measure of cost and benefit can override any decision.

Some hold to the code, "Death before dishonor; Integrity above all." So the question is what do you value and how do you make the choices? The problem is that the outcome can always vary and each person has to look at things for him or herself. Are you a risk taker, or do you prefer to play it safe? Do you follow rules or play fast and loose with the rules? Though there are so many little things that you can consider for yourself that go into your choice, the most important thing to consider is that you are responsible for whatever happens when you make a choice or decide not to act at all.

EXAMPLE 3.2
Review of Decision-Making Concepts

The following Web pages give a more in-depth discussion about and theories of decision making. Take a minute and review what each has to say and then compare them for yourself to see what you feel is the best way to consider when making decisions.

http://en.wikipedia.org/wiki/Decision_theory

http://www.decision-making-solutions.com/ decision-making-theories.html

http://www.au.af.mil/au/awc/awcgate/awc-thkg.htm

Stop and think about what your first inclination was when and if you read the instruction and URLs above. Did you ignore this exercise and move on? Did the stop sign make you at least consider the section? Did you read the links and wonder what they contained? Did you consider different choices and then make a decision about the course of action to take? Did you look at the topic and decide to come back later or wait until you had a computer available to follow the links? Did you just move on without thinking?

These questions deal with critical thinking and decision making. For now, it is important to stop after a choice has been made or a situation experienced to allow time to review what has happened and learn from it. Eventually, it is hoped that the thinking will happen ahead of time and eventually become second nature so that it is not a deliberate step but rather something that happens naturally.

Measuring and Evaluating

An important part of critical thinking, decision making, and many of the other skills listed in the text is the ability to measure and evaluate reliably. Reliability in measurement and evaluation means being both accurate and precise when examining something. This, of course, requires the definition of accuracy and precision.

When attempting to reach a goal or make a measurement, accuracy means attaining the goal or measuring the actual value within an acceptable level of correctness with regard to a standard. Precision, on the other hand, means the ability to reproduce the results of an attempt to reach a goal or make measurements. If each time an attempt is made, the same outcome is attained, it can be said to be precise. Accuracy judges true outcomes while precision judges consistent results. Having both precision and accuracy makes something or someone reliable.

Usually, an external measure of correctness or agreed upon truth is used. Official organizations or some body of experts can set external standards. In other situations, participants or judges can agree upon the standards for judging or criteria. This brings into question how to judge fairly. First, a list of criteria for judging equally must be chosen. Criteria are the measuring sticks by which the attempt will be judged. Selecting and weighting criteria is important because that is what allows the judge to separate reliable outcomes from ones that fail to meet the desired standard in the evaluation process.

When judging actions to take or making decisions using rational assessment and evaluation, eliminating personal bias toward particular outcomes as well as utilizing consistent sets of criteria to evaluate all outcomes fairly is vital to achieving the goal. Three ideas that are sometimes confused are prejudice, bias, and weight. Though often the standard for measuring fixed items such as size and volume can be easily agreed upon, other concepts such as success and failure are less clear-cut. Having an agreed upon standard that is not dependent upon subjective judging is necessary to facilitate good decision making and many of the other skills discussed in this work.

Prejudice is a conscious or unconscious opinion or decision made with insufficient knowledge of a situation that can be based on faulty logic, irrational feelings, or inaccurate stereotypes. Bias, is similar to prejudice but not as severe. It is an unfair preference shown toward one choice or criteria in the process. Though not always negative, bias is usually showing discrimination against something, such as race or color, in making decisions. In other cases, bias can be the favor shown to a particular sex or nationality. If bias and prejudice are not recognized, they can lead to faulty evaluation of outcomes.

Finally, weight is the relative importance given to one criterion over another. This weighting will allow each criterion to be shown as relatively more or less important. By giving one criterion a higher weight than another, the first is shown to be more important for determining the correct outcome.

The terms discussed previously are well suited for scientific study or amoral discussion. However, many decisions must be made based upon incomplete information and among choices that do not have some absolute right answer that needs to be found. Philosophers have been putting forth arguments about different methods for judging the correct decision, especially moral and ethical ones, for thousands of years. It is impossible to review all of the ideas put forth, but three general concepts are important to our discussion: subjectivism, relativism, and objectivism. When making a decision, these three concepts will help clarify discussion and allow more productive use of time. The easiest to understand might be objectivism, or the idea that there is some universal truth or correct answer that can be found through sufficient observation and reasoning. This idea deals with the concept of a set of facts that can be determined with enough effort or correct tools. Conversely, subjectivism puts forth the idea that all judgments are based upon individual experience and personal assessments. There is no one right answer because each person judges each question independently. Lastly is the idea of relativism. This concept states that there is no absolute correct answer but must be judged based upon the circumstances in which the question arises and those that face the decision.

All three of these concepts are most usually applied to ethical and moral questions that pose complex questions with numerous mutually exclusive opinions about the correct course of action. Knowing how these conceptual frameworks affect one's own thoughts is important when confronting these types of questions. This will become of greater concern during the problem-solving process especially when discussing social issues that do not have a single clear course of action specified as the best solution. Arguments often hinge on the judgments made by the problem solver of what is the best course of action, and these judgments can be colored by the subjective, relative, or objective learning of the problem solver him or herself.

Applications of Basic Concepts

Often, different parts of the whole are present at one time. Awareness of the ideas discussed previously will assist in clarifying a course of action and make the more complex situation easier to deal with. The person should identify facts and other information given to better understand the situation. Moving beyond the given information, it is important to understand the constraints that exist for both the situation and the individual by examining the parameters and assumptions at work. Next, it is useful for the individual to know the perspective and perceptions of themselves and others involved as well as have an understanding of the goals and purposes of all participants.

Understanding the initial conditions at the beginning of the process will allow for more efficient and effective thinking. Next, it is necessary to identify the questions or problems being examined so that thought processes can be brought to bear upon them to find a solution. Identifying a concise, clearly delineated question is one of the most difficult and vital parts of the process. Once this is done, the concepts to be applied, the information that still needs to be found, and the effects of any decisions and the path to the solution can begin to be uncovered. As the thinker moves forward, the implications of decisions, the consequences of actions, and the need for more resources—whether intellectual, physical, or other—can be seen. All of these areas work together as the person reasons through the thinking process to propose and test solutions, either on his or her own or with others.

Unfortunately, this is not an easy task. One of the most difficult parts of this process is knowing what you don't know. Also, many times, there is so much uncertainty that finding answers to the questions created by the concepts listed is impossible or would require more time than allowed by the situation. However, being aware of what areas might pose problems for you as you work through the process is useful. Awareness of one's own cognitive processes and how these factors can affect or hinder that process is the first step to eliminating these obstacles. To help improve your own thinking, the use of critical thinking is vital. Consciously working to improve how you approach, think about, and solve problems can be helped with the critical-thinking exercises; however, that is only the beginning. All of the concepts in this and the previous chapter are only meant to highlight methods that can be used by individuals to improve themselves. It is up to you to actually select those things that work for your situation. Studying oneself to know what is needed is at the heart of this text and must be done by research into your own particular circumstances.

So what do you think about when you want to do something? It is often hard to know what you want to do or what option to take. Part of what's been given so far is designed to help clearly identify what the situation looks like and what options exist. Other concepts discussed have helped to clarify thinking, define terms, and organize items into groups. What you need to do is use all of these basic skills to make decisions and find answers to the question. Many times you do not do things on a grand scale. Rather than look at everything at once and decide based upon all the aspects of each option, you compare one aspect of two things and pick the best one. Each person makes hundreds of little decisions based upon incomplete information and gut feelings. Often these decisions are made without knowing the big picture or even all the facts. What happens in many cases is that to arrive at a good general decision, each person just compares what they know or feel and then settles on something that seems best. What the basic skills ask you to do and what the rest of the book builds upon is the idea of becoming more aware and knowing more about that big picture. To do this, you do research, so now we will examine that topic.

Research

Both critical thinking and decision making are vital skills in the processes of approaching and solving problems, communicating, as well as leading. It is important to connect these general terms to the specific process of problem solving by giving a clear methodology for how problems need to be approached. In many cases, research and problem solving are confused and the process involved in one is thought to be the other. To help clarify what these two areas mean, let us begin with some definitions.

Problem solving can be defined as the ability to follow a systematic method for examining a situation, determining a course of action to reach a desired outcome, and justifying that decision. This skill includes several abilities needed to carry out the process of problem solving. These other skills include: critical thinking and decision making, which were discussed previously, along with research. Research is investigation either through the review of others' published work (literature search) or direct/indirect observation (surveying and experimentation) to gather information, test hypotheses, and assist in the evaluation of choices. It is important to note that both research and problem solving involve asking and answering questions. However, problem solving includes a recommendation for a course of action that should be taken while research seeks to find an answer to the question that is agreed upon as correct and/or verifiable.

Underlying the process of both research and problem solving is a series of learned, interconnected skills that serve as a foundation. In order to think critically and make good decisions, it is vital to be well informed. Thus, research is needed to inform the decision makers, and good research skills are necessary to find answers to questions and help support the decisions made. Though all these skills are important, we need to have a better understanding of what research is and why there are different types of research methods.

Generally, research is investigation aimed at creating a better understanding of a subject. This process of gathering information can be through introspection, self-analysis, thought, observation, experimentation, or a review of existing literature and past research. Three major categories of research used in the sciences are experimentation, survey, and literature search.

One typical type of research conducted by students is a literature search. In this case, a researcher reviews published documents to see what others have observed, gathered, or proposed. Without the research accomplishments of previous scientists, continued advancements would be far more difficult or impossible. However, literature review is only the first step. Practitioners of science must do more. It is important to define what the word *science* means. In this case, science, in its most general sense, is the systematic examination of phenomena in the pursuit of knowledge and truth about a specific subject through observation, description, classification, discussion, and experimentation of those and related phenomena. Science is an attempt to describe and explain things to better understand how things work and define the laws and principles of that inner working. Science is both the body of knowledge created by the process as well as the process itself—science is knowledge and method. Through survey and experimentation, science works to understand and articulate the laws and principles of a particular area of study. Many fields commonly referred to as "the sciences," such as chemistry and physics, could be more correctly named natural sciences or the study of the laws and inner workings of the natural world. In a similar way, the science of biology could be named a life science. With this understanding, we can see that social sciences are then the study of the interactions between and within societies or, more specifically, how people act and interact. This definition and many others will be explored more completely later.

No matter what science is being discussed, once a person moves beyond the review of others' work, they have entered the realm of scientific investigation. This is accomplished through surveying and experimentation. Surveying is the process of gathering information through observation and careful inspection. The facts and information gathered are referred to as data and can be of various types depending upon the method of collection and the discipline of study being employed.

Generally, there are two types of surveys that can be conducted—quantitative and qualitative. Quantitative surveys produce results that can be converted to numerical values and reduced to mathematical relationships for analysis. Qualitative surveys yield nonnumeric results that can provide understanding of complex systems that are not easily reduced to mathematical relations. Both quantitative and qualitative analyses are important to research. A good example of these two types of surveys can be seen on a test that students might take. Quantitative questions tend to have one answer or set of answers that can be broken into a correct or incorrect answer, such as multiple choice or matching questions. The answer given can be reduced into either a one or a zero and be figured into a mathematical equation to find the grade. More open-ended questions, such as short answer or essays, tend to be more qualitative and leave the interpretation of the results to the researcher or, in this case, the professor.

Both types of surveys use questions administered through a variety of instruments and utilizing a wide range of methods to ask the questions, observe the subjects, and record the results. Surveys may contains a mix of narrow, focused questions designed to yield a small range of answers and more open-ended questions designed to yield a wider range of answers. When designing a survey, it is vital to choose the questions carefully and be sure that the results obtained from asking the question will yield a result that is usable.

Beyond the simple collection of data is the use of that data to make predictions and thus run experiments. Experimenting is a set of trials made to gather knowledge or make a test. Often scientists try to control all but a specified set of conditions in order to test a predicted outcome or gain more knowledge about a more narrowly defined phenomenon. At its most simplistic, an experiment is observation made to confirm or disprove something unknown or discover some unknown principle or effect. Experimentation requires data collection, as does surveying, but experimentation goes one step further by creating a situation in which predictions are made and then the outcomes tested. The goal of the experiment is to see if an outcome can be predicted or test whether an observation or data can be obtained or replicated.

Whether surveying or experimenting, it is necessary to formulate a clear research question that sets parameters and predicts an outcome. The research question is based upon the interconnection of independent and dependent variables to determine a connection and make a prediction. A variable is anything that can change or vary within a defined system. The aim of any experiment is to create a situation that allows for the research question to be answered reliably so that others can repeat the experiment and verify the results. The fewer variables that exist, the easier it is to test outcomes and verify the predictions.

So why are there two types of variables? Independent variables are those characteristics of a person or thing in a system that can vary freely. Dependent variables are those characteristics of a person or thing in a system that change as a result of the independent variables. As the independent variable changes, the dependent one changes as well. Finding the connection or lack thereof between dependent and independent variables is the intent of much research. To reiterate, not all experiments produce results that say the prediction was correct. Many times, the experiment shows that no correlation exists at a level of confidence that can be accepted. Depending on the field being studied and the amount of data available, differing levels of error are acceptable to say that results are reliable. In this case, error is how far from a true value a result can be and still be considered correct. The smaller the error the more accurate a measurement is and so the more reliable and reproducible.

One of the most commonly discussed and employed methods of experimentation is the scientific method. Though the scientific method is a popular and useful means of conducting research, many other methods of research are also employed. In general, all of these methods share the common idea of systematically examining a situation to find common trends that can be understood by others. Also, any theory needs to be reproduced by others, as they look at similar subjects in similar conditions.

The Scientific Method

The scientific method is defined as the logical approach to the solution of problems that lend themselves to investigation by observing, generalizing, theorizing, and testing. It is a research method focused on experimentation to derive knowledge about occurrences. Though often associated with the natural and physical sciences, the method can be used with any experimental science including those in the humanities and social sciences, such as psychology.

The method itself is often explained with steps but is not necessarily meant to be used in a strictly linear fashion. As with any problem-solving process or research method, iteration is vital to attaining usable and valid results.

FIGURE 3.1
Steps of the Scientific Method

1. Identify a problem or gap in knowledge
2. Collect relevant information
3. Formulate a hypothesis
4. Experiment to test the hypothesis
5. Observe the experiment
6. Organize and record data from the experiment
7. Draw conclusions based on experimental facts to confirm or refute hypothesis
8. Communicate research methods, findings, and conclusions

Figure 3.1 shows the steps of the linear Scientific Method that is often used by research scientists.

Each of the steps listed has specific methodologies related to them in order to achieve a final solution or valid conclusion. The way each of these methodologies is set down and carried out depends upon the discipline utilizing the method. For example, the way in which a chemist creates and runs an experiment may be different from the process used by a physicist or a biologist. Though all three may look at the same occurrences in an attempt to gather information, the scale of the experiment, the process examined, and the hypothesis tested can be completely different. Each discipline has its own set of tools, processes, and guidelines by which experiments are carried out. Despite these differences, the reported results have a systematic way of being tested and reported so that all those who understand the method used can understand and utilize these results whether or not they are within the discipline.

In many cases, the type of questions that are answered and the perspective from which these answers come change. Even so, the same basic steps of the scientific method are used to systematically and rationally research so that others can understand and duplicate the findings of researchers. A specified research method allows for various disciplines to speak a common language. Although the tools and particular processes may change, the underlying methodology of research should remain the same.

At the heart of the scientific method is clear, rational thought that examines its own assumptions, parameters, and decisions to justify choice and conclusions. Utilizing faulty logic or experimental methods may produce results that might be only partially applicable or even invalid. As a result, the iterative process of the scientific method as well as other research methods is only as strong as the underlying critical thinking that underpins the research design. The abilities of the research to be organized, thorough, and clear during all phases of the research process are vital to good results. A good research method is centered on good thought processes.

Though the scientific method is a popular and useful method of research, many others are also employed. In general, all of these methods share the common idea of systematically examining a situation to find common trends that can be understood by others. Also, any theory needs to be reproduced by others as they look at similar subjects in similar conditions.

When examining the actions of people, methods other than the scientific method may be employed. Looking at cases, conducting personal interviews, and examining the overall picture can find insights. Many social science texts and disciplines give other methods for conducting research into various areas. No matter how it is accomplished, the idea that problem solvers and decision makers must have information to assist in the work they do is clear. More importantly, everyone should be exposed to these skills early in their academic lives rather than later. Knowing how to find answers and do research in order to make informed decisions and solve problems is not part of any one discipline, but rather necessary to all.

In order to do research, everyone must begin with questions. Asking questions may at first seem simple, but it is not always easy to find the correct question to ask and then ask it in the correct way to generate useful answers. Chapter 4 will look more closely at the practice of asking and answering questions.

SUMMARY

This chapter focused on the terms and concepts related to thinking skills. It then moved to a discussion of decision making. This included an examination of different aspects of the process of evaluation necessary to make decisions fairly. Finally, the topic of research and different research methods was covered. Bringing these two ideas together, creativity was reviewed.

Terms from This Chapter

Critical thinking: The ability to objectively examine a situation, understand motivations behind decisions, and rationally evaluate different facets of a problem and its solutions.

Decision making: The process by which informed choices are made in order to evaluate, narrow, refine, or choose between alternatives.

Uncertainty: The lack of knowledge of the future outcome of an action that a decision maker faces.

Risk: The potential loss related to taking an action.

Probability: A measure of the likelihood that an attempt will result in the outcome that is desired.

Science: The systematic examination of phenomena in the pursuit of knowledge and truth about a specific subject through observation, description, classification, discussion, and experimentation of those and related phenomena. Science is an attempt to describe and explain things to better understand how things work and define the laws and principles of that inner working.

Research: The investigation, either through literature sources or direct/indirect observation. It is used to gather information, test hypothesis, and assist in the evaluation of potential solutions.

Surveying: Process of gathering information by observation and careful inspection.

Experimenting: The process of making trials to gather knowledge or make a test. Often, scientists try to control all but a specified set of conditions in order to test a predicted outcome or gain more knowledge about a more narrowly defined phenomenon.

Problem solving: Systematic method for examining, considering, and determining a potential solution for a dilemma.

Questions and Exercises

1. How do you make decisions and judge things? Find out from others if they use the same methods for arriving at decisions.
2. How is critical thinking related to decision making, and how is it practiced?
3. What are the types of research? Which of these do you use regularly? How do you use critical thinking when researching?
4. Keep a Decision Diary of your thoughts about some decisions you made. Be sure to start with the situation you faced, the factors you knew about, and the selection of alternatives you had. Explain what you did as you made the decision. Afterwards, comment on the outcome of the decision and what you might have done differently. Try to see other options that you did not know about. Was there some piece of information or knowledge that would have helped you make a better decision? Keep a log of the decisions you make in the diary, and after several weeks look back over what you have done to find trends or see patterns of interactions in which one decision had an effect on future decisions you made.
5. The fishbowl exercise is a useful physical representation of critical thinking and examination of one's own thoughts in a situation. This exercise can be used for many reasons in many situations in the classroom, but it is described generally here so that whenever you

find yourself in a situation, you can see how both reflective and analytical critical thinking can be accomplished and utilized. To create the basic fishbowl, arrange the desks or tables in the classroom into a circle with at least two chairs in the middle and space around the outside. The idea here is that the tables around the outside create a fishbowl to watch interactions. Usually, role-playing exercises or other types of encounters can be shown in the middle of this ring while others watch and make comments. This can be analogous to a person watching a fish in a fishbowl; the person can observe things closely without being involved.

More important than just seeing the actions is the commentary that can be made about the actions by those watching. The idea here is that when you are in a situation, often you do not stop to thinking critically. However, if you can remember the fishbowl, you can reflect on what you did and work to improve the interactions in which you take part. By thinking of yourself sitting in the circle watching the actions happen in the fishbowl, you are using reflective critical thinking. Beyond that, if you can also step back and think of yourself standing behind the seats outside of the circle and analyze what you saw, what you thought about it when you observed it, and what could have been done better, you are using analytical critical thinking. The fishbowl helps you see the situation as well as learn from it so that you can improve outcomes in the future.

References and Other Resources

Rusbult, C. (2001). Creative Thinking: in education. Retrieved on January 5, 2009, from: *http://www.asa3.org/ASA/education/think/creative.htm*

CHAPTER 4

Focus on Questioning

Key Ideas of This Chapter

■ What makes good questions?
■ What are some common pitfalls in asking and answering questions?
■ What is creativity?
■ How do you improve your thinking with good questions?
■ What is lateral thinking?
■ What are essential and leading questions?
■ What are the types of questions used for assessments like tests and surveys?

Introduction

Throughout the previous chapters, thinking skills and some basic skills were presented much of which was based on asking questions. This chapter takes a closer look at this skill to assist you to become better at recognizing what makes a good question and help you find answers to them. Many people are familiar with the simplest types of questions—who, what, where, when, how and why. The first four of these seek factual answers while the last two how and why are usually more involved. How and why were discussed in various ways earlier related to issues of GOOP and critical thinking. When the question asks for more than simple recall or description of a process or motivation, advanced skills come into play.

FIGURE 4.1
Bloom's Taxonomy Questions

Level	Bloom's Taxonomy	Anderson Revision
1	Knowledge	Remembering
2	Comprehension	Understanding
3	Application	Applying
4	Analysis	Analyzing
5	Synthesis	Evaluating
6	Evaluation	Creating

Figure 4.1 shows two versions of Bloom's Taxonomy. For more discussion on these versions see:
http://epltt.coe.uga.edu/index.php?title=Bloom%27s_Taxonomy

To assist with these more advanced questions, this chapter focuses on questions specifically to point out common pitfalls and provide practice in understand what to look for. A good place to start is with Bloom's Taxonomy. In the 1950's Benjamin Bloom worked with a group of educators and others to outlined a hierarchy of skills related to learning such that a lower skill is built upon to attain the higher levels. Since that time the taxonomy has been refined and reworked but the essential levels are still used. The table above shows the original taxonomy (left) with a modern version in which skills are shown as actions to be taken (right). At level 1, items are known or are able to be recalled. This is part of each of the higher levels to be attained and serves as a basis for that attainment. As one moves on to the higher levels, it can be seen that more advanced skills and abilities are called upon. These relate back to what was discussed earlier in the text.

The taxonomy is at the heart of many educational curricula and is used to help specify the goals and objectives sought and the outcomes produced in education. A good discussion of this can be found at: *http://www.nwlink.com/~donclark/hrd/bloom.html*

It is important to see that asking and answering questions that are more than just judging factual recall are part of a system of research and assessment that rely upon many things. It is important to know the context, the depth of knowledge sought, the purpose and many other things. Some common terms are associated with this process of questions and answers. At the heart of it is the idea that a question is posed to identify a need, that need is satisfied with data that is gathered which must be reduced and analyzed to transform it into information and eventually knowledge and understanding. That is then the answer to the question but only if that data is reliable and valid for the question asked. Just saying that you have asked the right question or arrived at an answer is not enough. All steps along the way must be judged to see if they are working together to arrive at the correct answer for a good question.

FIGURE 4.2
Questions Yielding Data leading to Answers

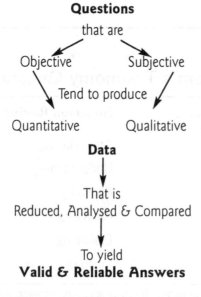

Figure 4.2 shows a Concept map of the process for questions producing data that leads to answers.

Generally, there are two types of questions objective and subjective questions that are asked. Objective questions have a specified set of right answers and tend to be more narrow and closed. Subjective questions tend to be more open-ended with answers that depend upon argument, evidence or a larger set of correct answers. These often require more involved answers to explain the argument and evidence as part of the process of answering.

Though you might not have thought about it, you are probably familiar with these types of questions from tests you have taken. The objective questions are the ones you can memorize the answer to and are tied to the lower levels of Bloom's Taxonomy. Subjective questions also require the recall of knowledge but then ask you to use your higher level skills in the taxonomy to provide more than just a right answer. Your answers to both of these questions yield data about your knowledge and understanding which can be quantitative or qualitative depending on how the data is processed. For tests, this data is used to generate a grade and provide you feedback in the form of a letter grade, comments or score on a rubric. The process is shown above.

A vital part of the process is for the questions to match the situation and goals of the way it is to be used. Only valid and reliable measures may determine correlations and trends that yield information about what was studied. If the questions on a test do not match what was taught your answers do not tell us what you learned. If your method of research does not provide an answer to your research question that is valid and reliable, the result is not trustworthy. The next part of the chapter examines questioning in more detail.

Basic Questions

The following exercise will assist with the process of research by highlighting many of the most common problems that are faced when considering and working to find answers to questions. Each question may at first seem simple but has hidden pitfalls. The critical-thinking skills mentioned discussed will assist with assessing questions and researching to find answers. The awareness of the pitfalls coupled with practice in considering questions is key to effective and efficient research.

One problem that cannot be addressed in a text that is more easily handled in the classroom is the desire of students to have answers to questions. For years, students have been trained to find the answer, and many times this makes working through problems difficult. Rather than consider the thinking processes at work, an answer is sought and once found, the next question is attacked without consideration of the quality of the answer or the processes related to deciding upon it. To help lessen the allure of just looking at answers, the explanation of the answers to the exercise that follow are presented at the end of the chapter. Hopefully, this might help the reader resist the temptation to short-circuit the learning process and obtain the answer.

EXERCISE 4.1

Research Questions

Please give the response you feel most appropriately answers each of the following questions. This exercise is designed to highlight critical thinking, decision making, and research skills.

1. After the new Canon Law that took effect on November 27, 1983, would a Roman Catholic man be allowed to marry his widow's sister?

2. A child is born in Boston, Massachusetts to parents who were both born in Boston, Massachusetts. The child is not a United States citizen. How is this possible?

3. Before Mount Everest was discovered, what was the highest mountain on Earth?

4. In what year did Christmas and New Year's fall in the same year?

5. Which is correct to say: "The yolk of the egg are white" or "The yolk of the egg is white"?

6. A woman from New York married 10 different men from that city, yet she did not break any laws. None of these men died and she never divorced. How was this possible?

7. Why are 1990 American dollar bills worth more than 1989 American dollar bills?

8. How many times can you subtract the number 5 from 25?

9. If, having only one match, on a freezing winter day, you entered a room that contained a lamp, a kerosene heater, and a wood burning stove, which should you light first?

10. Cathy has six pairs of black gloves and six pairs of brown gloves in her drawer. In complete darkness, how many gloves must she take from the drawer in order to be sure to get a pair that match?

An important note to make here regards the idea of trial and error. Often a solution to a question is found by guessing repeatedly until the right answer is found. Unfortunately, repeated attempts cannot always be made. Unless there is an answer to check against and/or experts to consult to determine if the trial is correct, guessing may not always lead to an acceptable answer. In the real world, this is not always possible so randomly guessing is not always acceptable or able to provide the best answer. Also, being satisfied that you have the answer is not the goal of this and the other exercises that follow. These questions are intended to point out common problems that are encountered when answering questions by demonstrating common pitfalls and assumptions that are made in thinking, research, and working towards solutions. Knowing that a "trick" might be present is helpful, but more important is the idea of being aware of the faulty logic that these common mistakes represent. The idea here is to apply the mistakes in reasoning that are highlighted to future questions so that the same mistakes are not made. Also, giving a reason for the answer you supply is as important as getting the right answer. As can be seen from Exercise 4.1, more than one correct answer can be found if the question is not worded correctly or narrowed sufficiently. Trial and error is an excellent way to learn from one's mistakes. However, learning by thinking ahead and thinking critically about one's experiences can provide a better route to future success.

Though trial-and-error and repeated guessing may be necessary in some cases, it is always better to have thoughtful, educated guesses motivated with reasoning that can lead to a narrowing of the category. This type of reasoning takes practice.

This process relates to the concept of ambient knowledge. This is the range of knowledge and understanding that is readily accessible to the thinker. Many times, a person will attempt to tap this easily accessible resource first. Afterwards, the next level of assistance often comes from either asking a nearby person or searching the Internet. In any event, the goal of the process is to arrive at the best answer. Starting with what one knows is always good. Thus, enhancing the ability to access and use ambient knowledge is useful for increasing the effective use of time and resources.

Now that the basic skills have been presented, it is possible to apply these to questions to give the reader practice and explain the topics in greater detail. Exercise 4.2 includes questions that provide practice with specific skills related to all of the items discussed thus far. Again, the explanations of the answers have been provided at the end.

EXERCISE 4.2

Exercise for Thinking

Please give the most appropriate answer to each of the following questions. This exercise is designed to highlight critical thinking, decision making, and research skills.

1. Two fathers and two sons go hunting. Each shoots a duck and none shoot the same duck. When they get home and cook them, there are only three to eat. How is this possible?

2. A cowboy rides into town on Friday, stays three days, and leaves on Friday. How is this possible?

3. Mom, Dad, and two kids have come to a river, and they find a boat. It is small and can only carry one adult or two kids at a time. Both kids are good rowers, but how can the whole family reach the other side of the river?

4. Three friends check into a motel for the night and the clerk tells them the bill is $30, payable in advance. So, they each pay the clerk $10 and go to their room. A few minutes later, the clerk realizes he has made an error and overcharged the trio by $5. He asks the bellhop to return $5 to the three friends who had just checked in. The bellhop sees this as an opportunity to make $2; as he reasons that the three friends would have a tough time dividing $5 evenly among them. Therefore, he decides to tell them that the clerk made a mistake of only $3, giving a dollar back to each of the friends. He pockets the leftover $2 and goes home for the day! Now, each of the three friends gets a dollar back, thus they each paid $9 for the room,

which is a total of $27 for the night. We know the bellhop pocketed $2 and adding that to the $27, you get $29, not the $30 that was originally spent. Where did the other dollar go?

5. Because cigars cannot be entirely smoked, a hobo who collects cigar butts can make a cigar to smoke out of every five butts that he finds. Today, he has collected 25 cigar butts. How many cigars will he be able to smoke?

6. Two planes take off at the same exact moment. They are flying across the Atlantic. One leaves New York and is flying to Paris at 500 miles per hour. The other leaves Paris and is flying to New York at only 450 miles per hour (because of a strong head wind). Which one will be closer to Paris when they meet?

7. Maker doesn't want it; the buyer doesn't use it; and the user doesn't see it. What is it?

Creativity and Working with Others

Much of what has been presented thus far deals with an individual becoming aware of and improving himself or herself. One fundamental skill that is perhaps the most difficult to identify and work to improve is creativity. However, being creative is important when trying to find novel solutions to problems or creating a new way of thinking for oneself or a group. Creativity has many different meanings depending on the context in which it is discussed. For some, creativity is associated with art, music, or other 'creative' endeavors. In other circumstances, creativity simply means making something up to fit a situation such as "creative bookkeeping." For this work, creativity is the idea that a person can integrate or connect two previously unrelated ideas in a new way. For many people, however, if they had not been aware of the connection beforehand, any connection that is made is new and thus creative. This distinction will not be drawn too finely at this point. If a connection already existed and could have been found through research, a person is not really being creative. The question is then, "Is any idea really new, or has someone already discovered it and all that is done is remembering or rediscovering the idea?" This debate is beyond the scope of this text. What is important is to see that there is a line to be drawn between thoughtful investigation and creation from remembering an answer or finding one from a source. Only the individual thinker can know what was done to arrive at the answer—was it thoughtful creation or researched and remembered.

When discussing creativity, words like introduction, imagination, innovation, and invention are often used. Creativity or to create is generally associated with bringing something into existence First, let us begin with the idea of introduction, or being the person who brings an idea to the group for the first time. Often, even if the idea is not original, if you are the first person to introduce it to a group, you may be seen as creative. This can be seen with many television shows that have not been seen before in your group. For example, the person who first presented the idea of *American Idol* might be seen as creative even though the show existed in England before. Many companies are the first to introduce a new technology even though other companies have been working on similar ideas. To introduce something is one facet of creativity, though it is much more than just bringing something to the attention of others.

Beyond introducing something is actually making something new or changing something that exists so it is a new version of an old thing. The first step in this is using your mind to envision something new. Imagination is related to envisioning something that does not exist in your mind whether or not it can even be realized. Creativity may lead to the creation of a new item, and so be associated with invention, while thinking of a new way of doing something or changing the present situation is innovation.

This overall concept of creativity has several aspects. One part deals with envisioning new things that have never been thought of before, and the other brings two existing things together in a new way or adds to an existing idea or item to create something new. Ultimately, to move something from the theoretical to the practical is also being creative but in a different way. All these types of creativity are necessary and are useful in different situations. The idea of newness and adding something through thought and effort are at the heart of creativity. When thinking of being creative do not limit yourself to the idea of an artistic expression since there are many types of creativity and many avenues by which it can be expressed.

One important aspect of examining thinking has not been discussed yet. Often it is helpful to work on a problem by oneself first and then consult others to gain a different perspective on both the answers obtained and the methods used to obtain those answers. Working in groups can provide new insights that had not been obtained previously. The distinction between groups and teams as well as many other relevant topics dealing with leading in these groups and teams will be handled later under the topics of communication and leadership. However, at this point it is necessary to say something about collaborating with others to accomplish goals and increase learning.

EXAMPLE 4.3

The following web pages discuss creativity, critical thinking, and decision making. Reviewing these will allow the reader to have a deeper understanding of what has been presented thus far as well as provide other resources for further study.

Creative Thinking: *http://www.asa4.org/ASA/education/think/creative.htm*
Introduction to Creativity: *http://www.ascd.org/publications/books/196073/chapters/Introduction @-Theory-of-Creativity.aspx*

These pages give reasons why creativity and thinking are so important to students and all people in general. For now, it can be said that there is a great deal to investigate beyond what has already been said. Hopefully, what is written in the text and presented on the web pages helps to increase the awareness of the reader as well as expand his or her ambient knowledge to make all the processes of education easier and learning more effective.

Though an individual can accomplish a goal and be creative, often working with others can allow the individual to accomplish far more in far less time. This is often stated in the clichés: "Two heads are better than one" and "the whole is greater than the mere sum of the parts." This is intended to convince people to work together to achieve something greater than they could achieve by themselves.

An important aspect of creativity and thinking that deals with incorporating the ideas of others is called lateral and parallel thinking. To this point in the text most of the concepts presented dealt with improving the individual. These other concepts also can improve the individual but incorporate others in the process. These ideas deal with shifting one's thought process to see alternative ways of approaching processes and seeing the situation from another thinker's perspective.

To assist with these skills, the following set of exercises has been provided. Many other thinking exercises such as these can be found on the web. Links to these pages are given at the end of the exercise.

EXERCISE 4.3

Questioning Games

To complete this exercise, it is best to assemble a group of people and designate one person as the question answerer. The rest of the group must determine what is happening or answer the specified questions by asking True–False style questions. The designated answerer will respond with "yes," "no," "maybe," or "irrelevant." Group members should take turns being the answerer as long as they can be trusted not to look at other answers. The intent of these questions is to practice all of the skills discussed so far through the use of defining, thinking, and narrowing the situation based upon ambient knowledge of the group.

1. A man leaves home, walks a short distance, turns left, walks a short distance, turns left, walks a short distance, turns left, and returns home. Who are the two masked men waiting for him when he gets there?

2. A man stops at the red hotel and realizes he has gone bankrupt. What's happening?

3. A man lies dead in a room surrounded by 53 bicycles. Why is he dead?

4. A man walks into a bar and asks for a glass of water. The bartender pulls out a shotgun and points it at him. The man says, "thank you" and leaves. Why?

5. The music stops, a woman dies. What happened?

6. There's a man lying dead in a forest wearing scuba gear. What happened?

7. Four people are dead in a cabin at the top of a mountain. What happened?

8. A man lies dead next to a rock. What's happening?

9. Ned and Stacey. What's happening?

10. A man dies of thirst in his own home. How is this possible?

http://rinkworks.com/brainfood/latreal.shtml

It is difficult for most students to imagine a class in which lateral thinking questions would be used to measure learning and assign grades. However, many real-world situations do not match the types of questions that are asked on many of the assessments given in class leading students to ask "when will I even use this?" Often objective questions are used on tests because of issues of time to administer and grade as well as to ensure fairness. More subjective questions can lead to misunderstanding or bias. In order to assess the skills in the higher level of Bloom's Taxonomy, it is necessary to use performance based or authentic assessment.

Judging Performance and Arriving at 'Right' Answers

In order to gain a picture of the attainment of the higher levels of the taxonomy, different types of questions and methods for gathering data are needed. A performance or authentic assessment does this by having the student answer the question in context of the related task. A good example of this is the driver's test. Just asking you multiple choice questions about the rules of road is not sufficient. You are asked to actually drive while being observed. However, just driving once is not sufficient either so both parts of the test are necessary to assess your readiness to drive. Everyone is also given an eye exam to ensure that a minimum level of vision is present. The written test measures knowledge, the eye test ensures baseline acceptable ability and the driving test is a performance indicator of the needed skills for driving. None of these alone is sufficient to give a picture of attainment. Even when taken together, the listened driver still needs practice to move from novice to expert often signified by learner permits or provisional licenses.

Not all tasks can be nor should be measured in this way. For example, it would not be a good idea to see if you know how to skydive by throwing you out of a plane and seeing if you land safely. Similarly, throwing someone into a pool to teach them to swim leads to an all-or-nothing, sink-or-swim mentality. Performance assessments must be used after instruction that has prepared for that specific task with clearly specified goals, objective, outcomes, and performance indicators. Many examples from education can be identified. Debates, lab practicum, Oral reports, class projects and many other assignments that ask students to apply what they have learned to create some product or perform some task are all examples of authentic assessments.

This leads to the need for good assignments based upon good questions that lead to an effective method for judging student learning. In order to specify the task Essential and Lading questing should be identified for the task.

Lading and Essential Questing

Asking good questions is not easy and can be approached in diverse ways. Good questions are clearly expressed and ask one thing that leads to a desired direction of inquiry. This does not mean that it has only one answer or that there is a specific answer to be sought. Good questions allow the person answering to understand what is asked and allows them to be on the right track towards finding an answer without any distraction or unintended obstacle. The full extent of this discussion goes well beyond this introductory text but the material presented earlier about definitions and reducing ambiguity is meant to have you consider what you are presenting and how someone else will interpret that. In the same say, when you are asking a question, it is important to consider how the one who will be answering it might misunderstand what was asked. As students, you also need to consider this as you read questions to be sure you are providing and answer to what is requested or expected.

Only you will know if the teacher will be receptive to you asking a question about the question. In other cases, the answer you know to be correct may not be the one the teacher expects. This may be due to a poorly constructed question or inaccurately taught material in a text or class materials. These situations are beyond what is being addressed here, but I hope that you are able to ask for clarification or can provide an argument for the answer you provide.

This brings us to the ideas of leading questions versus essential ones. Leading questions are meant to direct inquiry to a specific end or piece of knowledge or set of skills to be learned. The objectives set out for learning are often phrased as leading questions and are tied to content to be taught and outcomes produced by students. In most textbooks, chapters open with leading questions like those at the beginning of each of the chapters in this book. By reading the answers to these can be found within the content presented. Similarly, many leading questions can be searched for with an internet search and the correct answer found. Leading questions are often used to identify the key pieces of material to be learned and so be on a test. A good test should ask all the right questions to cover what is laid out in the goals and objectives for the material to be covered and so a food set of leading questions is very helpful.

Leading questions can also identify basic skills needed such as how to use a microscope, how to cite properly in your paper, or when to use proper evidence. Sets of leading questions can be used to establish a foundation for larger overarching questions which leads to the essential questions. Depending on the scope of the content being covered, a mix of leading and essential questions are often specified in a continuum such that the leading question establish the fundamentals on which a larger discussion of the topic is based.

So what are Essential questions? In his book Understanding by Design, Grant Wiggins presented the idea of Essential questions. He explained that this term has several different meaning depending on context. In our lives in general, the essential questions are the ones that are not easily answered, may change over time and that are open to debate and reconsideration. Within a discipline of study, the essential questions are the controversial topics and key research challenges and debates that exist at a given time. In education, the essential questions are those aspects of the body of knowledge that are fundamental to learning each subject in the curriculum. In short, Essential questions are the big questions that need to be considered and do not have simple answers that can be looked up or searched for on the internet.

For us, the essential questions depend on context and are really related to a discussion of level. Leading questions are ones that are smaller and Essential ones are larger and overarching. In any subject, you will have specific pieces of information or skills that need to be mastered. These should be learned in order to assist with answering the large Essential Question. If you look back to Bloom's Taxonomy, Essential questions are the ones that ask you to use the higher levels to arrive at an answer by using your own input. Though there may not be one right answer, the essential questions are the ones that allow you to show your own thoughts, opinions, attitudes and personal insights.

So why is this important to you as a student? This has two answers. First, based upon your own learning style and other personal preferences, you will naturally be more accustomed to and probably partial to either leading or essential questions and will need to be able to identify the distinction. Secondly and more important, Essential question require more thought and engagement by you as the student and so you need to be prepared. This also means that you may have to ask more questions to clarify the scope and nature of an essential question. To help identify an essential question, the following sty of characteristics will help:

Essential questions:

- Ask you to go beyond simple answers and vague statements to engage with the big ideas and fundamentals of what is being studied
- Requires more critical thought and reflection, discussion and sustained action

- Lead to understanding promoting further questioning and research
- Utilizes the skills of Information Literacy to find and assess sources to support arguments with evidence
- Leverages prior learning and personal experience to have you make claims and put forth your own perspectives and opinions that need to be discussed and defended
- Continues learning beyond a single class or subject to connect learning to past lessons form a variety of subjects
- Connects to future learning and makes it relevant to aspects of the learner's ongoing life.

Much of what was given above dealt with the ideas of your need to clarify the questions you were given or helping you identify how the course materials is laid out and tied to tests. One other practical application of Leading and Essential questions deals with the assignments that will be done in many classes throughout the years of education. When you are actually writing a paper or conducting research, you will need to create a question that is at the heart of your work. In papers, this is called a thesis. In research this is a hypothesis. This question must be at the correct level of specificity and be clearly stated to allow you to accomplish the work successfully. Asking the wrong kind of question for your given situation or one that cannot be answered within the constraints of the task assigned will cause problems.

There are different types of papers each with their own type of these. If you are to present facts or a review of some written work, a leading question will be better as it will specify a narrow scope of work. Whereas a more essential question would be better for persuasive papers or ones that have a larger scope or ask for you to present an argument with evidence. For a hypothesis, asking too large of an essential question will usually lead to a study that is very large in scope and thus require a great deal of time and resources to accomplish. On the other hand, if the questions too narrow, it may not be sufficient to satisfy the goals and objective set for you by the instructor. Even if the question itself is good, knowing how to adjust the specificity and scope is why is important to see the range of questions that exist and be able to adjust what you are asking. More on this decision process is given in the next few chapters to assist you to effectively communicate to meet the needs of your target in a situation to accomplish your goal.

SUMMARY

This chapter focused on the basic of questioning. It began with an introduction to Bloom's Taxonomy and the use of questions and the process of questioning and answering to generate data related to subjective and objective question types. An examination of several exercises was given to highlight problems with thinking and decision making. All the examples were intended to highlight tricks of reasoning and problem solving as well as provide an opportunity for you to practice and hone your skills. It concluded with a discussion of essential questions and how they are used for assessment.

References and Other Resources

Additional examples and explanations are provided on Dr. Lipuma's web page at
   http://njit.mrooms.net/course/view.php?id=14403
Rusbult. C. (2001). Creative Thinking: in education. Retrieved on January 5, 2009, from:
   http://www.asa4.org/ASA/education/think/creative.htm
Stoddard, S. (2008). Realistic Lateral Thinking Puzzles. Retrieved on January 5, 2009, from:
   http://rinkworks.com/brainfood/latreal.shtml

Bill Gates: "How Do You Make a Teacher Great?" Part 1
  http://www.youtube.com/watch?feature=endscreen&v=OnfzZEREfQs&NR=1
Bill Gates: "How Do You Make a Teacher Great?" Part 2
  http://www.youtube.com/watch?v=BCSdlRNZmHw
Essential Questions
  http://www.greenville.k12.sc.us/league/esques.html
Leading Questions
  http://www4.uwsp.edu/education/lwilson/learning/quest2.htm
Review of Bloom's Taxonomy
  http://epltt.coe.uga.edu/index.php?title=Bloom%27s_Taxonomy
Review of Learn gin Assessment and Bloom's Taxonomy
  http://www.nwlink.com/~donclark/hrd/bloom.html
Test questions creation
  http://oct.sfsu.edu/assessment/measuring/htmls/objective_tests.html

Questions and Exercises

1. What is Bloom's Taxonomy and how does it relate to learning and questioning skills?
2. How is data related to questions and answers?
3. What type of creativity do you exhibit?
4. What are Essential and Leading Questions?
5. Make a square consisting of nine (9) dots arranged in three lines with three evenly spaced dots in each line. Connect all nine dots using four or less straight lines. Once you have started drawing, you may not lift your writing utensil or retrace any of the lines. Find more than one way to do this. As you create new ways of doing this, are you giving the same answer in different ways or truly new answers?

More Questioning Games

- A man is lying dead with a backpack on, face down in the desert. What happened?
- A man is found hanging in an otherwise empty locked room with a puddle of water under his feet. What happened?
- In the middle of the ocean is a yacht. Several corpses are floating in the water nearby. What happened?
- Bob, Carol, Ted, and Alice all live in the same house. Bob and Carol go out to a movie, and when they return, Alice is lying dead on the floor in a puddle of water and glass. It is obvious that Ted killed her, but Ted is not prosecuted or severely punished. Why?

Answers

Exercise 4.1

1. After the new Canon Law that took effect on November 27, 1983, would a Roman Catholic man be allowed to marry his widow's sister?

   The first inclination of some people who cannot think of a valid answer is just to guess. The most correct answer is 'no' because the man is dead. In order to have a widow he must be dead. This first question highlights misdirection and habits that one might have. Since the Cannon Law was mentioned, many people ignore the facts given in the question and start researching in order to find the answer in the law itself. This can lead to wasted time and effort.

   There are other answers that solve this by making the argument that in some other society a person can marry a dead man. Another one is that he faked his death or died medically but then was brought back. These answers are possible but not as acceptable as the first and require justification to be accepted.

2. A child is born in Boston, Massachusetts to parents who were both born in Boston, Massachusetts. The child is not a United States citizen. How is this possible?

   The suggested correct answer is that Boston, Massachusetts was founded before the United States was established. In order to know this, it is necessary to have knowledge about the history of America and its settlement. Without this knowledge, students often put forth alternatives that try to find reasons this could happen based upon the different key parts of the question—parents having human children born in the United States. Some say that the question is not about people. The people could be aliens from another planet or animals so that the rules of citizenship would not apply.

   Another possibility relates to the location Boston, Massachusetts. Some argue that the people having the children are in an embassy and so that citizenship does not apply. Along these lines Boston, Massachusetts could be in another country so none of the people would be citizens.

   Any of these answers could be acceptable. The most plausible is the first one, but this does not mean it is the only correct answer. In the end, convincing others of the correctness of the answer you provide by giving reasonable arguments is the only true test of correctness.

3. Before Mount Everest was discovered, what was the highest mountain on Earth?

   The suggested correct answer is that Mount Everest was still the highest mountain even though the fact was not known. The misleading part of this question is that people think of the second highest mountain in the world, such as K2, which was replaced by Mount Everest. They assume that the question is looking for another mountain and so look for the second highest mountain today without really working through the problem or trying to envision what mountains were known when Mount Everest was discovered or Mount Everest was labeled the highest.

Other answers also exist depending on how the words *before* and highest are interpreted. If highest means most amount of rise from the base and surrounding area, then Mount Everest is not as tall as many other mountains, such as Mount Kilimanjaro in Africa. Since Mount Everest is part of a range, the surrounding mountains are also very tall, and it is only the small peak of Everest that reaches to the higher level. Kilimanjaro was created by volcanic action and has no other peaks around it. In a similar fashion, how height is measured with regard to this definition is vital to the answer given. If, rather than just looking at height above sea level, it is measured from the initial rise from base; the volcanic islands of the pacific are far taller than Mount Everest. Mauna Kea, if measured from the bottom of the ocean, would be the tallest mountain on earth. (For more details on mountain heights see: *http://www.peakware.com/encyclopedia/highest.htm*

Another definition that can lead to differing answers is that of the word *before*. Since the length of time is not specified, it is difficult to know how long before the discovery the question is asking about. Depending on what theory of geological action or divine creation is used as authority, different mountains have risen and fallen over the past eons. Knowing which one is being referred to by the ambiguous term *before* is all but impossible. This question highlights the need to ask specific questions that avoid ambiguity in order to arrive at solutions that are clear and workable.

4. In what year did Christmas and New Year's fall in the same year?

The suggested correct answer is every year because New Years Day of 2004 and Christmas day of 2004 are both in 2004. This question tries to take advantage of a person's tendency to view things in the order they are given and so see that Christmas of this year is in a different year than New Year 's Day of the next. If one does not realize the fact that every year has a new year, then the trap works.

However, there is a subtler problem that this question illustrates. Having seen this trick, too often the search for an answer stops, and so a wrong answer settled upon. The answer "every year" does not work because of the situation that is specified by the question. In order for Christmas and New Year's Day to fall in the same year, both events need to have occurred. Christmas is predicated upon the celebration of the birth of Jesus. New Year's Day is predicated upon the existence of a calendar that has a New Year's Day that is celebrated. So the most correct answer is every year since both New Year's Day and Christmas have been celebrated. Do not stop thinking just because one pitfall or trick of thought was identified.

5. Which is correct to say: "The yolk of the egg are white" or "The yolk of the egg is white"?

The suggested correct answer is neither because the yolk of the egg is yellow. This trick seems straightforward; the question that is asked is wrong and looks for something that is misleading. However, since the question was not specific, it is impossible to know if the question seeks grammatical correctness or factual correctness. Grammatically, the answer is that the yolk is white. Factually, the yolk may be yellow if it is a chicken egg. Other eggs may have other color yolks. In either case, the meaning of "correct" must be specified. Once again, seeing the trick may satisfy the person seeking an answer. In this case, any answer should be qualified so that when it is given, the assumptions being made by the person giving the answer are understood.

6. A woman from New York married 10 different men from that city, yet she did not break any laws. None of these men died and she never divorced. How was this possible?

   The suggested correct answer is that she is the justice of the peace or the one performing the ceremony. The problem many face is that the word *marry* makes them think of the person participating in the marriage rather than the one conducting the ceremony. There are several other ways that this can be answered and often relates to the types of answers given for questions one and two. The most common answer relates to the idea that the women and the men are from another country or have moved to somewhere that allows multiple marriages. Others find a loophole by using annulment instead of divorce. One of the most creative answers given relates to the idea of a Broadway play in New York City that has a marriage as part of the plot. If an actress plays the part of the bride over many years and the groom is played by a number of different actors, she could technically marry 10 men. All of these answers can be deemed correct as long as a good explanation of the answer is given and all of the conditions of the question are satisfied. As with many of the previous questions, more creative explanations can be found that are different from the expected answer. This does not make the answers more or less correct, just different and more unique amongst the group that is providing answers.

7. Why are 1990 American dollar bills worth more than 1989 American dollar bills?

   The suggested correct answer is that there is 1 more dollar when you have $1990 than when you only have $1989. The trick for this question concerns how the numbers are read and how that changes the interpretation of the question. If the numbers 1990 and 1989 are read as years, then the word *dollar* is seen as $1. In this case, a much more complex answer must be found that identifies some economic rational for the variation in worth of money from one year to the next.

8. How many times can you subtract the number 5 from 25?

   The suggested correct answer is just once because then you are subtracting 5 from 20. The original creator of the question thought that many people would say 5 times because then the person subtracting would reach 0 and have to stop subtracting. Seeing this as the trick, many people put forth that the subtraction can be accomplished infinite times because you can use negative numbers. Another possibility also exists that would result in the answer "infinitely" since you can subtract 5 from 25 over and over again and each time arriving at the result 20 ($25 - 5 = 20$, $25 - 5 = 20$, $25 - 5 = 20$, $25 - 5 = 20$ . . .).

   There is a subtler trick to this question as well. If you examine the wording carefully, it asks how many times can **YOU** subtract. That is an entirely personal question. If asked to a two-year-old or someone who knows nothing about math, the answer may be none at all. For many students after subtracting once or twice, they might be tired or need a calculator or something else. Examining the question is vital to producing a correct answer, and in turn asking good questions is vital to obtaining a good answer.

9. If, having only one match, on a freezing winter day, you entered a room that contained a lamp, a kerosene heater, and a wood burning stove, which should you light first?

   The suggested correct answer is that you would light the match first. Ha ha . . . this seems like a ridiculous question. The trick is that the way it is asked, you are led to a choice between three alternatives, yet the fourth is the right answer. However, there is more at work here. If you look at the question, it leads you to many assumptions that are not necessarily true. Are any of the items operated with electricity? Is it dark out? Are you cold? Are any of them already lit? If it is dark in the room and the lamp is electric, you might light the lamp first just by turning on the switch. This question shows the importance of creating a good image of the situation before making decisions. Do not become misled by the way the question is asked, and do not simply accept things because the question gives a vague situation. Gathering accurate information can assist in arriving at the best answer.

10. Cathy has six pairs of black gloves and six pairs of brown gloves in her drawer. In complete darkness, how many gloves must she take from the drawer in order to be sure to get a pair that match?

The suggested correct answer is difficult to say because the definition of a matching pair is not given. This, like many other math questions, has a definite answer that can be calculated once the parameters are known and all the assumptions clarified. However, if different people define things differently, each answer may differ and still be thought of as correct. Assuming that you must have the same color to make a matched pair, then you must take three (3) gloves to get a pair. However, that is only one way of defining pair. What if you have left and right gloves that are different and must be taken into account when considering the idea of a pair. In this case, you must take out all the gloves that match one type and at least one of the other gloves to obtain a pair. This means that you must take out all of the left-handed gloves and at least one right-handed glove (or visa versa) in order to obtain a pair. This would be a total of thirteen (6 black left + 6 brown left + 1 more glove = 13 gloves)

The basic idea is that you must remove all the gloves that do not satisfy the condition plus at least one more to make the pair. The worst case would be if you wanted to obtain a pair of a specific color of glove with each hand being different. In that case, you would have to take out all of the other-colored gloves twelve (12); plus all of one hand of the color you wanted, such as the right-hand gloves, six (6); plus one (1), which equals 19 gloves total. As many students have pointed out, at that point just take the entire drawer or turn on the lights.

Exercise 4.2

The answers to the following questions are much more logical than the set presented in exercise 4.1. Reasoning through the situation presented and researching information can find an answer to each of these questions. There are still intellectual pitfalls to be avoided, but these questions have less tricks and more thinking dilemmas contained within each question. The wording and the image each question creates play a much greater part in the misdirection that each question presents.

There may be more than one correct answer. Each question is intended to assist the thinker in identifying the ways the answers are arrived at and different ways to examine a question and arrive at an answer. If an acceptable argument can be made for the answer given, it will be accepted, the answer given here is the most common given for each question.

1. Two fathers and two sons go hunting. Each shoots a duck and none shoot the same duck. When they get home and cook them, there are only three to eat. How is this possible?

The correct answer given for this question is that there are three generations present, a father, son, and grandson so that one member is both a father and a son. Other answers relate to the identification of one person that fits two categories. One such explanation is that the fathers and sons are not in the same family such that a father and his friend take the first father's two sons hunting. Though the second father has children, none came hunting that day. Though all shot a duck, the father and the two sons return to their home and cook the ducks while the other father returns to a different home.

Of course, some people try to find a way around this by saying that the people cannot count or that they lost a duck.

The reason for this question is to focus the thinker on asking why and how the situation could exist. Rather than try to find a way for four people to shoot three ducks, it is necessary to identify the assumption about the language and see where to focus thoughtful effort to find a solution.

2. A cowboy rides into town on Friday, stays three days, and leaves on Friday. How is this possible?

    The correct answer given for this question is that the cowboy is riding a horse named Friday. As with the first question, the assumption made by the reader regards the focus of this question. If you assume the wording "on Friday" refers to the day of the week, a great amount of effort is spent trying to figure out how that is possible. Some people try to say that there is a trick related to the calendar, the cowboy slept too long, or something equally as creative but not very realistic. If that assumption is identified early, then the somewhat more obvious answer can be found.

    Wording is very important and examining the wording of questions and rereading to be sure that the proper meaning is found is very important. Though this is simple, many mistakes, confusion, and wasted effort can be attributed to the lack of understanding between the questioner and the one seeking an answer.

3. Mom, Dad, and two kids have come to a river, and they find a boat. It is small and can only carry one adult or two kids at a time. Both kids are good rowers, but how can the whole family reach the other side of the river?

    The correct answer given for this question is purely mathematical and is the trick that exists in many different types of similar problems. Too often problem solvers look for direct paths to the answer. These types of questions require loops in which it is necessary to backtrack or even move in a sideways direction in order to finally attain the goal.

    The key for this game is to notice that the two children can each row the boat. Since there always needs to be a person in the boat to row it across the river or back, the first step is to get one child across the river and still have one in the boat to row it back; therefore, you send the two kids first and send one back with the boat. Then one of the two parents rows over and the other child returns with the boat.

    The next trick is that you have to repeat steps so that the solution will work. You need to send the two children over and send only one back with the boat again. Then sending the second parent over and repeating the steps from earlier will allow the four to make it to the other side of the river. To review:

2 children go across →	1 child rows back ←
1 Parent go across →	1 child rows back ←
2 children go across →	1 child rows back ←
1 Parent go across →	1 child rows back ←
2 children go across →	

Many times people cannot figure this out and try to find another answer. By avoiding the restrictions that are inferred in the question, other ways of getting everyone across can be found. Some say the parents should swim or have the kids hang on to the side of the boat. Others say that the parents should just shove the boat back across the river.

An important aspect of this type of problem is the ability to use the insights found here in other problems that are not exactly the same but use the same logical problem. Another problem like this deals with a farmer crossing a river. He has with him a hen, a fox, and a bag of corn. He can only take one over the river in the boat with him at a time. The problem is that if he leaves the fox alone with the hen, the fox will eat it; if he leaves the hen alone with the corn, the hen will eat it. Applying what was learned from the other boat problem, the farmer must find a way to keep the corn with the fox while he moves the hen. The only way to do this is to move things back and forth across the river, which includes bringing the hen to the far side, and then go back for the corn. Once the corn is over, the hen must be brought back. Though it is not exactly the same, the principle of moving things over and back or backtracking is essential to arriving at the solution. Just pushing forward does not always allow for a workable solution.

4. Three friends check into a motel for the night and the clerk tells them the bill is $30, payable in advance. So, they each pay the clerk $10 and go to their room. A few minutes later, the clerk realizes he has made an error and overcharged the trio by $5. He asks the bellhop to return $5 to the three friends who had just checked in. The bellhop sees this as an opportunity to make $2; as he reasons that the three friends would have a tough time dividing $5 evenly among them. Therefore, he decides to tell them that the clerk made a mistake of only $3, giving a dollar back to each of the friends. He pockets the leftover $2 and goes home for the day! Now, each of the three friends gets a dollar back, thus they each paid $9 for the room which is a total of $27 for the night. We know the bellhop pocketed $2 and adding that to the $27, you get $29, not the $30 that was originally spent. Where did the other dollar go?

   The correct answer given for this question is that there was no extra dollar. This question is asked incorrectly. It shows that math can be deceiving if the way the question is asked is itself incorrect. Too often people accept what is asked as it is asked and try to work within the restrictions without seeing if it makes sense. Many people try to put forth that there is some fraction of money lost or kept with one of the parties. The only real answer is that it is incorrect to add two dollars to the twenty-seven dollars paid. The correct way of calculating the price is to add two dollars to the twenty-five or subtracting the three dollars from the thirty dollars.

5. Because cigars cannot be entirely smoked, a hobo who collects cigar butts can make a cigar to smoke out of every 5 butts that he finds. Today, he has collected 25 cigar butts. How many cigars will he be able to smoke?

   The correct answer given for this question is that there are six (6) because each cigar smoked still leaves a butt and so five sets of five still leaves five butts that can then be smoked as a sixth cigar. This is another math problem that tempts you to find the easy answer and stop. By seeing that 25 divided by 5 is 5, many people stop. This seems very simple, but if you rush to find the answer without thinking the problem through and examining all the parameters and definitions, a mistake can be made.

Be sure to work a problem through long enough to arrive at the correct and most complete answer.

6. Two planes take off at the same exact moment. They are flying across the Atlantic. One leaves New York and is flying to Paris at 500 miles per hour. The other leaves Paris and is flying to New York at only 450 miles per hour (because of a strong head wind). Which one will be closer to Paris when they meet?

The correct answer given for this question is that the two planes arrive at the same place at the same time. Again, the math can be misleading because many people are habituated to respond to word problems such as this by calculating an answer. However, that is not what is asked. Common sense tells us that if two planes meet then they are at the same place and so neither is closer. However, this question depends on the concept of "meets." Once the nose of the Paris plane passes the nose of the New York plane, they have met. If this is accepted then, the Paris plane is closer because its tail is slightly less than one plane length closer to Paris at that point.

One important idea highlighted by this question is clearly defining terms and acceptable levels of accuracy. Not knowing what "meet" means leads to confusion. Also, is a few hundred feet compared to thousands of miles significant? In many situations, the degree of specificity or the significance of the measurements is vital to determining the correctness of answers. It is important to know how accurate to be in order to have your answer accepted as correct.

7. Maker doesn't want it; the buyer doesn't use it; and the user doesn't see it. What is it?

The correct answer given for this question is a coffin. There are other answers that also work. The important part of this question is to analyze the three clues "maker doesn't want it," "the buyer doesn't use it," and "the user doesn't see it." Each of these defines a broad category, and all that is needed is to determine something that can fit into all three. Though generally a coffin might work, the person who uses it may also be the one who bought it ahead of time so even this answer might not work. It all depends upon the way the argument for the answer is presented.

To find other solutions, some people look for things that the maker does not want such as pollution. Others find things that cannot be seen. In either case, the example must be tested by the other categories. All that is needed is an acceptable argument for any example that fits into all three categories and that answer is deemed acceptable. Pollution seems to work because it can be unseen by the user, but the problem arises when you try to justify the fact that the buyer does not want it. The argument put forth is that pollution is bought with any product that produces it, such as gasoline. As long as the one judging the answer agrees that pollution is not wanted by the maker and not used by the buyer, it works.

Thinking of things that cannot be seen is a good way to generate many different examples. To do this, it is necessary to think of various things that cannot be seen or reasons why a person using something might not be able to see it. If your eyes are closed, the thing is invisible, the item is imaginary, it's too small to be seen, and many other possibilities can be found for things that a user cannot see. Each of these can lead to examples to be tested. One of the most convincing ones is that the user is blind. If a sighted person makes a cane for a blind person and a sighted person purchases it as a gift for a blind person, then that cane could fit the question. Many other answers can be tested in the same way.

Questioning Games

For each of these there are some basic hints that will help. First, look for misleading words or phrases that make you assume something that is not true. Beyond that, it is important to narrow things by isolating what you know and identifying parameters of the situation. Recapping what you know can help. Finally, some of these things may not be real situations or may even be breaking rules assumed to be set for the game. Stepping back and thinking about the game, the situation and your own assumptions are vital to solving the problem. All of the questions can be answered with the yes and no questions, but it takes time, skill, and clear thinking.

1. A man leaves home, walks a short distance, turns left, walks a short distance, turns left, walks a short distance, turns left, and returns home. Who are the two masked men waiting for him when he gets there?

   The correct answer is that they are the catcher and the umpire in a baseball game.

   The problem for most people is that they think of a house when the word *home* is used. This question is easier to solve because it has many parameters that can be determined with yes–no style questions, such as the distance traveled, the type of mask, and other facts about the people. However, if a person has never seen a baseball game and knows nothing about it, the answer will be much more difficult to determine and the exact answer may never be found. Even so, just by asking questions, any person can determine a great deal about what is happening and then they would have to rely on YKWIM to connect the ideas he or she has with the actual situation.

2. A man stops at the red hotel and realizes he has gone bankrupt. What's happening?

   The correct answer is that he is playing Monopoly and has just lost.

   This is similar to the first one and leads to similar problems if the person asking the questions has never played or heard of Monopoly. Another problem arises from people who may have played another version of the game that uses different-color hotels as with the international version. In either case, the specific answer may differ, but the general answer given of a person playing a game can be arrived at.

3. A man lies dead in a room surrounded by 53 bicycles. Why is he dead?

   The correct answer is that he was cheating. Bicycles are a type of playing card and 53 cards means that there is one too many cards in the deck. One important concept that will help people is that "dead" can be different things. If a person dies accidently, then he or she is killed. If someone intentionally killed them, then it is murder. If he or she chose to kill him or herself, then it is suicide.

4. A man walks into a bar and asks for a glass of water. The bartender pulls out a shotgun and points it at him. The man says, "thank you" and leaves. Why?

   The correct answer is that the man has the hiccups and the bartender scared him with the gun. The shock cured his hiccups so he left.

5. The music stops, a woman dies. What happened?

   The correct answer is that the woman is a blind tightrope walker in the circus that does not use a net. She has been cheating on her husband, the Master of Ceremonies, and he has found out without her knowing. He plays the calliope and when the music stops it is supposed to signal to her that she has reached the end of the rope and it is safe to step off onto a platform. This time, he stops playing before she reaches the end so when she steps off the rope expecting to find the platform, she finds empty space and falls to the ground. She dies on impact.

This can be found out but takes persistent questioning. As the person answering the questions, you can adjust the details to make it easier or harder to find the answer as well as fill in details about who she is sleeping with and other less-important facts.

6. There's a man lying dead in a forest wearing scuba gear. What happened?

The correct answer is that the man was diving in a lake near the forest. There was a forest fire and a fire-fighting plane scooped him up when it drew water to put out the fire. He was scooped up and dropped on the fire. Supposedly this actually happened, but it may just be an urban legend.

7. Four people are dead in a cabin at the top of a mountain. What happened?

The correct answer is that the cabin is part of a small plane. The plane was caught in a blizzard as it crossed the mountain range and crashed into the side of the mountain killing everyone inside.

8. A man lies dead next to a rock. What's happening?

The correct answer is that the man is Superman, and the rock is kryptonite. An asteroid was headed towards Earth that would destroy everyone. He flew into space to destroy it. In the center of it was the fragment of kryptonite, which robbed him of his powers. After destroying the asteroid, he drifted to the moon and suffocated from the lack of oxygen.

This one is difficult because so little information is given and the story is about a fictional character. If the question askers know nothing about Superman this is much more difficult and may lead to vague answers.

9. Ned and Stacey. What's happening?

The correct answer is that it is not about anything. This is about the questions being asked. The person answering the questions should determine at the beginning what type of questions are answered with "yes" and which are answered with "no." Some common ways of doing this are questions beginning with a letter in the first half of the alphabet (A–M) are yes and the second half (N–Z) are no. Any type of distinction can be used. If the group is large and diverse, you can use all questions asked by women are yes and those asked by men are no.

The point of this is to show that sometimes the rules of the game are not exactly what you think. Do not get too focused just on the answers but look for a pattern in all aspects of the game and see if the answers make sense. It is necessary to always remain aware and test your assumptions.

10. A man dies of thirst in his own home. How is this possible?

The correct answer is that his house is a houseboat and he is in the middle of the ocean. A storm comes and disables the engine and the radio so he is trapped without enough water. After the first question, many may get caught trying to find another way to look at a home but do not think of a houseboat. Others may envision their home and try to find a way that he will die of thirst in a place similar to their own home. In either case, this makes the problem harder than it actually is.

Homework

A man is lying dead with a backpack on, face down in the desert. What happened?

The correct answer is that the man jumped from an airplane that was going down. He accidentally put on the backpack instead of a parachute.

A man is found hanging in an otherwise empty locked room with a puddle of water under his feet. What happened?

The correct answer is that the man was hung by a noose in the room standing on a block of ice by criminals to whom he owed money. As the ice melted he died from being strangled.

In the middle of the ocean is a yacht. Several corpses are floating in the water nearby. What happened?

The correct answer is that the people went swimming and the ladder was not lowered. They could not climb back aboard the boat and died of exposure.

Bob, Carol, Ted, and Alice all live in the same house. Bob and Carol go out to a movie, and when they return, Alice is lying dead on the floor in a puddle of water and glass. It is obvious that Ted killed her, but Ted is not prosecuted or severely punished. Why?

The correct answer is that Ted is a cat and Alice is a fish. Ted knocked the fishbowl off the counter that held Alice, who died on the floor.

CHAPTER 5

Basics of Effective Communication—Reading, Writing, Speaking, Thinking

Key Ideas of This Chapter

- What are the basic parts of the communication process?
- What are different ways of viewing the definition of communication?
- What are the areas to consider when communicating?
- How do you use words to create an illustration?
- What is tone, and why is the correct tone important?
- What is close reading?
- What are fatal errors?

Introduction to Communication

There are many different types of writing that can be encountered in daily life: letters, e-mails, memos, résumés, summaries, lab reports, essays, and research papers, just to name a few. The same can be said of types of public speeches: class presentations, interviews, news reports, seminars, and professional business presentations. Though all are written or spoken, they each take their own form and have their own requirements. In school assignments, all share similar methods for proper completion. This section gives some guidelines and pointers for working on these assignments. However one approaches the subject—making an outline, doing research, brainstorming, stream-of-consciousness writing, or improvisation—in the end, there has to be some thought given to the process to take this raw material and transform it into a finished product. This chapter begins with a common definition of communication and some insights into how each person might view it differently.

The term *communication* is one that is commonly used and is generally understood by most to involve the process of transmitting and receiving messages. However, the exact nature of what is communication changes as the perspective, level of detail, and situation change. By examining the process, we can reveal these levels of detail and present a new way of thinking about what is happening when people communicate, which is useful for understanding communication as a method of solving a problem rather than simply a description of a process of moving things, in this case a message.

Communication, in its most general sense, is the process of transmitting something from one place to another and usually involves conveying the message from one person to one or more other people. The process can be carried out in various ways. A good way to begin is to see that communication can be described as a process. A useful method to use when defining processes is to identify and name the parts of the process. Most people can easily identify the parts of this process and though the names may be different the concepts that represent the parts are usually the same: message, sender, medium, noise, audience, and feedback. However, just knowing the parts can still lead to a wide variety of definitions. Choosing a perspective from which to examine the process makes the process of defining and understanding much easier.

Due to the large amount of advertising and sales-driven communication in America, many students have become accustomed to being the target of messages and see communication from the perspective of the receiver. For our discussion, students will be creating the communication products so adopting the perspective of the sender is far more useful. In this case, the parts can then be defined as listed in the following paragraphs.

The sender is defined as the person or entity that is responsible for transmitting or is the source. The sender has a goal to be achieved and is the one that makes the decisions about what to send, how to send it, and if it has been received properly. This does not mean that other factors cannot affect the process, but the actions taken and outcomes reached are seen and measured from the perspective of the sender. Our entire discussion from this point on will focus on the needs and actions of the one who is transmitting.

From this perspective, the message is the thing to be transmitted such as information or data, but can also be emotions or other less tangible things. The sender is the one attempting to accomplish the transmission and is often the one who must craft the message.

The medium is the method used by the sender to transmit the message and can mean both the physical way it is sent, such as during a phone call, or the form that the message takes, such as written or spoken words. Once again, the sender is usually responsible for the choice of the medium that best serves to deliver the message so that communication is successful. Sometimes, the sender does not have access to the best medium and must use what is available. If you want to ask someone for a favor, you may think it is best to meet him or her in person. However, you may only be able to contact them by phone and feel that it is not as good. You might also be able to send them a text, e-mail, or even write a letter, but these seem like even worse mediums to use. For us, medium is the choice of how the message is conveyed (written, spoken, body language, etc.) and how that message is actually delivered to the receiver.

Noise is anything that interferes with the process of communicating. In a simple sense, this can actually be loud noises that are distracting or static on a phone line. These things keep the message from getting through in the way it was intended. In more complex situations, noise can be emotions, mental distractions, physical activity, personal interest, or any other factors that affect the way the message is transmitted and received. Many times, the sender cannot control the affects of noise but should anticipate these problems and craft the message and choose a medium that reduces the adverse consequences of noise. A good way to think about this might be to picture trying to talk to someone during a movie. If there are loud explosions, the message may not be heard. If the theater is too cold, the receiver may not focus on what you are saying so the message is not as effective. If the movie is so engrossing that the receiver does not pay attention to the message, the message may be ignored. All of these can be thought of as noise.

The term *audience* is a bit more difficult to discuss. As communication processes grew more complex and were studied, the term *audience* grew in scope. In its most general sense audience is anyone that the sender intends the message to reach or that receives it. However, for our purposes it is useful to break audience into several terms so that your job of communicating can be understood better and accomplished more easily and successfully. The first term is *target* or the specific person or group that the sender is directing the message towards and by whom the sender wishes to have the message understood and acted upon.

The bystanders would then be all those that surround the target at the place and time the message is directed toward the target, and usually the sender is aware of their presence. Receivers are anyone that the message successfully reaches independent of the sender's intent and the receiver's ability to understand the message. This can be seen in a classroom. When the teacher presents a lesson, the targets are all the students since that is who the message of the lesson is directed towards. If a student has brought a friend to class or someone else not in the class is in the room, they can be considered bystanders, who are part of the audience but not the target. If people are waiting in the hallway outside the class and hear the lesson, they would be receivers even though the message was not intended or directed towards them at all. In this example, some of the targets may not receive the message at all since they might be absent from class or just not paying attention. It is the job of the sender, the teacher in this case, to focus on transmitting the message to the targets in the way that is most likely to be received successfully.

Lastly is feedback, which refers to anything that the sender receives back from the recipients that is related to the message. This last idea is very important to discuss because many people feel that without feedback, communication is not happening. Feedback allows the sender to assess the effect of the message, the medium, and the process in general. For example, imagine you are sending a fax. If the sender of the fax does not receive a confirmation message, uncertainty may exist in the sender's mind. The feedback is not necessary for the audience to understand and act upon the fax, only for the sender to know it reached its destination.

Though the parts of the process have been described and a perspective chosen, the term *communication* can still have several different but mutually exclusive ways of being defined. To help better understand this, the following section discusses the transmission model applied to a radio station.

Transmission Model of Communication

The transmission model was designed around the concept of a phone call so that the system might be improved. If we imagine a radio station sending their signal to a group of listeners that might be in their broadcast range, it will assist us to see the levels of distinction that exist when different people think about what communication means. The station does not know if anyone is tuned in or listening. The question becomes how you see the process of communication with respect to this situation.

Listed here are five situations where you may feel communication is happening. If you are at level 1, then the other levels are more specified types of communication. If you are at level 5, then the other options are something less than communication and would be given a different name.

1. The radio station transmits signals and no one needs to be listening, tuned in, or even own radios as long as the station transmits. The core of this level is that as long as the sender transmits, then communication is occurring. However, some people feel more than transmission must occur.
2. Some feel the radio station must have radios in range that could receive, but they do not necessarily need to be turned on or tuned in for communication to be occurring. For this, the only difference is that there are receivers that might hear. The transmission must be sent and receivable but no real understanding is required.
3. For this, radios are tuned in but the language or the message may not be understood. Here the process of communication must be completed, but the receiver does not need to comprehend what is being sent. It is at this level where some will say that if the

receiver understands, then this is successful communication, otherwise it is communication but just not successful at what was attempted.

4. At this level, radios are tuned in and the listeners understand the message being sent. The idea that the receiver understands the message so there is a measure of comprehension in the definition is the key to distinguishing communication at this level.

5. At the last level, the radio station sends out a message and asks for listeners to call back. In this case, the feedback is vital to the process of communication. Without feedback, communication is not occurring.

Each person must decide for himself or herself which of these choices fits the conception of communication that he or she feels is best. There are, of course, other factors that can also be included in these five areas and the level of detailed increased. What is important to see is that each of these can be a valid way to define communication. If a person feels that number one is the way to define the term, then all the other things are some form of more effective communication. If someone feels that only number five is communication, then all the rest are something less, perhaps just transmission. What is more important than settling on a single right answer is having each person understand his or her own conception of the term and be able to see how others understand the term from their perspective. This common ground can then allow everyone to better understand one another.

Moving beyond the transmission model of communication, some see communication as a tool for accomplishing the goals of the sender. It is a means to a desired end—a method or tool for solving problems.

Communication as a Tool

If we move beyond the transmission model to a problem model of communication, the definition may be different. Communication may be a method or tool used to attain the goal of the sender by developing a package to influence a target. In this model, the package is the combination of the message and medium that will most effectively affect the target. The word *target* is used rather than *receiver* because in this view, the sender chooses the person or group to receive the message, anyone else is not an intended recipient and not really part of the conception of communication.

This may not be strictly a definition of communication but rather an interpretation for what communication is and how it is used. At its heart, this idea ties the many parts of the transmission model together and uses them to understand that communication is not static but rather a dynamic, continuous thing that must be used fluidly rather than understood at a single point in time. It is a continuous negotiation of shared meaning to achieve a goal that serves a purpose from the perspective of the sender.

Usually, the intent of the communication process is to have the message received successfully by an intended target, understood, and in many cases acted upon in the way the sender desires. Much of this all happens without conscious thought by you as a participant. However, using critical thinking can assist in improving your ability to communicate successfully and effectively. Knowing these aspects of the process is particularly important for you to think about when you are the sender. It becomes your responsibility as the sender to ensure that the process of transmitting the message to the audience is accomplished with the least noise and utilizing the proper medium. To do this, it is now necessary to examine writing and public speaking in more detail in order to increase your awareness of the types of things that you can do to increase the likelihood that your message reaches its target and is acted upon in the way you desire to accomplish your goal as the sender.

Moving from Creation to Completion

In order to communicate it is necessary to bring something new into existence and organize it so that the intended target will understand what you have created. There are many processes that can be used to create a message and also used to construct the means of delivery. These processes move the message from creation to the completed form of the product that allows the highest likelihood that communication will be successful. There are two major divisions, form and content. Form is the way the material is presented and the rules that are followed to give some uniform look to the work. Content is the ideas, facts, opinions, and other material that is used to accomplish the goal. There are four major steps under each of these two major divisions—creation, revision, editing, and proofreading—each focusing attention at smaller levels (see Figure 5.1). As one moves through the process from creation to proofreading, the message is moved from a personal set of decisions towards the criteria of outside judges.

More importantly, as you move from creation to proofreading, you move from a study that is more of an art towards one that is more of a science. Sciences tend to follow systems of rules to generate consistent outcomes. Many students are more comfortable with the science of writing by following the rules of grammar to ensure that the work meets some external standard. Others do not have the patience to follow all the rules or are not aware of how to use them so when the message is judged by the outside standards, problems arise. On the other hand, an art draws upon less-tangible, subjective criteria and personal judgment or a feel for the way to proceed. Arts are usually more personal and judged by different, less-objective criteria that change by each person's taste. The most difficult task for any communicator is to balance the personal tastes for the art and the more practical concerns of the science so that the target is most likely to receive the message while the sender can still satisfy the artful side of creating the message. Now, let us look at each of these in more detail.

Creation is the step in which material is generated. This material can be original work, experimental data, research, or any other message that is generated by the sender. The next step is to revise this mass of raw material. During revision, the materials that have been created are adjusted to help accomplish the sender's goal as well as make the entire work more

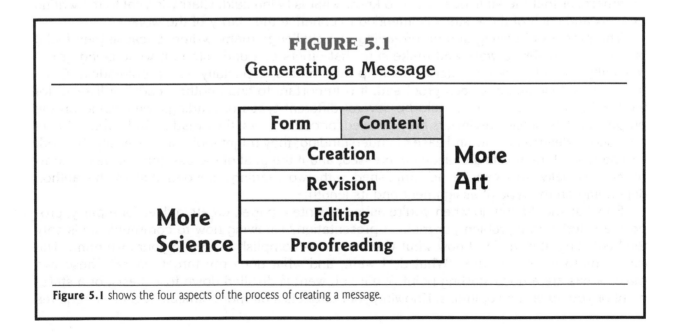

FIGURE 5.1
Generating a Message

Form	Content	
Creation		**More Art**
Revision		
Editing		**More Science**
Proofreading		

Figure 5.1 shows the four aspects of the process of creating a message.

easily understood by the audience. During the revision step some of the raw material is cut away and disposed of while others may be changed subtly to make it flow better or fit the purposes of the author. This step also highlights the areas where more raw materials must be created. Both creation and revision tend to be larger-scale processes that look at sections of a work and major ideas. These are more of an art and focus on the individual's expertise and personal choices. As one moves the finished product closer to completion and works to deliver it to an outside audience, the process moves more towards the science of communicating. The finer work of transitions, sentences, and detailed proofreading are worked on during the other two parts of the process that have more rules and guidelines to assist with this.

Once the basic framework of the package is in place and almost all of the necessary material has been created and organized, editing can begin. Editing is the process of examining the work at the level of sentences to correct errors and smooth out the flow so that the content can be understood more easily. During editing, areas that might need more revision can be highlighted. Editing can also involve movement and rearrangement of sentences within and among paragraphs to better accomplish the desired goal.

Lastly, proofreading is undertaken once the work is thought to be finished. Proofreading is the process of removing small errors in grammar, syntax, spelling, punctuation, or other such rules-related matters. It is at this stage that the little changes can be made to polish the work for final submission. During editing and proofreading, adjustments in word choice can be made to improve the clarity of the work to enhance the way the message will be received.

One good rule to follow is the Rule of 2. Each sentence must have at least two words to be valid, and each paragraph needs to have at least two sentences to be correct. In the same way, each section should have at least two paragraphs. If sub-sections are used there must be at least two sub-sections for each major section and so on. If the Rule of 2 is violated, material must be added, or the structure of the paper should be adjusted to fix the problem.

Another important item to catch with proofreading is lack of consistency with abbreviation and capitalization. It is important to abbreviate and capitalize words the same way throughout a paper. The first time an abbreviation is used the way it is to appear throughout the rest of the paper it should be included in parenthesis after the word. If this is not done properly, confusion can arise. For example, the United States (US) is how this might appear in the paper. However, if the words were not capitalized, the abbreviation would be very confusing (us). How and when you abbreviate is still the author's prerogative; however, it is important to remember that the audience needs to know what is being said. Clarity is vital to the writing process and each of these steps is intended to enhance the clarity of the work.

The process of editing and proofreading can challenge many writers because they feel it is difficult to review a work and make sure that others can understand it while being grammatically correct. Often a writer seeks help from others, especially with proofreading. Once the work is done and has been proofread, it is important to find another reader or listener for feedback. In general, there should be several different types of readings, depending on the purpose. Some outside reviewers may be used for correctness; they read to find errors. Others are used to determine flow and ease of understanding; they might look for how easily the work can be read, if the points are clearly expressed, and if the goal of the assignment was accomplished. Usually, this can be accomplished with two readings beyond that of the author, depending on the type of assignment and its length.

So what should you do when you're asked to write a paper, create a flyer for a party, propose a solution to a problem, or make a presentation? Knowing how to communicate is only the beginning. It is vital to know what you want to accomplish clearly in your own mind. The questions to remember are, "What do I want, and what does my target want?" These two major areas are a good starting point. What you want is distilled down to a thesis, or a statement of your ideas and opinions. Knowing your target is a bit more difficult because it requires you to think about how to transfer your message to another and have that person or persons understand and agree with them. This is easier said than done.

Knowing About MIMES and TRIBES

The place to start when communicating is to think about your goal, your target, and your package, which may be revealed by some simple questions such as: what is your message, who is the message meant to reach, how do you plan to reach the correct target, and what will increase the likelihood that the target will act on it in the way you want? The essential task is to increase the likelihood of getting your desired end-result. Once you have some idea of this, you can formulate your message more effectively and determine how best to deliver that message to your target. The combination of your message with the method of delivery (medium) is your end-product or package. By asking yourself several questions, you can begin to clarify the methods of persuasion that might work and what should be included in your package. The package is whatever you expect to send the target that accomplishes your goal. This process can be separated into two parts—what you know about yourself, and what you know about the target (the person or group with whom you are trying to communicate). When trying to communicate successfully and achieve a goal, it is important to remember that MIMES and TRIBE will assist in increasing the likelihood of successful communication. MIMES helps focus your attention on things you desire and can control or anticipate. TRIBE deals with information and decisions related to the target you identify.

Begin by considering MIMES—Message, Intent, Means, End-Result, and Success. The first step of the communication process is to think about these five aspects of the process, beginning with the message you wish to send. As mentioned, message can be whatever you want to transmit—facts, data, information, ideas, emotions, or anything else. The message can always be adjusted after considering the other aspects, but it is often easier to begin by knowing what you want to convey. The message is often the most creative part of the process since it needs to be generated in written or graphic form by you. Though many times parts of it can be found in templates or prepared materials, such as word processing programs, the final package is unique because you have adjusted the form and content to convey exactly the message you intend to send in the way you feel will best achieve your goal and influence the target. Though it may sound odd, the message is the first thing you can consider, and it will most likely continually change and be adjusted by each of the subsequent things you consider since how you say something affects how it is received and interpreted. Thus, it is important to always go back and check that the message is still conveying what you intended to convey at the end of all your changes and reconsiderations.

Next is intent, which has two parts—purpose (why you want to send the message) and target (who you think the message should reach). In its simplest sense, purpose is why you have decided to send the message. Often the reasons are not apparent without some reflection. Also, many times these reasons never are revealed to anyone but the creator and sender of the message. The other part of intent deals with your target and what person or group you intend the message to reach. It is important to think of all those that will come in contact with the package and know on whom you are focusing your efforts in order to ensure that target can access, understand, and act on the message properly. The message and surrounding package will have to be different for different targets in different situations. If the target is expected to hear the message, it will be different than another target that reads it via a computer program or on a sheet of paper. Knowing more about your target, his or her skills, and the way the package will be accessed and used is an important part of crafting it so the message is conveyed correctly and effectively.

The next thing to consider is means, or the methods you will use to deliver the message to the intended target. How you deliver the package is a key part of its successful reception. Sending a written document via FedEx is very different from giving a formal oral presentation utilizing PowerPoint and models, which is different from sitting in a bar talking to someone. Knowing how the message is to be sent is a significant part of the process of communicating successfully. The resources at your disposal, the message you are sending, your target's expectations, and your intent, among many other factors, can all affect the means used to deliver the message. In addition, the means chosen can convey more about you than just the message itself. Sending a great proposal in an unprofessional or sloppy way can lead to poor reception. This can be seen most vividly when submitting a résumé to a prospective employer. Not knowing the proper form or sending your message with mistakes or on inexpensive, unprofessional stationary can cost you the interview and the job even if you are highly qualified and have a great deal of pertinent experience. Some questions that help clarify means are, "what resources are available to create and deliver the message, what medium is best in order to convey the message to the target, and how will the package be delivered to the target?"

Once you have these ideas in mind, it is important to consider the ends you hope to achieve or the end-result that you hope to attain. Sometimes the communication is intended to persuade the target of something, such as to buy a product, while other times it is only to make the target aware of your existence or provide your opinion on an issue. Considering what type of feedback or response you hope to receive from the target is important when constructing the message and determining the method of delivery with some idea of what you expect the target to do and how you might know about it.

Finally is the idea of success—what you hope to get back so that you know the communication process was received by the target and acted on in the way you had intended. Considering what constitutes success will help you gauge if the message has reached the proper target and if that target is acting upon it in the way you intended. We all have seen many advertisements in our lives. They have a wide range of purposes and methods of gauging response. However, in the end, even if you enjoy watching an ad and remember it, if the ad does not make you buy the product or service, it has not been successful. Having a means for judging or knowing the amount of time to wait until a proper response is achieved is vital to the creation of a package. Sometimes, the sender needs an immediate response, while other times, the entire purpose of the package is to inform others, and the sender never knows the message was successful until a second, third, or more packages are sent far off in the future to the same target.

All of these considerations, with some more-detailed concepts that follow, help to determine what and how you handle the communication process as you create and send the package containing your message. However, there is more to be concerned with and other questions that must be answered. Now that you have an idea about what you want to send, it is vital to think about the target and what will be best received by that person or group as you create the final product. This includes all the aspects of what is being conveyed and how it reaches the target. You need to think about what the other person wants and how the target might respond. In order to do this you should consider your target and strive to find out more about how to construct the end product or package so the communication process will be successful. The key here is to consider how the target can be best reached and persuaded so that your own interests can be best served. One way to help this is to find out more about the preferences of the target and the exact situation that surrounds your target when the message is received. To do this, remember **TRIBE**—Target, Relationship, Influences, Background, and Environment.

We begin with the target you have chosen. It is vital to know the person or persons to whom you will attempt to deliver the package. Finding out the name and position of the correct person is vital in many instances because selecting the wrong target or just assuming that anyone who gets the message will be appropriate can lead to less-successful communication or even complete failure. The more details you have about the focus of the communication process, the more the package can be tailored to the target increasing your likelihood of success.

Next is the relationship you have established with the target. This may be considered networking or a working relationship. Having a clear picture of how you are viewed by the target and recognizing that, though you know the target, the target may not know you, are important to understanding how to craft an effective package. Another aspect of relationship is the connection you have with the message and how the target will perceive you as you attempt to deliver the package. In some cases, you are part of the package so the message will be colored by how the target views you, your purpose, and your overall competence; therefore, relationship becomes important to identify and utilize effectively.

Next, it is important to assess what will influence the target to do what you wish. The first thing to consider is what will help convince the target to receive the package, access it properly so the message has a chance to be delivered, and, finally, do what you want. Beyond this, it is important to choose your methods of persuasion wisely and appropriately for the target and the situation. Knowing when to use reason and when to appeal to emotion is vital to being able to influence the target. This will be discussed more when the topics of persuasion and tone are explained. Another thing to consider is the people that will be surrounding the target. Many people consider the important people in the audience stakeholders. A stakeholder is someone that has an interest in the communication process. The audience can be anyone that hears the message. For our purposes, the target is the person or group to whom you have chosen to send your message, whether that was the correct choice or not. Sometimes it is as important to sway those around the target, as it is the target itself. Audience, as it is used here, relates to the concept that the target might be part of a larger group that you are not thinking of reaching specifically but that can influence the target to react in the way you wish. Many times, convincing the larger audience is also important when trying to sway the specific target of the communication process. Think about a comedy on television; the laugh track is designed to cue you by having those around you laugh, thus making it more likely that you will laugh. Similarly, many live performers put people in the audience with you to engage you by having them cheer on cue or laugh at the right times. Knowing who will be with your target is useful and powerful information.

A vital aspect of research that needs to be assessed relates to the target's background, or the conditions that lead to the moment of delivery and the knowledge and abilities of the target. If you know the person you will be speaking to and he or she is expecting the message, the delivery may be very different from the case that arises when you have no idea who your message will reach or even if he or she is expecting it. What has proceeded the exact moment that the target is exposed to the message both physically and mentally? The time frame you had to prepare, the resources available, and many other factors concern the background of the package and thus change how it will appear and be received. If the target is expecting the package or perhaps has specifically requested it from you, the outcome will need to be different than if the target knows nothing about what is being presented. Another aspect of background deals with the knowledge, abilities, and skills of your target. If you send an e-mail to someone who does not know how to access the Internet or use color-coded slides with someone that is color blind, the package has less likelihood of being successfully received and acted upon. A third aspect of background is knowing if your target has been exposed to similar packages previously and how these packages have been acted upon by the target. Many times, your communication is excellent; however, three people before you have presented the exact same thing. In this case, knowing this piece of background knowledge could assist you by preparing you to give something of equally high quality but in a different form so it looks fresh to the target. It is difficult to know all of the background of your target, but the more research you can do and more information you can gather will help you as you craft your final package.

Finally, is the environment or the setting in which the package is received. It deals with the physical conditions and environment that will surround the target when the message is delivered. This can be the physical characteristic of the location: temperature, size, shape, lighting, and presence of windows. It is also related to anything in the space that has an effect on the target such as: available technology or equipment, time of day, food being served, or ambient noise. You need to plan for anything that affects the message and its delivery at the time it is being delivered. Really this question asks you to imagine where and when the message will be delivered and what the situation at that point looks like. These factors can have a profound effect on the way the message is received and acted upon. Imagine giving a presentation in a huge auditorium to hundreds of people; in a noisy, smoke-filled bar; or directly to the president of a company in his or her office. These three settings would demand different methods of delivering the message in order to increase the likelihood of success.

All of these questions may not ensure that you are successful, but knowing the answers can increase the likelihood that you will succeed. Taking the time to think about these aspects helps you craft the end product most successfully so that the message and medium work together to attain your goal in the way you wish. A good way to understand the audience of which your target is a part and find ways to adapt the package to that situation is to use audience analysis.

EXAMPLE 5.1
Thinking about a Homework Assignment

Look at a written homework assignment given to you in class. By looking at the assignment, you can answer many of the questions that have been raised. Using the questions discussed when considering MIMES and TRIBE, you will more closely meet what is expected and more effectively create and present your answers. In the end, this helps you become more successful. The process begins with understanding MIME. Some questions related to this ask:

- What message am I sending?
- Who is supposed to get the message?
- What, if anything, is my target expecting?
- When and where will they get it?
- How does it get to them?
- What does it look like when it arrives?
- What will they do with it?
- What do I get back if I did this correctly?

These are just some of the questions that help illustrate what needs to be asked. Fortunately, most assignments help the student answer these questions if time is taken to look at the instructions. The requirements are set down by the person evaluating it. Often these things are given in course syllabi or the assignment sheet itself. By understanding what is being asked for and what must be included in the written work, you can eliminate problems. The next step is to look at the target of the communication. Writing professionals call this audience analysis, and in this case the audience is your professor or the person grading the assignment. By stopping to think about who is going to read or hear what you have to say and then working to make sure those people receive the message properly, the entire act of communicating can be more effective.

Next you should think about your purpose. Most assignments are given to either teach or demonstrate how much has been learned. By knowing this and assessing your own purpose, the end result will be easier to produce. In many cases, the only purpose is to get something done so it is accepted. Honestly identifying the purpose and knowing what the audience will accept can allow for better results and less wasted effort.

Lastly is the package. Once the work has been completed, it is important to determine how the audience wants the message delivered as well as ensure that the proper message has been created. If the assignment asks for a research essay that is double-spaced and you provide a summary that is single-spaced, it is wrong. The package is vital to successful communication. Though all of the aspects are important, in the end, only the package—the blend of message and method of delivery—is helpful. It is the package that is being sent and is the thing that will be measured to see if the process is successful.

It is important to spend more time on the discussion of your target, known as audience analysis. Knowing more about both your specific target and the larger group that the target is part of is vital to increasing one's likelihood of success. To do this, many people have put forth things to consider about your target, much of which is covered by MIMES and TRIBE. The web page: *http://www.selfgrowth.com/articles/Laskowski4.html* gives a useful mnemonic device to assist with questions to ask about your target to increase your likelihood of success. You should always think about your **Audience: A**nalysis, **U**nderstanding, **D**emographics, **I**nterest, **E**nvironment, **N**eeds, **C**ustomized, and **E**xpectations. The more one knows, the better and easier it can be to craft a package that works, but nothing is a guarantee. These particular questions focus on oral reports but can also be used when considering written or multimedia delivery of a message.

So what does this all mean for you? The more you need to communicate and have your ideas understood by others, the more you have to think about what that other person might want. The more you know about all of these aspects, the better. Also, the less you know the more you may need to do ahead of time. Once you have some knowledge of what you want to convey and the target you are aiming at, it is necessary to begin creating the package. This will often start with the words you use and how you construct the meaning of the message in the mind of the target. In Chapter 2 we discussed the importance of words and the connotations and denotations of how you define them. However, words can be used to create images in the minds of the targets.

Using Words to Create Illustrations—Examples, Similes, Metaphors, Analogies, and More

Just as visual images can help to illustrate and illuminate a topic, so can words. Images are figures, and words that create images in the mind are figures of speech. Though there are many things to know about these ideas, for writing essays, it is more important to understand some aspects of figures of speech more than others. No matter what type you use, a figure of speech is intended to clarify a connection by using words to compare two things. The key is that the comparison being drawn is accurate, useful, and relevant. Accuracy means that the connection between the two things is correct as well as connects two things that are more similar than different. Useful means that the connection being drawn actually clarifies and does not confuse the connection being illustrated. Finally, relevant means that the target will understand the comparison and connection being drawn.

The first means of illustration with words is by example, or simply giving a typical representative of something. This does not always clarify things because examples can be difficult to find and not everyone is familiar with every example. Beyond examples, figures of speech, such as simile or metaphor, can be used to compare two things that are not alike. These both compare one thing to another directly: a simile uses "like" or "as" when making the comparison, whereas metaphors do not. Beyond this is the use of analogy, in which the connection between two known things is used to illustrate a connection between two other things. Many people are familiar with analogies from the SAT or other such achievement tests. There are many typical types of analogies, and all can be helpful when trying to explain something.

EXAMPLE 5.2
Analogies and Extended Metaphors

In a presentation, you can show an example of what you are trying to explain to the audience. In writing, you must use words.

Direct comparison: "The hat is as blue as a blue jay." This is a direct comparison because it provides a description of something I assume you know of and can relate to directly. As the connections move away from direct comparison, using analogy and metaphor can help clarify but must be done well.

Simple analogy: "He swallowed the hotdog like a snake swallowing a mouse." If you have no idea what a snake swallowing a mouse looks like, this makes no sense and does not clarify.

The following link has more information about analogies to assist you as you try to understand, create, and use them to clarify your communication.

http://www.fibonicci.com/verbal-reasoning/word-analogies/examples-types/

The most difficult figure of speech to create and use is an extended analogy or metaphor that tries to connect one complex situation or topic to another so that many aspects of the concept can be understood in more common and simple terms. Several parts of the topic can be connected to one large set of ideas so that the theme of the situation works to make the unknown topic more familiar. As the relationship grows more complex and the number of connections increases, so does the difficulty of creating a good analogy for your target to understand. Adding to the difficulty is the level of understanding and sophistication of the target. Just because the connection is clear to the sender does not mean it will be clear to the target. It is vital for the sender to put him- or herself in the place of the target and create connections that make sense to that target. If done well, an extended analogy can be effective and be used to tie an entire work together or illustrate a complex point to a less-advanced audience. Usually these types of analogies do not stand alone and are supplemented with explanations so that the illustration assists the target to understand the complex topic more clearly.

One simple example of this might be to compare the layers of the Earth to a peanut M&M. If I just say this, the connection I am seeking may not be clear. However, if I go on to say that each has three basic layers, it might be clearer. The candy shell is like the Earth's crust, the chocolate filling is like the Earth's mantle, and the peanut center is like the Earth's core.

Obviously, this is not a direct comparison, and it is not a perfect analogy. However, if my target is a group of small children, this connection can be enough for them to understand the idea of layers and to remember how the Earth is broken into layers. Unfortunately, if one is not careful, an analogy like this might lead some people to think the Earth is filled with chocolate and has a peanut at the center.

There are other figures of speech and ways to use words to create images that describe and explain. More than just making the connection or showing something, words must be used carefully and wisely to be effective. Beyond just creating figures of speech, words can convey feeling and emotion as well. Due to this, it is important to discuss tone of speech.

What Is Tone and Why Use It?

In addition to the methods previously listed to enhance your message, you can also change how the message is interpreted by changing your tone. *Tone* has many meanings, but, essentially, it is the words, repetition, voice affectations, and gestures used by the sender when conveying the message to the target, including choice of vocabulary, pauses, movement, and even physical gestures that give the target a sense of the sender's state of mind. It is as essential to the delivery of your message as the content itself. It is what gives the readers or viewers a true depth of the words, and helps them to visualize what is being said.

Tone is what differentiates a powerful message from a mediocre one by improving emphasis and the persuasive power of the package. Without a proper tone, however, the message might be less effectively delivered because what is being said does not match how it is presented within the package. This is key to both written and spoken messages. While presenters have the benefit of varying their style of presentation with physical gestures, writers have an even bigger responsibility for selecting proper tone. The key is that proper tone helps convey the message effectively and appropriately.

According to toolsforwriting.org, a website serving writers, "just as listeners make assumptions about your personality by observing how you dress and act and by listening to the tone of your voice, readers make judgments about your personality and feelings regarding a subject based on what and how you write." If an inappropriate tone is chosen, the entire message may be dismissed by the reader as being subjective or underdeveloped. Choosing a proper tone allows a writer to build a rapport with his or her audience by displaying the maturity and knowledge that is evident in writing style and presentation of ideas. Accordingly, tone also depends on the writer's knowledge about subject matter and his or her background.

How to Increase Emphasis and the Effect of a Message with Tone

There are several ways to achieve different levels of tone for the same message. The three major methods deal with the words used, the number of modifiers added to the sentence focusing on the problem, and the comments attacking the target directly. The first thing to know is the level of formality being used. For this discussion of tone, we will consider formal tones. If you are speaking informally, the word choice is the first thing to examine. One of the easiest ways to see this is with complaints you might make. When you are complaining about things, you can state your problem very directly:

Less formal: "I'm pissed that there ain't enough parking."
More formal: "There is not enough available parking."

The more formal simple statement conveys the message but does not reveal your emotion or the strength of your convictions. One of the first steps to aid in this is to add emotional words such as *angry*, *disappointed*, *dismayed*, or others conveying levels of disappointment. "I was upset to find that there is not enough available parking," is different from "I am horrified to find that there is not enough available parking."

You can also add more modifiers to each thing being modified and to other aspects of the sentence to strengthen the tone even more: "I was extremely upset to find that there is a complete lack of parking as promised." Taken even further, you can add multiple modifiers that reinforce the same feeling. This redundancy helps reinforce the strength of your words: "I was extremely upset and angered to find that there is a complete lack of parking as promised, causing me to become physically ill with outrage." Let us hope that parking is not such a big issue for you, but it is a way to let the target know your message is important to you.

Last is the idea of focusing on the target directly. Including personal words, such as *you*, or mentioning a personal responsibility, makes the tone personal and more serious or stronger: "Your inability to provide sufficient parking shows your incompetence."

When the three are combined, the complaint becomes extremely powerful: "I was incredibly shocked, angered, and outraged by your utter incompetence and flagrant disregard for your responsibility to provide sufficient parking, which obviously shows your lack of qualification for even this simple task." It is important to realize that sometimes if you move to a powerful statement when it is not warranted, the target may react badly and not read or listen further. How you use tone and level of formality is important because it can affect the way the message is received and acted upon.

Persuasion

One last thing that is related to both tone and your message is the ability to persuade with content and method of delivery. When attempting to persuade, finding the balance between appealing to the mind and reasoning of the target versus appealing to the emotions of the target can be useful. When appealing to reasoning, facts, arguments, and logical support are given to increase the weight of evidence through the large number and quality of reasons to do something. The greater the number of good reasons and the better each reason is, the more likely the target is to agree. On the other hand, if you are appealing to emotion, the power to persuade rests with getting the target to feel something that sways that person to act the way you want due to the consequences. The two most powerful emotions and means to persuade relate to fear and desire. When tapping into a target's fear of something, such as death, loss, or injury, the associated emotions can move him or her to act the way you want. The other emotion is desire or greed. By tantalizing a target with rewards, the target's desire will lead him or her to do what you want. In either case, the emotional means of persuasion is powerful and often what many advertisements aim to attack.

Both reason and emotion can be effective but have different situations that make them more or less so. Reasoning usually works best in settings that deal with arguments and debates that have a logical basis, are not pressed for time, and do not have emotional content. When you write a paper for class, logical arguments work well. Logical arguments, if accepted by the target, tend to be long lasting. Emotion works better when the issue has highly opinionated followers and can be related with passionate words and actions. Emotions tend to capture the target and move him or her in line with the persuader, but once the stimulus is gone, so is the persuasion. Unlike reasoned arguments, the emotional means of persuasion can lose effect much sooner, and the target can more easily revert to his or her previous feelings.

Conclusion

The material in this chapter was meant to introduce some general ideas and rules to follow. Each communication process needs to be undertaken by the individual. There is no one answer that can be memorized and then used every time. The act of writing is difficult because it begins with the art of creation. However, this can be made easier by practice.

As students, workers, and citizens, the need to communicate effectively is ever-present. Though not everyone needs to be spectacular at this skill, improving one's ability to communicate in all forms will assist you to be more employable and give you an edge in the information age. Moreover, if you become a more efficient communicator and spend a little time practicing now, you can complete the tasks of communication more quickly and effectively throughout your life. Rather than dread having to write and speak in public, you will know that you can do it effectively, and if you do not like it, be finished with it more quickly. If you enjoy it, the material here can help you see the distinctions in the various types of writing and help you to be more than competent in the processes of communication.

SUMMARY

This chapter discussed a variety of aspects of communication. It begins with a discussion of the process of communicating in all forms. It then moves to more specific details of how to create and send an effective communication package, combining the message with the appropriate medium. The mnemonic devices MIMES and TRIBE—Message, Intent, Means, End-Result, and Success; and Target, Relationship, Influences, Background, and Environment. were presented and discussed.

Questions and Homework

1. What are the different parts of the process for creating a message? What is the difference in the art and science of communication?
2. Why is audience analysis important? Perform an audience analysis for a commercial on television or in the print media. How are the audiences different? How are the approaches taken the same and/or different? Do you think the package was successful? Did you receive the message? What would you have done differently to send the message more effectively?
3. What does MIMES and TRIBE mean, and how can they assist in crafting a package to deliver your message? Use this to examine a class assignment.
4. What does each letter in the device A.U.D.I.E.N.C.E. represent? Why is that useful when analyzing your target?
5. What are typical assignments you are given in school? How are the requirements, purpose, and measurement of success for each different? Do you change your thinking for each type of assignment? How can thinking about this lead to better success on each assignment?
6. why are words and how hey are used important to communication? How can you use words to create images, enhance meaning, adjust the feelings of your target or persuade?

References and Other Readings

Additional examples and explanations are provided on Dr. Lipuma's web page at
http://njit.mrooms.net/course/view.php?id=14403
Selfgrowth.com. (2008). A.U.D.I.E.N.C.E. Analysis. Retrieved on January 5, 2009, from:
http://www.selfgrowth.com/articles/Laskowski4.html

Other Web Links

Choosing and writing for an audience:
http://facstaff.gpc.edu/~shale/humanities/composition/handouts/audience.html
Considering the gender difference of your audience and using humor to improve your
presentation.: *http://www.public-speaking.org/public-speaking-articles.htm*

CHAPTER 6

Written Communication

Key Ideas of This Chapter

- What should be considered when writing?
- How do you distinguish different types of graphics, and how do you use them?
- What are different graphical methods for conveying a message or representing data?
- What are the types and parts of different types of writing?
- How do you evaluate the quality and usefulness of different sources of information?
- What makes a good résumé and cover letter?
- What makes a good summary?
- What makes a good proposal?

What You Say and How You Say It

If you did not care about anyone else understanding what you meant, as long as you were happy knowing what you had in your own mind, you would be effective at communicating. But as soon as someone else is involved, the need to consider that person becomes important. At the heart of successful communication is the idea of picturing something in your mind and then finding a way to create that same image or understanding in the mind of the target. It is tough to do and most of the time there is no guarantee that you will be right. This is the art of communicating and why so many people find it difficult. Hopefully, knowing some of the things to ask and consider will help. Reading and following instructions and listening to others is a good start. In school, paying attention and asking a few simple questions like those listed previously should help reduce some of the uncertainties. Knowing the methods that follow for tailoring your package will assist you to be a better communicator.

The first step is to begin to craft the message. In order to do this, there are two parts to think about: what you say and how you say it. What you say relates to the content of the message and is dependant on the situation, the assignment, and the needs that the message has for its sender. Determining some of these questions of content will be addressed later in the chapter. In order to communicate most effectively what you say is as important as how you say it. By changing the appearance of text, and adding in visual representations of data and information, you can augment the communication process. Below are some of the tools you will need as you answer the question of how to send your message so that you can increase the likelihood of accomplishing your own goals.

The first means that people use to assist in delivering the message is to change the graphical style or appearance of the words themselves. Most word processing programs and other software packages come with a wide variety of fonts and other means of changing their appearance. The first column of the table below shows different font sizes. With current display and printer technology, a font size of 7 is the smallest people can read. Some material such as legal disclaimers, offer restrictions, and expiration dates are sometimes listed in even smaller font, but this is often an attempt to include them without them being recognized or read clearly (as can be seen in the 5-point font used in the first row of the table). In oral reports and presentations, text should rarely be smaller than 24-point font to be readable.

The second column of the chart talks about font style, or typeface. Most typewriters and old-style printing was done in Courier, which has a fixed width and looks blocky. This was done to increase readability and make setting the type easier since each letter occupied the same space. With the advent of computers, different standards were adopted and more options were presented. One thing to look for in the font is how readable the font is. There are three major types shown below: serif, san serif, and fancy or custom fonts. Serif fonts are those that have edging or little hanging lines so that each letter is more visible to the reader and more able to be distinguished at a smaller size. San serif means that these marks are not included. Fancy or custom fonts are not written in a plain style that looks like traditional typewritten text Serif fonts are considered more professional and formal. Times New Roman and Georgia are two very common serif fonts that are included with almost all software packages. Aerial and Helvetica are two very common san serif fonts that are included with almost all software packages. As can be seen there can be more than one option for a general font family, such as Aerial and Aerial Black. Finally, the fancy fonts that can be any style the creator wishes. These are used for special applications and can be extremely informal. For essays, research papers, and resumés, it is suggested that the sender use a serif font, but you must know your target.

The third column gives examples of text emphasis. Three that are used commonly today are bold, italic, and underline. Each one is a means of emphasis. Implementing more than one of these adds even more emphasis. The intent here is to draw the attention of the reader to the emphasized word or phrase. Too much emphasis can overload the reader and defeat the purpose of the emphasis, so use them carefully. The next example of emphasis shown is uppercase. This is used in headings or for acronyms. In the world of electronic communications, it has come to mean yelling or exclaiming something and should be used carefully. Rarely is uppercase combined with the other three examples of emphasis, as it becomes overkill. *'DON'T DO IT'* might seem out of place, even though your eye may have been drawn to it. Other less common types of emphasis can also be used. In the font window of word processors many things can be chosen, such as outline, emboss, shadow, or engraved. These should be used if you feel they add to the presentation of the material, but realize that they make the text harder to read and may be thought of as odd by the target. Lastly is the idea of highlighting or adding a colored bar over the text. In business communications that are passed among several users or designed to be scanned quickly, a highlight can be very useful since it draws the attention of the reader to a specific item and can remind him or her of a vital part that needs to be addressed. It is the electronic equivalent of the highlighter used by students marking important words in a textbook.

The last column of the chart shows some color text augmentation that can be done. It is important to choose text color carefully. Both the color of the text and the color of the background need to work together to make the text visible and readable. Since some text conventions, such as URLs being blue and underlined now exist, knowing how colors work together and look on different media are useful. There are texts and pointers that can be used, but for now, realizing that color choice can be very personal and a matter of trial and error is enough. The best contrast is black and yellow, while the worst is red on black. Today, billions of color combinations are available, so each subtle change needs to be judged by you as you work to craft your final package. Remember, what you like may not be liked by others and how you see it on the screen may be different from how it looks when printed or projected. Knowing the technology and the look of the final product will affect how you make your choices.

EXAMPLE 6.1
Analyze Audience—Orals and Others

Font Size	Font Style	Emphasis
Graphics (5)	Graphics (Times New Roman)	Graphics (Plain)
Graphics (7.5)	Graphics (Georgia)	**Graphics** (Bold)
Graphics (9)	Graphics (Aerial)	*Graphics* (Italic)
Graphics (10)	**Graphics** (Aerial Black)	Graphics (Underline)
Graphics (12)	Graphics (Helvetica)	***Graphics*** (Bold & Italic)
Graphics (14)	Graphics (Comic)	GRAPHICS (Upper Case)
Graphics (18)	*Graphics* (Script)	Graphics (Outline)
Graphics (24)	Graphics (Castellar)	Graphics (Highlighted)

Example 6.1 shows different examples of graphics that can be used to enhance message delivery.

Moving beyond just text, a useful method of conveying what you mean more effectively is to include a pictorial device used for illustration. There are a wide variety of different terms related to these ideas. The most important thing to remember is that anything you add should serve to make the message clearer and illustrate what you mean. Too often, people just add in graphics without a reason. A graphic is anything placed on a surface. This can be text, photographs, lines, or anything you wish to show things visually rather than with just words. For the purpose of this text, we need something more detailed.

Our first distinction is a figure, or an object that symbolizes something or is used as a representation for clarification. This can be anything that is used to help convey the message. There are a variety of different types of figures that each have a specialized use and help the sender to communicate more effectively if used correctly. The distinctions are usually based on the information being conveyed and the methods used to create and present that information. It is key to know when each is appropriate so that the content can be shown to the target in the way that you as the sender wish it to be seen.

The first way to organize data is in a table, which is the presentation of data, usually arranged in columns and rows in an essentially rectangular form with a label at one end for the row, column, or both. Each data entry is not necessarily connected with other entries in the row or column. The types of things you are comparing and how much data you have will change the way the chart looks. You should always present the data in a way that helps the reader see the relationships you are trying to present.

Generally, a table is built by creating columns (items organized vertically) and rows (items organized horizontally). The topmost column and the leftmost row are usually reserved for labels that describe the information that appears in the rest of these rows and columns. The intersection of a row and a column is referred to as a cell. Typical spreadsheet programs, such as Excel, format and organize data for you as you create tables. Formatting of tables and the way you change the appearance can affect how the reader interprets what is being displayed. The data in the table has varying degrees of connection with the cells around it. At the lowest level of connection, each cell is separate from all other cells such that it represents one point of intersection between the variable labeled by the row with the variable labeled in the column. This is true for many surveys in which each question is answered by a different respondent and answers are reported in a table. A higher level of connection exists when data in rows or columns are related so that movement from one cell to another is represented in the table. The more there is a connection between variables being discussed, the more a visual aid can assist and is usually accomplished by means of a chart or graph.

Example 6.2 gives several pieces of data in table form. For this example, imagine that two students kept track of how much money each spent on different things throughout the semester. These two students are at the same college in the same dorms with similar expenses. Just knowing a little about the life of a student, you can see some trends in the data. Things like travel to and from school, a vacation at spring break, lack of funds near the end of the semester, and more time needed to study for exams may not be stated but might explain some of the trends in the data. The way things are presented in the table helps the reader see the trends you are trying to show. A discussion of statistics can be found at *http://www .carillontech.com/QE.htm*

EXAMPLE 6.2
Data in Tables

Our first table shows the total expenses for two students for one academic year (4 months in both the fall and spring semesters).

Table of Total Expenses for Students A & B—1 Academic Year

	September	October	November	December	January	February	March	April
Student A	$1000	$725	$650	$400	$775	$525	$625	$550
Student B	$1000	$1200	$1525	$1600	$1100	$1050	$3525	$600

Though the information provided may be useful to prove some points and support some arguments, more detail may be needed. The following table shows what Student A spent on four categories of expenses during the spring semester.

Table of All Expenses for Student A for Spring Semester

Expenses	January	February	March	April
Food	$300	$400	$300	$400
Entertainment	$75	$100	$100	$100
Supplies	$300	$25	$25	$50
Travel	$100	$0	$200	$0
Total	$775	$525	$625.00	$550.00

Finally, our last sample table shows a comparison of the expenses for our two students for the spring semester. Each table should be used to illustrate a point being made.

Combined Table of Expenses for Students A & B for Spring Semester								
	January		February		March		April	
Expense	A	B	A	B	A	B	A	B
Food	$300	$500	$400	$625	$300	$525	$400	$475
Entertainment	$75	$300	$100	$400	$100	$1,500	$100	$100
Supplies	$300	$200	$25	$0	$25.00	$0	$50	$0
Travel	$100	$100	$0	$25	$200	$1,500	$0	$25
Total	$775	$1,100	$525	$1,050	$625	$3,525	$550	$600

Each table serves a different purpose and presents the data differently so that the reader can see it in the way you want. If you are comparing the expenses for student A and B, the last table is best. If you are only looking at one student, one of the first two might be better, depending on the information you intend to show. The additional information in the third table may distract the reader with superfluous data not related directly to your point.

Listing data in a table may not be enough for the reader to understand your argument or to be persuaded. By using a visual method of presentation, your argument can be strengthened and connections between data points can be more easily illustrated. If the data is presented so that it can be seen in relation to something, usually drawn on axes, it is said to be a plot, chart, or graph. A good way to decide on which of these visuals to use, relates to the connection that exists between data points and the variables. As with tables, knowing the best way to present the data often rests on the data itself and the argument you are trying to make. Knowing more about these different types of visuals will help you so we begin with the basic parts of most graphs, an axis.

An axis is a line that shows a graduated set of values. Usually at least two axes are shown and are drawn like an "L." Typically, the horizontal axis is referred to as the X-axis, and the vertical axis is termed the Y-axis. Any variable can be listed on the X-axis or Y-axis but some common conventions are typically used. The Y-axis is usually used to show the value or quantity of the things being listed, while the X-axis is used to list each distinct item or a progression of something (such as the passing of time.) The point at which the two axes meet is known as the origin. For the first table in Example 6.2, the cost or dollars would be placed on the Y-axis, and the month would be placed on the X-axis. If you are showing both positive and negative data, the X-axis and Y-axis will look like a cross rather than an "L."

The distinction between plots, charts, and graphs is based upon the data being presented and how it is presented. A plot simply places a point in a space according to the relationship of one variable to another as shown on each axis of the space. No connection is made between one plot point placement and another. One of the most common types of plots is a scatter plot, or histogram, which places points on an XY-axis. Each point is independent of the others on the plot and is often labeled individually.

When the data has a connection, a chart is used. A chart is an outline, map, or block on which specific information, such as scientific data, heights, or directions is show. Many times a chart will not appear on a set of axes (such as a topographical map) and gives a set of fixed relations in a visual form so it can be comprehended more quickly and easily by the reader. A common chart is one that shows heights or depths of a region using lines that represent differing fixed altitudes. This is usually used to present the data in a way that shows points of connection that are difficult to see without an overview or broader perspective. The data displayed on a chart are fixed quantities for a fixed variable so that when a XY-axis is used, the variable being shown is given in a static way (such as with a bar or line).

For data that is to be presented on a set of axes, there are various types of charts and graphs, but the three most common and distinct are pie, bar, and line. A pie chart shows a percentage of a total amount. Each point in the set is compared to the overall total of data in the set. This is to be used when the given data are related to parts of the whole. The percentages need to equal 100% for the pie chart. Next is the bar chart that shows fixed quantities that are related to other fixed quantities. Each bar is measured against an independent scale on one axis. Charts can become graphs if they are intended to show movement over time or connection of the variables on one axis to those on another as a continuum. Charts that show a dynamic relationship become graphs of those things by plotting movement.

Example 6.3 uses the information in the tables provided to show the different types of figures. An attempt has been made to show various types of charts and graphs along with common additions that make it easier for the reader to read them. Besides how the data is shown, these graphs and charts should have additional information included to make it easier to follow. Each figure should have an overall title that is descriptive of what is in the figure. Furthermore, each axis should be labeled if the variable being shown is not apparent. Beyond this, a legend that explains how the data is presented can give further clarification. In extremely complex situations, data points can actually be labeled within the figure itself. Some figures will include gridlines (straight lines that show the level of the value of a variable) to make the values easier to read. Other display techniques, such as color schemes, contrasting backgrounds, three-dimensional bars or lines, or other pictures in the figure are used to enhance the look of the graphic. A balance must be struck between giving more information and visually presenting the material effectively. Insufficient labels make things hard to understand, while too many labels clutter the field. Do not put too much or too little on the figure. As you begin crafting these figures, a trial-and-error approach may be the best means to see what looks best. Over time, you will be able to get a feel for what works best. Luckily, programs such as MS Word and Excel make it easy to create and edit all the figures discussed here with autoformatting and wizards.

A graph is a pictorial representation of a relationship, usually mathematical, between two or more numbers or sets of numbers, shown as a set of points. The graph shows connection and dynamic situations that connect the various data points. The most common types of graphs plot a variable versus time or represent an equation that has two or more variables. Though each point is fixed, the reader can see movement over fixed intervals. One of the most common graphs is a line graph that shows a connection between one data point and another. The idea of this is that though data points were taken at intervals, the line shows where other points would most likely be seen if the sampling was more frequent. All of these move along a continuum from one point taken separately from all others to the connected sets of points that constitute a line or curve. Many times graphs are used to compare separate sets of data for the same variable in order to draw comparisons and reveal trends and similarities. Example 6.4 uses the information in the tables from Example 6.2 to show a graph.

EXAMPLE 6.3
Charts

Using the data from Example 6.2, the following bar chart of monthly expenses for Student A for the year can be generated.

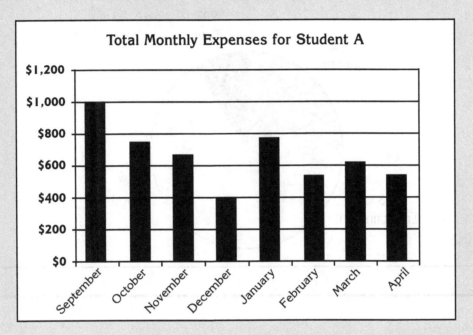

If a comparison of each expense for each month was desired, the following chart could be created.

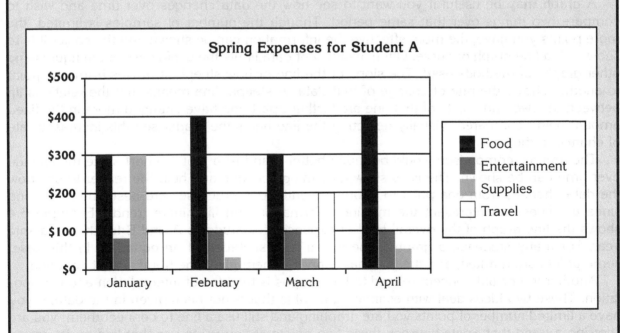

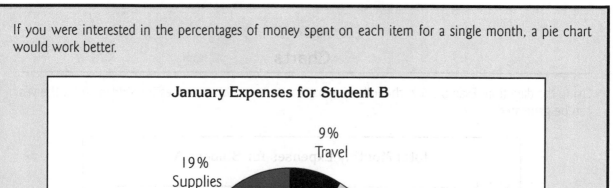

If you were interested in the percentages of money spent on each item for a single month, a pie chart would work better.

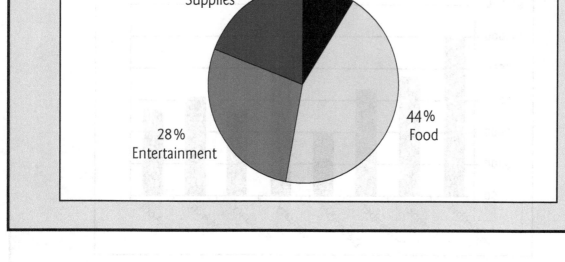

January Expenses for Student B

9% Travel

19% Supplies

28% Entertainment

44% Food

A graph may be useful if you want to see how the data changes over time and wish to compare two things over that same period. Though the number of samples is limited, the more points you have, the more effective the information can be shown and the easier it is to show with a line graph or curve. Often insufficient data limits the usefulness of the figures and other graphical methods used. The slope of the line or how steeply it moves from one point to another shows the rate of change of that data. A steeper line means that the relationship between the two end points of that line are further apart and have changed more in the fixed amount being compared. Visually depicting the line helps the reader see this increased rate of change in the line.

The graphic comparison would be much better than just a plot or chart since the change over time can be shown. The lines show how things change and help the reader to see how the data changes from one point to another. Continuous processes are best when graphing since the lines can represent the missing information and illuminate trends. Example 6.4 shows the line graph of the overall total of expenses for Students A and B for the academic year. For many students, a graph is the visual representation of an equation. In this case, some points are marked, and the line that connects them gives the trend of that equation.

Another important concept related to line graphs is the idea of interpolation and extrapolation. These two ideas deal with estimating a value that is not been given in the data. If you have a limited number of points you are graphing and still use a line to connect them, you are showing a trend that exists between these two points. If you try to use that line to determine a value that would exist between the two known points based on the trend of the line, this is interpolation. In another case, you might have two or more lines that represent a regular data set for a series of values. If you try to estimate a value that falls somewhere between these lines, this would also be interpolation. If you see a trend in the data and move the line back

EXAMPLE 6.4
Graphs

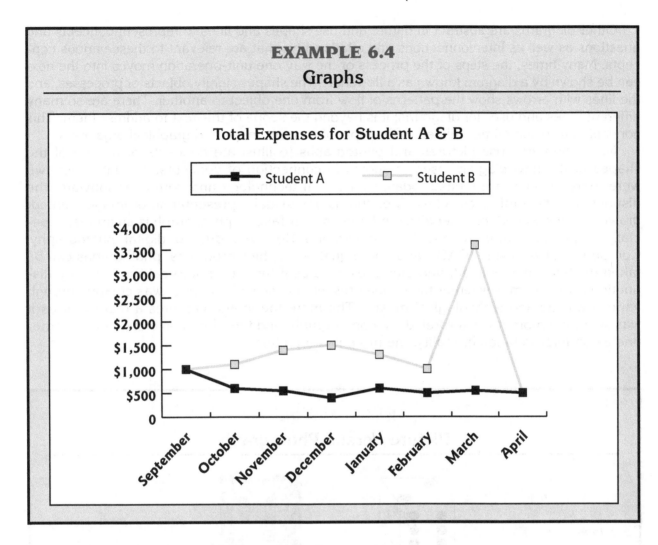

beyond the first point, out farther past the last point, or above or below the existing set of data, this line does not have values associated with the line that is created. If a value is then taken from a point on this line, you are extrapolating the data to find that value.

In many situations, interpolation and extrapolation are necessary, but you must be aware that they are not guaranteed to be accurate, and the points you find are a guess at what the value would be for the data. It is best to interpolate or extrapolate when you have good data and a sufficient number of data points to make the guess a good one. These two methods of data extension are usually only valid when the data is regular and uniform. As the lines become less uniform and regular, the estimated values become more unreliable and can be trusted less as actual values. For more on these points, you should refer to a statistics text or consult someone from the field related to data being discussed.

Moving beyond data, a diagram is a means of showing plans, processes, or outlines designed to demonstrate or explain how something works, the steps to be followed, or to clarify the relationship between the parts of a whole. Diagrams can be literal representations of something that uses figures and labels to explain how it fits together. Literal diagrams often employ an exploded view of the object. An exploded view takes a small part of the entire figure and magnifies it so that a close-up of that part can be seen in greater detail. These types of diagrams are typically utilized in mechanical applications and as part of process descriptions to aid users. If you have ever assembled something, you most likely have seen diagrams with exploded views.

Other diagrams are abstract in nature and use shapes and lines to represent concepts and questions as well as interconnections and relationships that are relevant to these various concepts. Many times, the steps of the process or the way one unit-operation moves into the next can be shown by a diagram known as a flowchart. The shapes signify objects or processes, and the lines with arrows show the patterns of flow from one object to another. There are so many different types and uses for diagrams; it is beyond the scope of this text to address them. This concept is also sometimes related to the topic of concept maps and graphical organizers.

Many diagrams use pictures and photographs to illustrate concepts or as one of the shapes of the flow diagram used to show the connection of concepts. Though these two were more distinct in the past; today, with digital technology and computer software, the distinction is becoming less clear. A picture is any visual representation or image painted, drawn, photographed, or otherwise rendered on a surface. A photograph is an image, especially a positive print, recorded by a camera. However, due to digital photography, Computer Aided Design (CAD), and photo quality graphics programs, photographs can be taken digitally, manipulated, and then presented as if they are photorealistic. The key distinction now becomes whether the image presented a view of reality or was created through various artistic and technological means. The more the image captures a real event as it was seen, the more it is interpreted as a photograph, and the more it is a creation of someone as an interpretation of reality, the more it is a picture.

EXAMPLE 6.5
Picture Versus Photograph

These figures may be more or less difficult to distinguish as pictures or photographs. On the left is a drawing done with Microsoft PowerPoint. It appears cartoon-like. The other, a scanned image of a real die, is considered a picture. However, without knowledge of the original photographer, it may have been created using a computer.

Example 6.6 gives a summary of the most common types of figures.

When using a figure, it is important to include information to assist the reader to understand what is being presented and how it fits into the overall work. By including a label, a title, and a description, the reader can better understand the figure. A label is a marker that tells the reader how to find the figure in the text and is usually included in a table of contents. Also, this label can be referred to in the text so that the reader knows what you are speaking about when you mention it as well as helping to direct the reader's attention to it. Throughout the text, the figures are labeled with a word such as "figure" or "exercise" followed by a number. This allows the reader to find these inserts more easily. Next is the title of the figure, which tells the reader what the figure is about. Finally, a caption with a brief description should follow figures so that the reader can gain some insight about what the figure shows, why it was included, and where the information was obtained if it needs to be cited.

EXAMPLE 6.6
Summary of Types of Figures

Table	This is a presentation of data, usually arranged in columns and rows in an essentially rectangular form with a label at one end for the row, column, or both.
Plot	A point is placed in a space according to the relationship of one variable to another as shown on each axis of the space. No connection is made between one plot point placement and another.
Chart	This is an outline or map on which specific information, such as scientific data, heights, or directions are placed.
Graph	This is a pictorial representation of a relationship, usually mathematical, between two or more numbers or sets of numbers shown as a set of points. The graph shows connection and dynamic situations that connect the various data points.
Diagram	This is a means of showing plans, processes, or outlines designed to demonstrate or explain how something works, the steps to be followed, or to clarify the relationship between the parts of a whole.
Picture	Any visual representation or image painted, drawn, photographed, or otherwise rendered on a surface.
Photograph	A photograph is an image, especially a positive print, recorded by a camera.

Example 6.6 shows a summary of different figures.

Though all of this information is not necessary, it is helpful to the reader, especially when it is being accessed without reading the entire text that surrounds it. As a good rule, figures should be placed as close as possible to the material it relates to in the text. This may not always be possible, but if a figure is too far away from where it is referenced, the connection can be confused or lost. Labeling figures is especially helpful if they are included in an appendix. An appendix is used when the material being presented is not directly related to the understanding of the material in the text but might be useful, or when including a figure will draw too much attention from the reader. It is up to the writer to decide how best to use figures. Once again, your job is to enhance understanding by including these figures.

Writing Tasks

Now that we have explained the process of communication, identified key questions, and specified many of the elements that might be part of making a package, it is time for you to take control. If you are trying to communicate and you have done some investigation or reflection, you will usually know how to answer the next question—is the package mainly written or an oral presentation. Even if you are going to present the package there are often graphical elements and written components in it so we will start there with our discussion. Chapter 7 will discuss public speaking in detail but for now we need to consider the many different types of written packages that are typically encountered. Of course, all of this is meant to prepare you for whatever you will need to do but much of the groundwork has already been laid out for you so you can have a head start.

The rest of this chapter focuses on various types of formal and informal writing undertaken for a variety of purposes meant to accomplish personal goals in a wide range of situations for many distinct targets. It will be the responsibility of the sender to make choices and identify preferences in order to arrive at the correct final package. What is presented are guidelines and descriptions that will help with the process of selecting the most effective writing form as well as provide insight into the distinctions that exist to highlight how to use each more effectively.

Summaries

One of the most common types of tasks is writing summaries. This is very different from a paper or essay assignment because it has the purpose of reviewing what someone else has written or said. One common summary that many students write is the minutes of a meeting or the notes from a class. In this case, the most complete form of the summary would be a verbatim record of everything that happened. A video of the class would allow for everything that happened to be reviewed later. This is not what most people think of when they take notes or minutes of a meeting or class. Less rigorous is the idea of listing the major points of the meeting or class. Audiotapes or other recording material can be used to reference, but a written report that gives the major ideas put forth and the participants of the meeting is enough.

Moving outside of the meeting room or classroom, other summaries are also expected as part of your academic career. These summaries are usually related to the research papers or articles that are to be used as sources for papers or projects. These summaries should begin with the citation of the piece being summarized. This can be put into the first paragraph or listed separately under the title. Next, a review of the main idea of the article and the facts and arguments given to prove this thesis should be provided. For many assignments, this may be enough, especially if the summary is to be used as part of a larger research assignment. However, more can be included. After the review, several other topics can be covered. One of the most important is the view of the opinions put forth in the article. Along these lines, inclusion of counter arguments or contradictory facts can be included along with the summarizer's opinion of the article. Finally, depending on the class, a discussion of how the article relates to the material presented in the class can also be included. In the end, the minimum a summary must do is briefly cover the material that was put forth in the original article. However, a good summary can give much more than that.

Several common ways of creating your summary are to outline everything that was said or to list out the topic sentence or thesis for each paragraph or conceptual section that was presented. For shorter works, this is usually very effective. However, if you are summarizing a large work or were asked to distill down the larger work to its essential elements, the outline or topic sentences are only a diary of what occurred rather than your review. Thus, it is necessary to present only the most vital parts of what was being presented to allow the target to understand the given situation, follow the argument, and have a clear picture of the conclusions reached along with the methods and evidence used to arrive at the at conclusion. The distinction here is that the first type of summary is just recounting the original presenter while the second is your voice explaining what was presented. To assist with the second type of summary, you should present the following items:

- What are you summarizing (cite the original source)
- Describe the purpose
- Present the thesis
- List the initial assumptions and parameters
- Provide the methods or argument

- Explain the conclusion(s)
- List the key evidence used

You may not use all of these items, but this will assist you to reflect on the work to be summarized and preset it in your own words.

Letters, Memos, and E-mails

Some of the most common writing tasks for students today are e-mail and text messages. Unfortunately these are not usually approached in a formal way. As a result, students may have difficulty seeing that a different level of formality, tone, and measure of professionalism is needed when e-mailing a professor, school official, or potential employer. Even though the same basic aspects of communication apply, students do not often use critical thinking and analysis for these less-formal writing tasks. This is not really an issue until the student's attempts to shift writing towards a more formal situation. Since the practice of writing is not normal, many default to writing the way they speak to one another or the way they write in e-mails and text messages. Once again, unless the focus of their attention shifts to giving the target what he or she wants, this self-centered communication process will tend to be less successful.

Generally, the basic forms of writing will be in letters, memos, and e-mails today. All three of these have similar form and must contain the same common information. Usually the level of formality shifts from less formal to more formal as you move from e-mail to memo to letter. However, as electronic communication has become so prevalent these days, this is not always true. The blurred line between work and home as well as formal and informal can lead to problems as students write e-mails to friends and then shift right into a formal letter to a professor or employer. This leads to problems, especially when the target does not accept this less formal tone and demeanor.

Many guides exist for the form of letters and memos. The basic information needed on each is the same. There needs to be a date, a recipient, and a sender. Memos are given the heading of "memorandum" and a subject is added similarly to an e-mail. Memos tend to be less formal and are seen as internal communication so that they can be more direct. On the other hand, formal letters or business letters are usually external and more formal. The form of business letters has evolved with technology. With the advent of typewriters, the form reflected the needs to the typist. Today, with word processing programs and color laser printers, many of these demands on form are not as needed, but a consistent easy-to-read form is the best. For students who read this text, the most important type of letter is a cover letter usually associated with a résumé. These are the first two writing tasks that will be discussed in detail, as they provide a good view of how to apply the concepts listed previously in this text.

Résumé and Cover Letter

One important written work for almost everyone is a résumé, and its accompanying cover letter. There are many types of résumés that can be used for specific reasons. At the most general level, a résumé is a picture of you and your past that highlights certain desired aspects of your life. All résumés are intended to provide others a glimpse into your life and will introduce you to the reader. Its major purpose is to inform someone about your strengths and convince him or her to make further contact with you. It is not, as some people think, to get a job. The résumé is the first step in the process, and the better it is crafted the more likely you will be contacted. You might think of your résumé as a movie trailer. You are not expected to give the entire movie in the trailer because you are trying to interest them in seeing the movie. The résumé gives them an idea of who you are and what skills you have related to their needs. It does not tell them your life story or show them everything you have ever done. Most résumés are read for between 5–15 seconds when first examined. If it does not impress the reader, he or she will not continue reading, and if it is not made clear and direct, the reader may not look further. As a result, it is vital to put the most impressive and persuasive information near the top and to the left of the page. Using clear headings and using emphasis will assist you to get your message across.

One thing to note is that the use of white space is important. Having too much cluttering the page is as bad as having not enough. Try to fill the page but not to make things too packed. It is better to say less in a larger font than more in a smaller, hard-to-read way. If you find that you do not have enough to put on your résumé, it is a good idea to go out and do things to add to your worth rather include put less impressive things. Including information about your high school is usually only acceptable for first- and second-year college students unless the activities continue or the school is somehow important to the target reading the résumé. Looking at samples and seeing what you feel works best for you in your field of study is a good way to start. However, using a template or something that looks like everyone else is not the best idea. You want to be distinctive without being too different.

The cover letter is the opportunity for you to engage the target in a conversation about you and is the bridge between how you know about the position and the résumé that shows you are qualified for that position. If you have a job posting, you should use terms and wording from that in the letter. If you are just sending the letter and résumé without a posting describing the position, you need to think about those things that the person reading the résumé wants to see so you can mention that in the letter.

The most common and the one that most college students should have prepared is known as a functional résumé. It should be one page and utilize the graphical method discussed such as fonts, bolding, italics, and, if needed, bullets. At the top should be your name and contact information. After that many people recommend an objective of the résumé worded in a short but informative way that explains the type of position sought, the level of employment, and the future desires you have in that company. Do not be vague or too general as it wastes time and space. Below that should have a series of headings that cover the major aspects of your history that will interest and impress the readers. Some of these headings might be education, work experience, volunteer work, community service, activities, projects, research, awards, or honors. The most important of these is education and work experience. At the university level, school is a full-time job. Both of these should be listed in reverse chronological order, or put the most recent higher up on the list so that is viewed first. The balance that must be sought is between a full page versus a readable page. Blank space must be offset by small fonts, but the most important thing to remember is that only the things that will impress the reader should be included. Some tips to help make a good résumé are listed here.

- Do not use less than 10-point font on anything you would like read on your résumé.
- Put the most important things at the top and as clearly as possible.
- Order things so that the reader follows them clearly and can access them easily.
- Use white space to separate different things, but connect items together when they are to be looked at together.
- Be sure to list activities you completed at work as active verbs in the past tense.
- Tailor the objective to the job.
- The résumé must be free from mistakes.

- Always be truthful, but do not include everything you did. Only give those things that impress and that you want others to know because you might be asked about anything on the résumé.
- Use a professional e-mail address, and don't put your work phone number or work e-mail on your résumé if it is not appropriate to receive phone calls at work from other potential employers.

One thing that can help with a résumé is a cover letter. The cover letter is your opportunity to focus the reader on the most appropriate or strongest parts of the résumé as well as give more information about yourself. In addition, the cover letter can help the résumé reach the right target. Often if a cover letter is included with the résumé, the objective can be removed, but it always depends on what you feel is best and the specific situation you face.

There are many different professional forms for letters, and it is up to you to choose the one you think looks best. If you are not sure, it is best to use the block left form that aligns everything along the left and is single-spaced with an extra space between paragraphs. All letters, memos, and other such communications can use the basic block left format. As mentioned, it is assumed that most students are familiar with e-mails and that is a good place to start. At the top of the e-mail is the header information that helps ensure it arrives at the right place. A cover letter is the same. You should include the date and the recipient's title and address information.

After the formal recipient address should be a greeting such as Dear Sir. The body of the cover letter typically consists of three paragraphs: introduction, focus, and call to action. This is the same for almost any formal letter you might write. The first paragraph in the introduction directly gives the name, purpose of the letter, and some information about your connection to the recipient and the reason you are writing the letter and sending the résumé. The second paragraph focuses the reader on the area of the résumé you want him or her to focus on and that will impress the reader. The paragraph can give more about your reasons for applying for the position as well as generate more interest in the reader to delve further into the résumé. Finally, the last paragraph should give a call to action. This means you should thank the reader for his or her time and suggest what you want to happen next. This can be a request for more information, an interview, a visit, or whatever you deem appropriate; be careful not to be too passive or too assertive when making the call to action. The letter should end with a closing such as "sincerely," followed by several blank spaces for a signature, which is in turn followed by your full name typed and your contact information.

This is a general form for letters and can be seen in many places on the web. The key is always to think about what the reader wants and to try to provide that to him or her. The more you can impress, the more likely you are to succeed. To assist you, a sample résumé with two styles of cover letters are given at the end of the chapter.

Formal Writing and Citing

When writing a paper, it is important to begin by understanding the purpose or the goal of the writing assignment. Papers can be written to explain, inform, impress, or persuade a reader. Every paper has different lengths, targets, intentions, and many other factors that must be considered. Once the goal of the paper is understood, the process of writing can begin. Many times, when writing a paper for a class, the form is specified and a word processing program provides the template to use. Things such as margins, font size, line spacing, and even language are provided without thought. This eliminates most of the process for the selection and completion of the form. However, it is useful to think about your target and the type of writing you are undertaking before going further.

By thinking about the MIMES and TRIBES of the situation, you can gain insights into how to better construct the paper so that your message is most effectively delivered. The handout given at *http://facstaff.gpc.edu/~shale/humanities/composition/handouts/audience.html* provides a discussion of some of the basic questions to consider as you use the information from your analysis. The handout uses the term *audience* instead of target to describe the focus of the writing assignment. However the ideas and advice given are useful to consider when trying to improve the quality of your writing. In the end, knowing the rubric for assessment that the teacher is using and the goal of the assignment will assist you to create a better end-product and hopefully earn a higher grade.

In the same way, some students try to eliminate the process for content. This is plagiarism. Plagiarism is submitting someone else's work as your own, whether intentionally or unintentionally. This can be copying others' work, misquoting, missing or misleading citations, or having someone else do the assignment for you. Any work handed in must be of your own creation. If material is taken from some other source, it must be properly cited using a specified format, such as Modern Language Association (MLA) or American Psychological Association (APA) format.

It is difficult sometimes to see when and how to cite and quote. The key to remember is that anything you have not written yourself or ideas you have not generated yourself need to be given credit. It is not a bad thing to have many citations, as it shows that you have done work reading the work of experts, finding supporting research for your ideas and incorporating the ideas of others into your own work. Quotation marks are used to show the reader that the words are those someone else wrote somewhere else. If your words are taken in part or in total from another source, credit must be given to that source. The next level down is paraphrasing. If you change a few words or change most of them but keep someone else's idea, a citation is required. Citations or footnotes are used to tell the reader where the material was first found or explained by someone else. The trouble arises when material written by another person is read, changed slightly, and rewritten. How much needs to be cited to make it not plagiarized? This question is a difficult one to answer. If no citations are given, you are putting forth the idea that the writing is your own and the ideas presented were yours. Any time you have taken specific facts from some source, you must cite this because the material could not have been obtained without the outside assistance. The test usually put forth is the common knowledge test. If you feel the facts being given are easily accessible and understood by anyone, then they do not need to be cited. For example, the fact that the population of the United States in 2002 is 280 million people does not need to be cited. However, if the fact used in the paper was more specific—for example that the population of the United States in 2002 was 280,573,819 people—a citation showing where this number was found would be necessary. This is so that the audience can understand how the fact was arrived at and see the methods and reasons behind its creation.

The citation and corresponding entry on the reference page tells the reader where the material came from. This helps the audience judge the worth of the ideas as well as allows them to find the original material and read more for themselves.

Many times, people write without any outside sources and do not have any citations. This is not necessarily a bad thing depending on the type of writing being done. If you write an e-mail to a friend and bring up something, a citation would be absurd. However, when asked to write a research paper at a university, students are being asked to put forth more effort and be more professional as they conduct a higher level of research. As a result, clear and correct citations are expected as well. There are many types of writing assignments between e-mails and formal research papers. It is up to the writer to decide how much effort and how formal and professional to be when submitting an essay.

Evaluating Sources

Even if you cite everything you use in your paper correctly, this does not guarantee that what you used was any good. When researching, too often, the first thing that agrees with what you want to say is accepted as a good source. This may not be true. Just because something was published in a textbook or article, the content may not be valid, useful, current, or authoritative. Moreover, anyone can post things on a web page and make it seem factual and persuasive even if no evidence supports what is being said. This section gives some questions to ask about sources to help determine if what you find is worth using in your assignment. In the end, it is up to you to construct a paper from your own thoughts, supported by the thoughts and work of others in order to accomplish the assignment you were given or achieve your purpose.

There are many considerations when judging the quality of a source to be used to support your ideas in a paper. How relevant is the material, when was it written, is it based upon studies, is the author an expert, and many more. Only you can judge the quality of the specific material being presented and determine if it is useful and timely to meet your purposes. However, there are some general things to consider when assessing a source.

First, the creator, editor, or distributor of the work needs to be assessed. Asking about the quality of the information being given and who is giving it to you is necessary to determine if the work is worth citing or using. Usually, if the author is scholarly, seen as an expert, or has some experience in the field being discussed, the quality and worth of the author is more likely reputable and can be relied upon. Next, it is important to see how and where the material being reviewed was published or distributed. In general, a scholarly journal is more reputable than a weekly news magazine or a personal web page. Knowing the way the article was published is an important consideration. Some people feel that because something is published, it is of quality but this is not true. Just because material was published in a book does not make it more true, and just because something was posted on a web page does not make it of less quality. However, as a rule, knowing the person who generates the material and where it was distributed is helpful when measuring the quality of the work. This leads to a last area, which asks you to examine how you came to find the material. Just because you used a database to find an article does not make it of quality. Databases and other library resources are intended to help you narrow your search and save time. However, just as the library can buy any book and list it in the catalog, the database provider can include material from a variety of sources that range in quality. Nonetheless, knowing about the method you used to obtain the information is useful to ensure the information has not been changed and the quality of the source and other measures you consider are accurately represented.

Beyond questioning the source are other considerations. As stated, the usefulness of the material is key to creating good final products. Just because you find material does not mean you can use it to support the points you want to prove in your essay. In addition, you have to be aware of how persuasive the target will find the information you have identified in the source. Even the most accurate and high-quality information that is pertinent to your topic may not be useful in persuading someone that does not give credence to that source. You have to consider the information in the context of your argument as well as the person or group the argument is intended to convince.

One last concern deals with how current the information is that you have found. Even if the material found is of the highest quality and is relevant and useful to persuade the target, if it is not timely for the topic, it is not useful. Imagine you find an article telling you which brand has the best television. If you do not check the date of publication, you cannot know how accurate that information is and how well it might persuade. An article from the 1999 Consumer Reports Magazine about televisions will be useless when discussing current plasma televisions. However, the opposite situation might exist. If you are researching some problem or issue from the past, more recent articles may not have the same perspective or give any useful information on the topic. It is up to you to judge how recent the material needs to be in order to support your topic. Along these lines, it is important to note that books take time to publish and tend to have information that is dated. Even a book published in 2008 might have study data from 2004 or earlier. Sometimes, the most recent data is from the last census, so the 2000 census may be current even though it is already 2009. Newer is not always better, but sources that are relevant and current for the topic of study are key to picking good sources.

Parts of a Paper

Though every paper can be broken into form and content, it is important to understand that most, if not all, follow a similar outline. Though the specifics of the form and content vary, the sections listed in the following sections will appear in most papers. It is also important to realize that as the length of the paper increases, the requirements change. Though any paper may have section headings, once the paper reaches a length of six pages, they are usually expected, and beyond 10 pages almost always required. As the length increases beyond that, an abstract and a table of contents are usually included as well. All of these features are intended to assist the reader to follow the material being presented and help to make the work be accepted and understood more easily. Following are some brief guidelines for sections that should be found in your papers.

There are many ways a paper can be broken down. Each person can organize the work he or she creates in any way deemed best. Many times, professors expect certain common things to be present in a written report. However, this is not a fixed rule, but rather a way to make the paper flow and the ideas easier to understand. Many professional societies and journals provide the rules for organizing a paper. Some of the common parts are title page, abstract, table of contents, introduction, background, body, conclusion, and references.

Every paper should begin with information about the author and the assignment. This can include the author's name, due date, class, professor's name, and many other things. On longer assignments, such as term papers and those written by multiple authors, a separate cover sheet is used. The title of the work should be centered below this heading. For works with a separate title page, the title may be centered vertically on the page as well. Be sure to use a title that gives insight into the topic being covered in the paper (do not use "Assignment #1"). Sometimes pictures, photographs, or other graphics are also included on this page at the author's discretion.

The abstract is a summary of the paper written in the past tense once the work is completed. It is intended to review the thesis and the major points of evidence used to support that thesis, not an introduction to what is being presented. It is usually only included with a larger writing assignment and is normally no longer than 250 words. In reports prepared for businesses, government agencies, or other committees and organizations, an executive summary is often substituted for the abstract. The executive summary gives the project that was originally assigned, the assumptions and parameters made by the author, and the conclusions that were found.

In large papers, there is a need for a table of contents that helps the reader understand how the work is organized. Each heading in the text should be used as an entry in the table of contents along with any other graphs, tables, figures, or other inserts.

The introduction is the opening of a paper. It is intended to catch the audience's attention and focus it upon the main idea or thesis of the paper. It may also contain an outline of the evidence presented in the paper that supports the thesis being discussed.

Next the background can be presented. This section is not necessary for every paper but helps the audience understand what is being discussed and provides useful definitions and other materials that appear in the body.

The main part of the paper is the body, which logically develops the topic specified in the thesis statement and supports it with evidence and examples.

Finally, there is a conclusion. This section draws the paper to a close by summarizing and bringing together the relevant facts and arguments that were presented earlier in the paper. It concisely crystallizes the significant points of the paper. It can also give the audience insight into how the topic is connected to other areas or has implications for further exploration and research.

After the paper, there must be a list of works that are referenced. Throughout the paper, references may be used to support the arguments given. These citations can take many forms, but at the end of the paper there must be some complete list of the sources from where the material cited in the paper was taken. Each different citation format has a set of rules. All are intended to make it easier for the reader to find the source of the material being cited and follow a similar uniform set of guidelines. All citations usually have the name of the creator, the date of creation, the title of the work, and the source of publication.

Proposals

A proposal is one important type of written work that is a specialized type of paper that students may need to create when in school and long afterward. There are a wide variety of proposals that people might be asked to make, and they are both in written and oral forms. In any event, it is useful to know more about the parts of a proposal and how to create it. In school, most students will be asked to create a research proposal though some may need to create a sales proposal for some classes. All proposals identify a problem or need that someone else has and presents a solution along with a list of costs for generating those solutions. In a research proposal, the focus is on some new research that is needed to further understand the area under discussion or open an entirely new area. This type of proposal usually asks for resources (time, money, facilities, etc.). The other type of proposal is a sales proposal that offers a particular item or service. In this situation, the intent of the proposal is for the target to purchase the proposed item or service. In some cases, money may not be the only reason for writing a proposal. Though there are many reasons for writing a proposal, some include: seeking recognition for others or yourself in the form of an award, obtaining permission to pursue personal interests or make changes in the way things are done, or even just to let others know what you think about topics or their ideas.

When thinking about your proposal, it is important to keep some things in mind. Is the proposal solicited or not? This relates to whether or not the target of the proposal knows it is coming. Sometimes, the solicitation is direct in that you have been asked to write a proposal, while other times it is an open call to anyone. Open calls for proposals are known as Request For Proposals (RFP). In some contracting work, asking for a proposal is known as bidding to do work. The other concern is how formal you should be when writing the work. This deals with your knowledge of the target generated by using MIMES and TRIBE. In some cases, you are asked to write a short letter describing what you want, while in others you and a group of others will be asked to make formal presentations and submit large documents detailing work plans, costs, and liabilities. Formality is important for you to judge so that your proposal does not seem too far off from the expectations of the target.

To help you see how this fits together, think about one of the most common proposals that you come in contact with—your résumé and cover letter. Essentially, this is a proposal for the target to provide you an interview and eventually a job. Depending on how you found out about the opportunity and how well you know the person, the level of solicitation and formality changes.

The more you know, the more effectively you can tailor your proposal to the desires of the target. If you send a résumé to a company knowing nothing, this is very unsolicited. If you read an ad for the job, this is more solicited. If you worked for the company during the summer, and the manager told you to send him a résumé so he can give you a job, this is highly solicited. The same is true of judging formality. The more you know who you are targeting, the easier it is to write, speak, and look appropriately formal for the situation. Example 637 below provides more information about the parts of a proposal and how to go about creating one to increase your chances of being successful.

EXAMPLE 6.7
Characteristics of a Good Proposal

A good proposal:

- Considers the target(s) to make a good impression by giving them what they want.
- Presents a clear, concise, and focused message concerning a subject of value to the target.
- Is presented at an appropriate level for the target in the situation it is being received.
- Is truthful, accurate, and actionable by the target.
- Meets expected form and organization for the situation and target

Not every proposal needs to include every section listed. The key is to determine what will work best for your project and include those things that make you more likely to successfully get your message to your target and convince your target to say "yes." Usually, a proposal is based upon research and work you have done before you even know if you are going to be given the go ahead. Depending upon the project, you may invest resources that might complete 5–15% of the work before you even know if you will be chosen. As a result, you have to be aware of what you do as you work. Do not promise too much, and do not do too much work if you are unsure of the success of your endeavor. The reason for the investment is because a proposal will make promises that you will have to keep if you are given the go-ahead. You need to be sure that you can do what you promise and are willing to deliver it in the way your proposal states. Each proposal must be adjusted to fit the target and intent of the communicator so that the message is successfully received and acted upon. Usually the end result of a proposal is that the target says "yes" to whatever was requested. Therefore, the proposal must make the request clear and give the necessary arguments and evidence to convince the proper target.

Links to assist with proposal writing include:

Proposal: Getting results: *http://www.nightcats.com/sales/proposal.html*
Proposal: How to write bids: *http://www.marketProposal:ingprofs.com/ea/qst_question.asp?qstID=2892*
Proposal: Layout and examples: *http://www.mcf.org/mcf/grant/writing.htm*
Proposal: Web business proposal: *http://www.pegaweb.com/articles/business-proposal-writing.htm*
Proposal: Writing a request for proposal: *http://www.internetraining.com/6art2.htm*

Example 6.7 lists the good characteristics of proposals.

Conclusion

As students, workers, and citizens, the need to communicate effectively is ever-present. Though not everyone needs to be spectacular at this skill, improving one's ability to communicate in all forms will assist you to be more employable and give you an edge in the information age. Moreover, if you become a more efficient communicator and spend a little time practicing now, you can complete the tasks of communication more quickly and effectively throughout your life. Rather than dread having to write and speak in public, you will know that you can do it effectively, and if you do not like it, be finished with it more quickly. If you enjoy it, the material here can help you see the distinctions in the various types of writing and help you to be more than competent in the processes of communication.

SUMMARY

This chapter discusses a variety of aspects of communication. It begins with a discussion of the process of communicating in all forms. It then moves to more specific details of how to create and send an effective communication package, combining the message with the appropriate medium. The mnemonic devices MIMES and TRIBE—Message, Intent, Means, End-Result, and Success; and Target, Relationship, Influences, Background, and Environment. were presented and discussed. After this discussion, specific forms of writing and citing were discussed, with some focus on common writing tasks performed in educational settings. Finally, the chapter discussed oral reports and provided general guidelines to assist with the process of creating and delivering these types of packages.

Questions and Homework

1. What are typical assignments you are given in school? How are the requirements, purpose, and measurement of success for each different?
2. Do you change your thinking for each package you are creating? How can thinking about this lead to better writing?
3. How are oral and written reports different?
4. How are different graphics and figures important to your delivery?

References and Other Readings

Additional examples and explanations are provided on Dr. Lipuma's web page at
  http://njit.mrooms.net/course/view.php?id=14403
OWL at Purdue. (2004). Purdue Online Writers Lab—Writing helps.
  Retrieved on January 5, 2009, from:
  http://owl.english.purdue.edu/lab/owl/tutoring/faq.html
Selfgrowth.com. (2008). A.U.D.I.E.N.C.E. Analysis. Retrieved on January 5, 2009, from:
  http://www.selfgrowth.com/articles/Laskowski4.html
Taflinger, R. F. (1996). What is Evidence? Retrieved on January 5, 2009, from:
  http://www.wsu.edu:8080/~taflinge/evidence.html

Other Web Links

Create charts and diagrams in PowerPoint 2002: *http://www.microsoft.com/office/*
  previous/xp/columns/column09.asp
General chart and graph info: *http://www.42explore.com/graphs.htm*
General information on charts and graphs:
  http://www.cs.iupui.edu/~aharris/mmcc/mod6/abss8.html
How to use tables: *http://java.sun.com/docs/books/tutorial/uiswing/*
  components/table.html#selection

Links for understanding and writing procedures, policies and process descriptions: *http://www.bizmanualz.com/articles/04-06-05_control_procedures.html*

Making a table and figure: *http://abacus.bates.edu/~ganderso/biology/resources/writing/HTWtablefigs.html*

Pictures and presentations: *http://www.findarticles.com/p/articles/mi_m1563/is_n12_v11/ai_14756955*

Proposal: Getting results: *http://www.nightcats.com/sales/proposal.html*

Proposal: How to write bids: *http://www.marketProposal:ingprofs.com/ea/qst_question.asp?qstID=2892*

Proposal: Layout and examples: *http://www.mcf.org/mcf/grant/writing.htm*

Proposal: Web business proposal: *http://www.pegaweb.com/articles/business-proposal-writing.htm*

Proposal: Writing a request for proposal: *http://www.internetraining.com/6art2.htm*

Samples of different common forms in school

Below are the three common forms of writing that most students will encounter—Essay, Memo and Letter. Though each target might specify different elements of form, these basic templates will provide an example to follow unless directed differently. Though all are listed on the same page, each would start at the top of the first page of you document

Essasy

Name
Class-section #
Due Date

Descriptive title (Centered)

Heading
    The body has double spaced paragraphs with a half-inch or one tab indent at the start of each paragraph and 1 inch margins all around.

    There is not an extra return between paragraphs or between headings and the body paragraphs. Essays usually also have the following:

- page numbers
- Use headings when 5 or more pages with an associated table of contents and title page
- Give references to research that are cited in proper MLA format as shown on the Purdue OWLsite
- MLA format for citations means parenthetical citations within the text with a reference page in alphabetical order at the end of the document

Memorandum
(The word Memo or Memorandum is centered at the top)

To: Recipient name or names with titles if appropriate (CC line can be added below if needed)
From: Your name, Title or relationship if appropriate
Date   Date written
Subject: provide a brief detailed note on what the specifics of the memo are about

---

The body is single spaced, with no indent and an extra return between paragraphs.

Letter

Date

Recipient Name
Recipient Title
Recipient Organization
Organization/ Recipient Address

Dear Recipient Name:

The body is single spaced, with no indent and an extra return between paragraphs and 1 inch margins all around.

Typically you should use the 3-paragrpah form given in class materials for cover letters, complaints, thank you notes, letters of transmittal, recommendations. Etc.

Sincerely,

Your name
Your contact information

Enclosure: (Used when something is sent with the letter)

Sample Cover Letters and Résumé

Following are two cover letters showing different styles of presenting the material to impress the reader. Both are similar in following the proper form, but the first uses a focus paragraph, while the second employs a chart to make the information stand out as well as make it easier to read.

After the cover letters is a résumé that gives a general, functional form of a résumé in reverse chronological order. The résumés do not relate to the cover letters but can show some of the typical ways to present your information.

February 3, 2009

Employer address
Line2
Line3

Dear Employer name (or Recruiter if not specified)

I am writing regarding the position posted on (give location) on (give date). I am a computer science student at the New Jersey Institute of Technology graduating in December 2006 and am sure that my skills and qualifications match your position well.

As you can see from the attached résumé, I meet the requirements listed in the job request. In particular, I am a creative, self-motivated, bright, adaptable worker, experienced in a broad range of programming languages and styles. My training is strongly rooted in object-oriented programming and design, with over five years of programming experience in the C++ language. I have a strong interest in applications of computer graphics and am experienced with both the Microsoft DirectX and OpenGL graphics packages.

I would like to discuss my qualifications for this and other positions available at your company. Please feel free to contact me at the address listed below. I look forward to hearing from you and thank you for your time and consideration.

Sincerely,

Your Name
Employer address
Line2
Line3
(908) XXX.XXXX
email@njit.edu
http://web.njit.edu/~address/

Sample Cover Letters Style 1

February 3, 2009

Employer address
Line2
Line3

Dear Employer name (or Recruiter if not specified)

I am writing regarding the position posted on (give location) on (give date). I am a computer science student at the New Jersey Institute of Technology graduating in December 2006 and am sure that my skills and qualifications match your position well.

Requirements	*My Experience*
Maintain existing code Properly propagated change through AEC	
Develop new functionality and new enhancements	
A Bachelor's Degree in Computer Science, Math, or Physics.	
2–3 years of programming experience in C++ with CAD system development.	
Experience in math—geometry.	
Understand customer requirements and propose effective solutions.	
Work well in a team environment.	
Ability to learn quickly	
Excellent skills of manipulating with complex data structures and C++ classes.	

I would like to discuss my qualifications for this and other positions available at your company. Please feel free to contact me at the address listed below. I look forward to hearing from you and thank you for your time and consideration.

Sincerely,

Your Name
Employer address
Line2
Line3
 (908) XXX.XXXX
email@njit.edu
http://web.njit.edu/~address/

Arthur T. Student
123 Bogus Blvd.
Newark NJ 07102-1982
973-555-1234
ATS123@njit.edu
http://web.njit.edu/~ats123

Objective: Obtain a full-time, entry-level position in Chemical Engineering with opportunity for advancement and the ability to contribute to a strong team environment

Education

Stanford University, Stanford, CA 94305
Bachelor of Science in Chemical Engineering,   Conferred: 2008
Areas of focus: Environmental Science

Experience
2008–present New Jersey Department of Environmental Protection, Trenton, NJ
Bureau of Standard Permitting Officer,
- Performed Quality Assurance/Quality Control on the Acute & Chronic Biomonitoring program
- Researched background and bases for new regulations
- Developed spreadsheets to organize and collate information on Stream Studies; wrote complete documentation for spreadsheet program
- Assisted permit writers in formulation and writing of facility-wide permits and general permits

Internships
2007–2008 Campaign '07, Edison, NJ
Communication Intern, Coordinated Campaign Office
- Recruited and organized volunteers to assist with campaign
- Composed news articles and press releases
- Designed leaflets, posters, and other materials

Computers
Programs MS Office Word, Excel, & PowerPoint, Adobe Acrobat & Photoshop
Web page HTML, Java, Dreamweaver, FrontPage

Societies American Institute of Chemical Engineers (AIChE), Member, 1991–present
Beta theta Pi Fraternity, Social Chair, 1990–1992t

Volunteering *Tutor,* Colonia High School, Colonia NJ 07067

Activities Intramural sports

Interests Fiction Writing, Screenwriting, Coin Collecting, sports

References Available upon request.

CHAPTER 7

Presentations

Key Ideas of This Chapter

- What should be considered when making an oral presentation?
- What are the parts of a speech?
- What are the different conceptions of the role of the presenter?
- What are the essentials of formal presentations?
- What are Handouts and why are they used?

Public Speaking

Many people dread or even fear public speaking. A survey done of the biggest fears of people has public speaking ranked above death because you only die once but can be made to give a speech over and over again. One of the most important things to realize is that the fear or nervousness about public speaking is in the mind of the speaker. When asked, people say the hesitation comes from the fact that they are being judged, are the center of attention, and have only one chance to do it correctly. Rather than see an oral report or speech as an opportunity to succeed, it is seen as the potential for failure. It is this mindset that must be overcome. The audience does not know what you are going to say, and you have the opportunity to lead them along the path of your report. By practicing, knowing what to do ahead-of-time and preparing, you can spend less time worrying about the speech and more time working on your delivery. To assist with this, some basic tips for public speaking are given in this chapter. To ease concerns, especially for oral reports in school, it is helpful to embrace them as a way to practice for when you have to present in a more official setting where the stakes are higher and consequences greater. By changing your mindset from something to endure or finish to one of an opportunity to share your ideas and practice, making speeches may be easier. The key to improvement is practice and self-awareness of what needs to be done to improve. Knowing your material well makes it easier to deliver it more effectively. Knowing how to deliver material orally makes it easier to focus on what you say. As a result, the more you prepare and practice, the better you will be and the easier the task will become.

When presenting material orally, there are many factors that must be considered. Generally, you must work on what to say and how to say it. Both are important and so the less you need to concentrate on one of them the more effort can be focused on the other. Eventually, as speaking skills are improved through practice and the content is known better, both aspects will be mastered. To help with this, you should remember the three C's of presenting: Confidence, Composure, and Connections. Confidence deals with knowing your strengths and weaknesses, your audience, as well as your material so that you can feel comfortable with it and feel you have a mastery of the situation. Remember that no one knows what you are going to say or what the speech is about. You are the expert and the one in control. You are guiding the audience through the material in the way you wish to present it. Having confidence in yourself and your ability to present along with the strength of the material you are presenting will make giving the speech easier. The second C is composure, or remaining calm and in control throughout the presentation. Murphy's Law says that if something can go wrong it will go wrong. Being prepared for problems and knowing that things might not go as planned can help you stay in control and react more effectively to problems. Having confidence in your ability and knowledge helps you to be prepared and remain composed. Nervousness is the major obstacle for many people as the presentation progresses. Though unavoidable, being nervous is something that can be minimized, and exhibiting composure makes your speech seem more authoritative and you more prepared and expert. Finally is connection, which reminds you to make contact with your material and your audience. You are the conduit via which the ideas and content are transmitted to the audience. Being sure to connect with the audience on their level and conveying the material to them in the best way for them to understand and act on it is essential. Being confident and composed will assist with making the connection. Always working to keep your audience in mind as you make the speech and working to complete the speech will help make it successful.

Most of us can quickly bring to mind examples of people who are excellent public speakers and even more that exhibit poor public speaking skills. This can be true in our everyday encounters with people but is brought into greater focus in formal speaking situations like class presentations or even instructor lectures. Better speeches are organized, easy to follow, and easy to listen to without distractions. Poor speakers do not seem to connect with the material for the audience seem unprepared, are difficult to understand and generally cannot get their points across. In the end, the goal of the oral presentation must be to have the message received by the target with as little noise as possible.

The formality of the speaking situation is often the most important to identify as it brings with it a sense of judgment and pressure. Regardless of the level of formality, the value you give to the assessment others have of you may impact your final package. Speeches, unlike written work include you as part of the package and allow for instantaneous feedback as you see the reaction of the audience as you present. It is important to realize that your view of your role when presenting and your assessment of the situation are two major factors that affect the outcome and your ability to improve your public speaking. If you are giving the speech as part of a class, you will be judged on some common areas. Even if you are not, these same areas will be the ones that affect how well your audience is able to understand what you are saying and react to how you are saying it. Too often speakers only consider the elements of good content and delivery when standing in front of the class as the focus of the activity or feel the presentation is being assessed. However, if you see every time you speak as an opportunity to work on good basic skills of speaking and an obligation to delivery your message effectively to your target, you will become better at your delivery and thus improve your overall public speaking when the time comes for you to stand up and lead.

For the content or what you say, the following areas are important both in speeches and in written work. First, was the proper topic covered? Along with this is the idea of a good thesis clearly expressed and supported throughout the entire work or speech. No matter how well written or spoken something is, if the topic covered is wrong or a clear central idea or argument is lost in a jumble of facts or distracting images, the entire work will not be successful. Moving to the smaller level of examination, it is important to clearly express oneself, especially with regard to proper word choice and the use of elaboration and supporting evidence and materials. Having accurate facts and figures along with a sufficient number of points to support the main point carried through the paper is essential to a good speech or paper, as it convinces the audience by proving the argument with the weight of good evidence. Lastly, with speeches, it is important to handle questions effectively and be able to give answers concisely, clearly, and accurately.

For the delivery of the speech or what you say, the following areas are important. First is the attitude of the speaker. If you do not take the speech as seriously as it should be or appear to trivialize what you are speaking about, problems can arise. There are so many small things that can be misinterpreted by the audience that the appropriate attitude is essential when giving a speech in order to maintain control of the situation and connect with the audience. One of the most difficult aspects of how you present relates to the rate and volume of the speech. The speed at which you speak and how you vary the level of your voice is key to good public speaking. Both of these aspects of the speech can give emphasis, hold audience attention, and provide many tools to the speaker. Unfortunately, these same aspects, if not handled well, can distract or even deter the audience from getting the points being made. Along with this is the need for good pronunciation of the chosen words and elimination of as many pause words as possible. Mispronunciation and using pause words distracts the audience and weakens the delivery of the content as well as the audience's impression of the speaker. This can also be carried to body language and gestures. Used effectively, gestures can enhance a speech and drive home important points. However, used incorrectly, the effects can be counterproductive by distracting the audience and confusing the message. Overall, the delivery seeks to have a professional look and feel so that the speaker presents a neat and appropriate presentation for the circumstances. If any are used, the visuals should be appropriate and augment what is spoken and not used to distract the audience or replace the speaker. Visual aids are just that, aids to help the audience follow what is being said.

Turning our attention to the situation in which you are asked to deliver content about some topic to a group, it becomes important to ask you to reflect on your view of what you are being asked to do. The following section discussed the different roles a speaker assumes when leading the presentation.

Conceptions of the Role of the Presenter

When you prepare for an oral presentation, the way you prepare and think about what is to be done will reflect your view of your role. Everyone starts as some level of novice and many stay there even if skills are added and speaking improves. However, by seeing different classifications of the roles speakers play and the skills used in each of these roles the beginner can work to attain high levels of competency and become a better public speaker. Good speaking starts with good listening. As you listen and watch public speeches, you can begin to see those aspects you feel were better and those that were worse. You should note what aspects fit your own style of presenting and so might be added to your repertoire. Active listening will assist you to be more engaged in the experience and allow you to get more out of the presentation as well as see ways you might improve your own abilities.

Though some people may be able to naturally be better presenters, being consciously aware of the typology listed below will help those who want to work to develop a specific style and be more prepared for different speaking situations. Remember the acronym BASIC which stands for:

- Beginner
- Administrator
- Script Reader
- Integrated Presenter
- Coordinator of Experiences

The beginner is where most people start when planning and presenting a speech. He or she usually sees speeches as a more formal version of what is done in daily life when talking with anyone else though there is pressure from accountability and so exhibits many of the common flaws in both the content and delivery. The beginner's mindset often sees the risk of failure rather than opportunity for success and so is nervous and relies heavily on the coverage of materials with reliance on facts or the words of others. Tools and technology are used to draw attention away from the speaker rather than to make the speech more effective for the targets to understand the message being presented. The beginner is not aware of or misuses techniques of oral oration and does not link what is said with how it is being said. The content is often poorly organized for the listener and the target is rarely the focus of decisions about the presentation.

As the beginner becomes more practiced at speaking and works to improve their skill, two common means of improvement are often utilized. They become an administrator of the presentation or a script reader. Both the administrator and Script Reader still relies on the content being covered but approach the delivery in two different ways. The Administrator organizes the material to be presented and manages the interaction so the content takes center stage. They will often prepare a PowerPoint or use other technology to deliver the content so it can be shown to the audience. Rather than hold the attention of the group on themselves they direct it to the visuals and make statements that move the presentation forward rather then keep control and guide the listeners through the content. At its highest level, the administrator can be removed from the presentation without any loss of content. On the other hand is the Script Reader who as the name suggests, prepares a script to read. Every word and gesture is planned out and delivered. Some will read from a paper or note cards while others will memorize the material. Even so, like the Administrator, the Script Reader steps back and allows the content to be the center of attention so that they are just the one orchestrating the presentation rather than a vital part of it.

Both of these roles can yield effective presentations, especially when the goal is to convey content or review the work of others as in many classroom presentations. It is important to note that using technology or referring to notes or a script is not necessarily a bad thing. However, if this creates a barrier between the presenter and the targets is weakens the presentation. These two roles are often seen as better then the beginner but are only steps on the way to highly effective presentations.

If the beginner can recognize those aspects lacking in their work and transforms their thinking to do what is not being done above, he or she can become more accomplished. To move to the next level, it is important to see that the content and delivery must work together in the presentation. This integration is what the next role is able to do. The Integrated Presenter (IP) recognizes and considers target and stakeholders as well as the tie between content and delivery to make the presentation more effective. The IP is focused on the best way to deliver the content so it attains the goal and conveys the core message. He or she is tied to the target or at least considers the knees of listeners and makes attempts to increase the likelihood of success. IPs gain depth of knowledge about content to increase the ability to deliver it effectively and allow targets to internalize the materials. With the integrated approach, technology and other tools of presenting become the means to effective delivery of the message and a way to keep the targets engaged rather than distracted. Most speakers who are seen as good or excellent envision themselves in this role and plan for an integrated approach to the content being presented.

So why is there another role? What is beyond the integrated presentation? Only a few people move beyond the first four levels identified and will have a specific reason to do so. It is usually tied to the situation in which the presentation will be made. The Coordinator of Experiences sees his or her role as creating an experience for the targets. If you think of an accomplished actor performing, they are not just delivering lines. It is their job to make you believe that they are the person they are portraying. This is akin to what this highest level of presenter is doing. Within this highest level are three different types of presenters: Master of Ceremony (MC), Eloquent Specialist (ES), and Director of Experiences (DE). Not everyone will seek to attain these levels of ability or ever need to assume these roles. However, if you have seen experts in these roles presenting, you will most likely identify them as some of the best presenters. Moreover, you may feel as if the experience you had was more than just a means to have content given to you so that you were being connected with on a personal level.

The MC is usually more disconnected from the material and is more involved with the orchestration and organization of the presentation. A MC has excellent oration skills and does not need to be concerned with the content being presented. Engaging the audience and keeping them focused while the material is covered is more important than deep knowledge of the material. In school, many students might see someone who is an MC as being a great speaker but experts in what is being presented might see that the content is lacking even though it was presented well.

ES bring together the MC and IP to be able to speak effectively and persuasively about advanced contend that is delivered to the level of the target. Often the ES makes some connection with the group but the targets may recognize a feeling of distance between the speaker and the audience. This might be seen in larger lectures or video presentations. Though things are done to attain goals effectively a great deal of time and effort is typically needed ahead of time to allow the ES to make the oration happen.

Lastly, the DE transcends the levels by mindfully constructing experiences for the targeted groups and those that are around and might influence them in order to create an experience that accomplishes the desired goals. The DE can work at the level of Individuals or masses of people. This can be in person or via synchronous or asynchronous media. The DE creates an experience and understand how all aspects of the process of oration can impact and influence the targets. Often the targets feel a personal connection with the speaker and are fully engaged with what is being said. Few attempt and even fewer are able to attain expertise at the DE level since this role relies on many intangible to allow the DE to generate buy-in and enthusiasm in the targets. Many charismatic leaders and effective salesmen work to assume this role and be highly effective at creating a planned experience for the audience even if the targets are not aware of it.

Formal Presentations

Though every speech can be broken into form and content, for beginners it is important to understand that most, if not all, speeches follow a similar outline. Though the specifics of the form and content vary, the sections listed below will appear in most speeches. Also, remember that every formal speech should begin with a salutation such as "hello" followed by the name(s) of the speaker(s) as well as the topic to be discussed. In most cases it is also a good idea to instruct the audience how questions will be handled. The three most common ways to handle questions is to let the audience ask them throughout the speech, ask them to wait for planned pauses, or to have the questions held until the end of the speech when there will be time for questions and answers. Though accomplished presenters adopting the advanced roles might not follow the outlines below, for beginners, the scheme is provided as a good starting point.

Many times there will also be visual aids that accompany the oral part of the presentation. The visual aids can be in many different forms: PowerPoint slides, maps, handouts, overhead projector transparencies, slide projector presentations, or many other systems for displaying visuals with the oral presentation. All of these aids are intended to make the message easier to understand. In all cases, visual aids should be used to help make things easier to follow or understand. Do not use aids to distract from your speech and your message. It is assumed that most people will use some type of technology to aid in presenting such as PowerPoint

The first thing spoken or displayed during an oral presentation should be the title or title page. This is similar to the title page of an essay and should contain the same information. The presentation title and presenter's name may be larger and placed in different locations on the screen. This page can remain posted until the speech begins. While this page is posted, instruction to the audience can be given. For example, handouts can be distributed and equipment checked.

Immediately after the title page is usually an overview of the speech. This is similar to the abstract of a research paper. It is intended to give the audience an idea of what to expect in the presentation and how it will proceed. It outlines the flow and pacing of the work. Usually items that are mentioned in the overview are the major topics covered in the presentation and may appear on slides as the presentation moves forward. During the overview, explanation of how to use handouts, types of multimedia devises to be used (video, audio etc), or other instructions can be given to the audience. The overview usually ends with instructions about questioning such as, "Please hold all questions until the end of the presentation." Depending on the situation and the length of the speech, you may not have a formal overview. It is up to you to decide if it is appropriate but remember that any visual is meant to aid the targets to understand the structure of the presentation, easily access the content, and get the message.

Next an introduction is presented. This is similar to the opening of a paper. It is intended to catch the audience's attention and focus it upon the main idea or thesis of the speech. It may also contain an outline of the evidence presented in the speech that supports the thesis being discussed.

As the speech begins, the next thing that might be given is background on the topic. This section is not necessary for every presentation but helps the audience understand what is being discussed and provides useful definitions and other material that appears in the body, which logically develops the topic and supports it with evidence and examples.

Finally there should be a conclusion. This section draws the speech to a close by summarizing the points made and restating the thesis. It can also give the audience insight into how the topic is connected to other areas or has implications for further exploration and research. This section usually ends with some statement of conclusion and movement to questioning if it is to be allowed. For example, "This concludes my presentation, are there any questions?"

After the speech is concluded, time should be given for questioning. This is the time for the audience to interact with the presenter and ask questions or make comments related to the speech. The presenter should mediate this and remain in control of the situation.

As mentioned earlier, handouts are an effective way to augment a presentation. Good handouts can reduce the amount of content that needs to be presented, allow visuals to be accessed more effectively, and provide the targets with something to take with them. The first thing to consider when developing a visual to be used in the presentation or handout is the ideas of legibility and readability. Legibility is how well an item can be distinguished from one another and from the background. This was discussed in the previous chapter when discussing graphics and fonts. Readability is how easily the visuals can be accessed to gain the intended meaning. For example, at the level of words and sentences, legibility deals with the fonts used and the way letters are able to be distinguished while readability deals with the layout of the text in sentences and paragraphs so it flows well and can be grasped easily by targets. For images, the density of material, size, resolution, and other characteristics determine how legible and readable the image will be.

Effective handouts must be designed, distributed, and utilized to aid the presentation and not replace or distract from it. Planning is key to proper use of handouts. Handouts should provide:

- Important terms and concepts
- Any essential illustrations or graphics, if appropriate
- Your contact name, title and contact information, if appropriate
- Content that supplements your presentation if needed
- Connections to the presentation content
- Space for notes.

It is important to design the handout so it supports what is being said and does not replace it or conflict with it. You do not want people to be reading instead of listening to you. If you need the handout to be used during the presentation it is important to identify where it fits and when it is to be used. If it is a takeaway then you may want to hold it until the end of the presentation to use as reinforcement during your conclusion. The style of the visuals in the presentation should be consistent with the handout. Handouts are just another tool you should use to increase the effectiveness of your message. Two links to tips for effective handouts can be found at: http://www.rethinkpresentations.com/how-to-write-a-presentation-handout-5-effective-ideas/
http://www.wittcom.com/index.htm

Conclusion

Oral presentations and public speaking are one type of situation that everyone will face and being prepared for it can improve your effectiveness. Though there is much more that can be discussed, the key is to practice and reflect on your own presentation and those of others. If you can recognize good aspects that can be added to your own style and worked on to improve them, you will be able to present more effectively whenever you are asked to do so. Though not everyone needs to be or even wants to become the best public speaker in the world, through some work and reflection anyone can improve to a desired level of proficiency.

SUMMARY

This chapter discussed oral reports and provided general guidelines to assist with the process of creating and delivering these types of packages. It also presented different levels of the role of the presenter and his or her relationship to the audience.

References and Other Readings

Additional examples and explanations are provided on Dr. Lipuma's web page at
    http://njit.mrooms.net/course/view.php?id=14403
Budiu, M. (2005). Making a Good Presentation. Retrieved from: *http://www-2.cs.cmu
    .edu/~mihaib/presentation-rules.html*
Demand Entertainment Inc. (2008). So You Wanna Deliver An Effective Speech? Retrieved
    from: *http://www.soyouwanna.com/site/syws/speaking/speaking.html*
OWL at Purdue. (2004). Purdue Online Writers Lab. Retrieved from:
    http://owl.english.purdue.edu/lab/owl/

Pearson Education Inc. (2008). Public Speaking Website. Retrieved from:
http://wps.ablongman.com/ab_public_speaking_2
Presentation Handouts
http://www.rethinkpresentations.com/how-to-write-a-presentation-handout-5-effective-ideas/
Tips for Handouts
http://www.wittcom.com/index.htm

CHAPTER 8

General Problem-Solving Process

Key Ideas of this Chapter

- What are the steps of the problem-solving process?
- Why is awareness so important to the process of problem solving?
- What are parameters and assumptions, and why are they both important to the process of problem solving?
- What are the parts of the problem question statement?
- What is the difference between criteria and parameters?
- How are solutions measured and compared?
- Why is it important to attempt to put the solution into action?
- How are the different concepts discussed earlier related to problem solving?

Introduction

The following is a general problem-solving process that characterizes the steps that can be followed by any discipline when approaching and rationally solving a problem. When used in conjunction with reasoning and decision-making skills, the process works well for one or more participants. Its main purpose is to guide participants through a procedure for solving many types of problems that have a varying level of complexity. Please note that this is a rational, thoughtful process based upon critical thinking, and so it takes time. Some problems need immediate action and thus may not lend themselves to being examined in this way. However, if an acceptable outcome is not reached, this process can be used to examine what was done to better understand where issues might have occurred. The process is both descriptive and prescriptive. This means it can be used to look at past, present, and potential future problems and their solutions in a clear, systematic way that is consistent and able to be generalized. At each step along the way to a solution, various types of research must be conducted to successfully accomplish the steps of the process and thus arrive at an effective solution that is viable. In problem solving, good research, decision-making, critical-thinking, and self-assessment skills are vital to a high-quality result. At each step in the process, the problem solver may need to go back to earlier steps and reexamine decisions made. It is this revisiting of earlier choices that makes the process iterative and allows for improvement of the final outcomes.

It is important to have a framework to approach, examine, and solve problems. The following section explains the process for examining the various aspects of a problem that you might confront. The steps of the process are:

1. Become Aware of the Problem
2. Define the Problem
3. Identify Parameters and Assumptions
4. Choose Particular Problem to Be Solved

5. **Identify Potential Solutions**
6. **Choose Evaluation Criteria**
7. **Explain Valid Potential Solutions**
8. **Evaluate Solutions to Identify Best Solution**
9. **Explain the Best Solution**
10. **Create Plan to Implement Best Solution**

The first step of any problem-solving process is becoming aware. This awareness can be generated from inside or outside the problem solver. Many times, the awareness is part of a stated task or assignment given to the individual by someone else. In other cases, a person can observe a specific problem or a clear gap in knowledge that they feel must be addressed. In the end, as long as someone perceives a problem, awareness of this problem is achieved. However, the level of awareness and the research associated with this level is vital to the initiation of the problem-solving process.

Going back to the case described earlier, feeling hungry might be the way you become aware of the problem of needing to get something for lunch. However, perhaps it is looking at the clock or having someone ask what you plan to have for lunch that makes you aware that you need to get something to eat. Having become aware of the problem, the next step is to define what exactly it is you are talking about. For some, lunch can be a snack-sized bag of chips. For others, a three-course meal might be barely enough. It is important to know what is meant by "lunch" and "food." These words can mean different things to different people or even make no sense to some.

You should stop for a moment and think about why the steps of the process are given. Often when you are made aware of a problem your first inclination is to jump to the last step and recommend what you feel is the best solution or at least something that will work. This chapter and the material presented earlier attempts to break you of this habit so that thoughtful effort can be employed to arrive at a solution that is justified by research and reasoned argument.

EXAMPLE 8.1

If I say, "I have a headache," what do you think of and what would you tell me? Many immediately suggest an aspirin, or some other pain reliever without asking any questions or thinking any further. Though this may be an answer, the problem-solving process will give more insight into why the person has the headache and if a pain reliever is necessary or will even be effective. Research is needed to determine if the suggested solution is a good one.

There are many reasons why a person might have a headache. Perhaps the person did not eat anything all day or is suffering from a cold. Many students say that just thinking about this hurts their head (or some other part of the body). Other reasons are less likely but still possible, such as they have a brain tumor or have been hitting their head against a nearby wall. Though an aspirin might work temporarily to help the person hitting their head against the wall, the better solution might be to stop hitting his or her head against the wall.

In the end, many problem solvers are seeking any solution so giving them an option that works is fine. For the process described here, especially when dealing with potential problems, the arguments for the course of action to be taken are as important as the best solution put forth. Since potential problems can be dealt with by a number of different solutions, each with varying probabilities of being successful, having a wide range of potential solutions to choose from and knowing more about the situation is a vital part of the process. Do not just skip ahead even though it is easier and faster.

Define the Problem

After the problem is recognized, research is conducted. Initially, research must be done to help define the problem as well as identify the assumptions being made and determine the parameters of the situation. The main purpose of this step is to evaluate the constraints on the problem and the problem solver to better understand the goals that are trying to be reached. Once these goals are identified, the objectives that must be attained in order to reach the goals can be specified and utilized to help narrow the scope of the problem. Once the goals and objectives are clearly understood, the problem to be solved can be decided upon.

Though knowing the goals and objectives of the process is necessary, equally as important is having a clear grasp of the terminology being used. Creating a list of definitions is a good idea. It is important for the problem solver to understand what he or she means by the terms being identified by research as well as those being created during the process. Just accepting what is said in a dictionary may lead to problems when information from a variety of sources is consulted and synthesized to solve the problem. In addition, when the problem solver communicates with others, confusion about what words mean can lead to misconceptions and misunderstandings throughout the process. Having a firm grounding in clear definitions is vital to assist the entire process to move smoothly.

Parameters and Assumptions

Next, it is important to discuss parameters and assumptions. Both parameters and assumptions are important because they help simplify the process enough so that a solution can be found. Real life is complex so knowing the boundaries of particular situations as well as how to make choices that lead to an attainable answer are vital to success. Once a conscious decision has been made to use an assumption, from that point on it is considered a parameter for the process and taken as true. However, if the solution does not prove to be successful, the assumptions can be examined and changed to lead to new outcomes. In many cases parameters, and sometimes assumptions, are supplied by outside sources such as the professor or a supervisor. In these cases, it is even more important to be able to distinguish what is an unalterable fact and what is just an assumption or suggestion.

Returning to the problem of having lunch, time, money, diet, season, location, and a host of other things restrict the problem of getting lunch and shade the choices. As a result, until the problem is more clearly defined and parameters and assumptions are set, it is difficult to know what to do. Suppose that you had only $1 and were restricted to the school cafeteria. The choice of what to eat would be very different from the situation if the parameters were that you had enough money to afford anything but only 15 minutes to get and eat it. Depending on the parameters, the problem question changes. For the first situation, the question might be, "What can I eat from the Café for $1?" In the second situation, the question becomes "What can I get and eat in 15 minutes or less?" In either case, the question would start out as "How might I get something to eat for lunch?" and then the parameters would change because in both cases the goal of getting lunch is the same. Once the question has been asked, it is important to generate a list of solutions that can be used to answer the question with a "yes" response. However, it is important to note that if the problem is not focused enough, too many solutions may be generated. If you simply ask "What can I get for lunch?" for example, the potential items are staggering. Even if you limit it to a place and time, the options may still be too great: pizza, burgers, chicken, pasta, hotdogs, tacos, and many more items. In this case, the criteria for evaluation might then just be "what do you feel like" or "what costs the least"? If the parameters had been more specific, the criteria in this section would be less important because the number of items to choose from would already be narrowed. After criteria are settled upon, they should be used to identify the best option. Finally, once you have decided upon something to eat that fits all the parameters and ranks highest for the criteria, the last step of the process asks you to actually try to get the lunch you decided upon. Suppose you decided that you felt like a burger and only eat Whoppers. The problem you might face is how to get to Burger King rather than what to eat for lunch. Often, though one problem is solved, others are identified in the process.

In the end, no matter what the problem is or how it is presented, a good problem solver using this process will be able to approach any problem logically. In addition, he or she will be able to utilize a wide array of skills and tools from many disciplines to assist in the researching and solving of the problems. The skills learned herein can be used in any discipline at any level to assist problem solvers to more clearly define a problem, evaluate options or decisions, as well as arrive at a justified solution.

Just as research might have been the impetus for engaging in the problem-solving process—it made the problem-solver aware—research is vital to the specification of parameters and assumptions. The heart of this step is the series of decisions made to narrow the scope of the problem made by the problem solver. Parameters are those factual boundaries and constraints set by the problem statement or discovered through research. Assumptions, by contrast, are those constraints that the problem solver sets without having incontrovertible factual backing for those decisions. A clear understanding of the assumptions being made when engaging in the process is important. If an unsatisfactory outcome is reached, it may be necessary to adjust these assumptions. Even if the final solution is arrived at, knowing one's assumptions assists the problem solver in explaining and defending their conclusions.

All of this has been very abstract so far. A more realistic example that most of us can relate to is needed to bring this into focus. I will use myself as an example to clarify the first few steps and how each might proceed.

EXAMPLE 8.2

Suppose I came to you and said, "I need help finding a date." This should initiate the problem-solving process because I have made you aware of my problem or lack of something—in this case, a date. What is your first inclination? Starting with what you think of first is a good way to begin because it taps into your ambient knowledge. However, be careful not to jump right to the last step and give me the solution. Doing some research will help. First, did you assume I wanted to find someone to take out, or that I was looking for a day on the calendar to do something? What was meant by the word *date*? If we agree I am looking for a person to accompany me, you can think about what you or people you know do to find a date. Also, you can consult dating pages such as Match.com. These types of sources will give background into dating and some overarching categories of areas to investigate.

More specific research may be more helpful. Asking me questions about my particular problem will help much more. What is my problem with dating? Am I not able to find a person to date, a place to go, how to ask someone, or something else? Each of these questions helps provide parameters that can focus the discussion of the problem I am having. Knowing more about the specific problem helps to narrow the problem and identify parameters. As you can see, the first three steps work together to clarify what is happening and how to proceed to the next steps. The problem will be very different if I need a date for some event versus finding a long-term companion.

Select the Problem to Be Solved

Once a goal and set of objectives has been specified and the parameters and assumptions identified, it is necessary to choose a particular problem to solve. Any large problem can be broken into smaller problems that are in turn broken into even smaller problems to be addressed. Each problem is an achievable goal that consists of objectives. Each of these objectives is a sub-problem that must be solved first in order to solve the larger overarching problem.

There are many different reasons to choose a particular problem to solve. It is important to do risk assessment on the problems involved and examine why the problem is being solved. For example, the problem might be the most important, most immediate, most far reaching, or most politically important at the moment. Whatever the choice, the individual or group must have clear reasons why they choose the problem to be solved.

Once the aspects of the problem are known, the problem must be phrased as a question that each solution can answer affirmatively. An example of a problem statement might be "How might I increase the use of problem-solving techniques by college graduates of four-year universities in America today?" This specific type of question has four separate parts: question statement, active verb, object, and parameters and assumptions.

The first part is the question statement that transforms the problem into a question to be answered. It takes the form "How might I" or "In what ways might I." If the process is being undertaken by a group, it should be phrased as "we" instead of "I." At times, an individual or a group may examine an issue concerning a third party. For example, students may work on problems facing their institution or that must be handled by the government. In this case, the question might become, "how might our school," or "In what way might the United States government." In all of these cases, the object is to create a question that must be answered as well as specify the group who is designated to answer it. Each solution must then apply to that group and be able to be accomplished by them as well.

Next is the active verb or the action used to solve the problem. Some of the most useful of these active verbs are the ones that describe change without specifying an absolute end or any one action. It is important to realize that the stronger the verb, the more difficult it might be to accomplish workable solutions. For example, it is easier to reduce crime than to eliminate it. Keep this in mind when choosing verbs because verb choice is vital to good solution finding. If necessary, two or more verbs can be used and should be separated by the following conjunctions: and, or, and/or. To assist in the verb choice process, some active verbs are listed in Figure 8.1.

The third part of the problem statement is the object of the sentence that relates to the problem being solved. The object states what is being acted upon by the verb to help solve the problem. Each solution must directly or indirectly affect this object. In our earlier statement, the object is "use of problem solving. techniques".

Finally, the parameters and assumptions that are bounding the solution are listed. These help to focus the solutions that are generated. Though parameters are not necessary, they are often useful to help limit and focus the scope of the process. Be careful not to leave too broad a problem. Broad problems lead to a wide number of solutions that can be difficult to choose between and implement with weak or ineffectual results. At the same time, an overly narrow problem statement can lead to a small number of solutions that provide few useable results. In our example, "college graduates of four-year universities in America today?" are the parameters. This is identified with the conjunction "by" and is used to mark who should have the use of problem solving increased.

FIGURE 8.1
Active Verbs

Accelerate	Compile	Evaluate	Introduce	Prepare	Revise	Systematize
Accomplish	Compose	Examine	Invent	Preserve	Schedule	Teach
Accommodate	Conceive	Execute	Launch	Prevent	Select	Terminate
Achieve	Conclude	Expand	Lead	Process	Serve	Test
Add	Conduct	Expedite	Locate	Program	Settle	Tighten
Administer	Conserve	Fabricate	Maintain	Promote	Shape	Trace
Advise	Consolidate	Follow	Manage	Propose	Simplify	Train
Alleviate	Construct	Form	Market	Protect	Slow	Translate
Analyze	Control	Formulate	Maximize	Prove	Stabilize	Trim
Arrange	Coordinate	Find	Minimize	Provide	Start	Uncover
Assemble	Create	Generate	Monitor	Publish	Stimulate	Unify
Assess	Define	Guide	Motivate	Recruit	Stop	Unravel
Audit	Demonstrate	Head	Negotiate	Redesign	Strengthen	Utilize
Avert	Design	Hire	Operate	Reduce	Structure	Verbalize
Broaden	Determine	Identify	Organize	Reorganize	Study	Verify
Build	Develop	Implement	Originate	Report	Summarize	Visualize
Centralize	Earn	Improve	Participate	Represent	Supervise	Widen
Change	Eliminate	Increase	Perform	Research	Support	Withdraw
Clarify	Employ	Initiate	Persuade	Resolve	Surpass	Work
Collaborate	Ensure	Inspect	Plan	Reverse	Survey	
Compete	Establish	Institute	Predict	Review	Synthesize	

Figure 8.1 is a list of action verbs that can be used when formulating a problem statement.

Once the problem statement is phrased properly, solutions can be generated. However, it is important to note that this statement might have to be modified as more research becomes available or as the remainder of the process is worked through. As the process is iterated, small modifications to the problem statement can be made and refinements in the scope and specificity accomplished through changes in the verb, object, and parameters.

EXAMPLE 8.3

Let's return to my problem, "I need help finding a date." After asking me questions, you determine that I am looking for a companion to go out with who is near my age and attends my university. It is now time to create a question that will assist in finding solutions to this problem. Knowing more about my background and my requirements is necessary. If I have no requirements, the only parameters might be someone who says "yes" when I ask them if he or she wants to go on a date. This is too broad and needs to be focused. Gathering information about the type of person I want to date is helpful. I am a man looking for a woman interested in going out who is near my age and attending or working at my school. At this point, I may also have preferences for the person that I decide to date; however, if these preferences do not rule the person out, they must be considered criteria for judging rather than parameters. I have set down some rules for the person I wish to date. She must be a woman who is willing to consider a relationship with me. These are the parameters. One of these terms is not well defined and must be further specified. What does it mean to be near my age? Am I looking for someone within one, five, or ten years of my age? This may not be easy to define, but when asking women if they are interested, knowing that I am looking for someone between 30–36 years old is very different than someone 21–41 years old.

Other parameters would be even more difficult to specify. What if I wanted a long-term relationship? For some, this might mean more than one or two dates while others think this means being married in a year. If I had a more specific goal, such as to marry the woman I date or to date for more than ten dates, the parameter and the pool of eligible women would change.

Other things are not so firmly set. Though I might have a preference for age, educational background, physical characteristics, and many other aspects, these aspects will be used later to identify the best woman to choose and not to limit the pool of potential women. For now, the question that these parameters specify can be worded, "How might I find a woman at my university who is age 31–41 and interested in dating me?"

Generating Solutions

Once the problem statement has been chosen, it is necessary to generate potential solutions. This is the most creative portion of the process. Even so, conducting research into existing solutions to the problem or similar problems is helpful to generate workable solutions. The main criterion for judging solutions in this step is simply whether or not they answer the problem statement with a "yes." At this point, it may also be possible to eliminate some solutions because they do not agree with commonly held moral and ethical guidelines. Even though not stated specifically, these guidelines are understood and assumed to be upheld when reviewing solutions. For example, a solution to global pollution might be to kill every human. This is obviously not a good solution even though it would give a "yes" answer to the question of "How might we minimize global air pollution caused by humans?" Nonetheless, it is important that the problem solver know why the solution is being eliminated and this elimination happens only after due consideration of scope and scale. Though the solution to kill all humans is not acceptable, restricting admittance to certain areas or limiting population growth can be seen as a valid solution. By examining the core idea and adjusting the way the solution is defined, the level of specificity and so the outcome of the solution can be adjusted to fit within the desired parameters of the problem.

When working in groups, it is important to work together to generate solutions. Also, it should be realized that the solution process takes time depending upon the problem complexity. At this point, do not judge solutions for more than their ability to answer the stated problem questions with a "yes" because they will be evaluated more closely in the next step. Many times it is possible to use discarded solutions to develop new ideas for solutions. However, it is important to be able to distinguish between similar solutions. Saying the same thing in 10 different ways may not be 10 different solutions. Try to group similar solutions together. An example of this is seen when discussing the problem of garbage or solid waste. If you list out the solutions of reduce, reuse, and recycle as separate solutions, recycling may be selected as best, but grouping them together as a system of conserving resources is a better way to present the solution. If all the solutions fall into one group, then perhaps the best solution is to implement that group with different variations for different cases of the problems. Just as there are many unique problems, the solutions to these problems are all unique and need to be adapted to the particular situations being discussed. This will be addressed in the last section of the problem-solving process.

Measuring with Criteria

Once a list of potential solutions has been generated, the evaluation process can begin. First, a list of criteria for judging all solutions equally must be chosen. Criteria are the measuring sticks by which each solution is judged. Since all the solutions will answer your chosen question with a "yes," all of them are valid. The criteria are used to separate better from worse solutions. It is not good enough to rest on trial and error in which each solution is tried until it fails and then another put in its place. Due to time, money, or other more important factors like human lives, some solutions are better than others. Choosing and weighting criteria is important because they are what allow the problem solver to separate out the most important measures and, therefore, the best valid solution. Deciding upon criteria is similar to the identification of parameters. The only difference is that parameters mark what is and is not a solution, while criteria judge which solution is better or worse based upon the characteristic being measured and are more dependant upon your research and personal opinions.

It is vital to eliminate personal bias towards particular solutions as well as to utilize a consistent set of criteria to evaluate all solutions fairly. To do this in the process, criteria must be weighted. Weight is the relative importance given to one criterion over another. This weighting will allow each criterion to be shown as relatively more or less important. By giving one criterion a weight of two (2) and another one (1), the first solution is shown to be twice as important as the second.

Some examples of criteria are: most cost effective, most socially acceptable, most easily implemented, most directly solves the problem, most far-reaching effects, most lasting effects, least government intervention required, least limiting to development, or quickest to implement. It is important to have research and logical reasons for the criteria chosen as well as factual support for the rankings given to a particular solution for each criterion.

Once the criteria are chosen, they should be given a weighting. In most cases, all the criteria have the same weight. However, it is possible to give other weightings to criteria so that a particular factor is seen as more important. Many times, the cost, time to complete, or political nature of a project is more important than other factors; therefore, that criteria may have a higher ranking than others being used to judge what is the best solution. When deciding upon criteria, be sure to have enough to separate out the solutions you have generated. If there are not enough criteria, it will be difficult to create a large enough difference in the solutions to know which one is best for the problem that has been identified.

With the criteria in mind, the larger list of potential solutions can be narrowed to those that fit best for the situation and the desired outcomes. The set of solutions for a particular problem statement will differ depending on how the answers are being evaluated. Clearly defining and justifying the criteria is essential to understanding why and how the best solution was chosen. The process of generating and evaluating potential solutions is often iterative. As a batch of solutions is identified, the criteria to judge them is brought into play to see how well or poorly the solutions will work. Once a set of solutions is deemed acceptable, the scope of the actions presented by these solutions is then assessed to see if more are necessary. In this way, a diverse and effective set of solutions to the specified problem can be generated. In some cases, more or different criteria are necessary. In other cases, the problem statement itself needs to be reworked to allow for a different set of solutions to be generated and evaluated.

Once the final set of criteria are chosen and weighted, all qualified solutions must be described fully to show how each would compare to the criteria. Once this is done, these valid solutions can then be ranked. It is very helpful to include summary charts of both the valid potential solutions and the criteria to be used to judge them after the detailed descriptions have been listed. Examples of this have been given in Example 8.8.

EXAMPLE 8.4

Back to my dating problem, finding a woman to date poses other problems. Hopefully, a large number of women have been found. As long as all of them fit my parameters, they can be considered. If there is only one woman who fits my parameters, then I am done and will ask her out. If I want more women to pick from, I have to change my parameters.

If the number is larger, it will be necessary to have a set of criteria for picking whom to ask. Asking me more questions can help determine these criteria. What do I want in a woman? Am I looking for an athletic woman, a religious person, an educated one, someone with a similar background, a woman I find attractive, or something else that separates my choices so I can judge one as the best to date? Going back to our general research into dating can assist in finding categories that exist to separate out one type of woman from another.

In the end, there is no guarantee that the right person will be found. One of the biggest problems facing a problem solver is uncertainty. Since the problems are only potential and often the subjects are people, it is not easy to narrow things down to easily quantifiable terms. If it were, dating would be easier and this problem would not exist. Even if I try to date the woman identified as best for me, it might not work out for some other reason not considered. However, thinking ahead increases the likelihood of making a match, and by the way, I do not actually do this when looking for a woman to date.

Evaluation Process

Now that the list of solutions to the specified problem and the criteria have been fully defined and explained, the process for picking the best solution to the problem, given the specified criteria, can be undertaken. Two types of procedures for ranking and comparing solutions exist. If the number of solutions is large, usually greater than ten, an independent ranking should be conducted first to narrow the number of choices. Each solution is listed along one side of a grid and then given a score for each criterion from 1–5 where 5 is the highest (other ranges can be used). The rankings for the various criteria are then totaled and a score for each solution is reported. These scores are compared to create a subset of solutions that have the highest score. Though all are valid, the top few move on to the comparative analysis that follows.

If the number of solutions is initially small or the independent ranking has been conducted, the remaining solutions are placed into a grid with the criteria for a comparative analysis. Though all the solutions may be seen as good, the comparative analysis gives the best solution by measuring each solution against the others with regard to each criteria. The total number of solutions listed gives the range of numbers for each criterion. For example, if there are six (6) solutions, then the rankings will go from 1–6 with 6 being the highest. Each solution is ranked for each criterion in comparison to the other solutions for that criterion. However, within a criterion set, two solutions should not be arbitrarily given the same number. If two are equal, the adjacent numbers should be added and then divided by 2. The result is then placed in the space for each solution. See the charts in tables that follow for an example.

It is important to note that the way the solutions are defined and grouped can greatly impact the results. The key is to group similar solutions together if they can be evaluated together. If the problems question statement was "How might we minimize gun violence in schools?" a number of similar solutions could be listed separately. Video cameras, metal detectors, scanners, and security guard searches could all be listed separately. However, all of the solutions could be grouped together under the title "Gun Detection Methods." Another grouping may put the technological fixes together as one solution and separate out the security guards as part of a solution related to increased supervision and security presence. Depending on how the solutions are defined and grouped, the evaluation of the best solution would change. If all of these were to be listed separately, all might be deemed nearly equal in effectiveness and greatly affect the ranking of any other solutions.

EXAMPLE 8.5
Example of the Solution Evaluation Process

If the topic that you started with was cheating at your school, the question you arrived at might be, "How might we minimize online plagiarism at universities in America?" The following charts might be created to summarize what was identified as criteria and solutions, as well as arrive at the best solution. Summary charts are a good way to present things so that the reader can review them quickly. These tables are only tools to help others follow your arguments. A full description of the process is given later. For now, these are only illustrations of one way to solve the problem. Each person must decide how best to present the argument being made and the reasoning behind it.

TABLE 8.1	Table of Potential Solutions	
#	*Potential Solution*	*Description*
1	Awareness to High School Students	Make students aware of plagiarism and its consequences
2	Awareness to University Students	Make students aware of plagiarism policy on their campus
3	Awareness to University Faculty	Get faculty involved in preventing online plagiarism
4	Ban Internet Sites	Enact a law to make downloading papers illegal
5	Eliminate All Papers	Eliminate paper assignments and replace with other classroom assignments, such as presentations and case studies
6	Plagiarism Software	Create software for students and professors to use for reports
Table 8.1 shows a list of potential solutions and short descriptions.		

	Name	Description	Weight
		TABLE 8.2 Table of Evaluation Criteria	
A	Effectiveness	Determine the most effective solution for minimizing online plagiarism	3
B	Directness	Find the best solution that directly affects the problem of minimizing online plagiarism	3
C	Implementation	Least amount of time to put solution into action	2
D	Social Acceptance	Solution accepted by both students and faculty	2
E	Cost	Least amount of cost to be paid by taxpayers and college tuition	1
Table 8.2 shows the criteria with a short description and weight.			

	A(3)	B(3)	C(2)	D(2)	E(1)	Total	Total w/weight
			TABLE 8.3 Table of Comparative Analysis				
1	2 (6)	1.5 (8.5)	5 (10)	1.5 (3)	3	13	26.5
2	2 (6)	4 (12)	3.5 (7)	1.5 (3)	1.5	12.5	29.5
3	4 (12)	1.5 (8.5)	3.5 (7)	4 (12)	1.5	18.5	37
4	2 (6)	3 (9)	1.5 (3)	5 (10)	5	16.5	33
5	6 (18)	6 (18)	6 (12)	3 (6)	6	**27**	**60**
6	5 (15)	5 (15)	1.5 (3)	6 (12)	4	21.5	49

Table 8.3 shows a comparative analysis of the potential solutions. A rating system of 1 to 6 was used, with 6 being ranked highest. Solutions are listed on the left side of chart with numbers (refer to Table 8.2) and criteria are listed on the top of chart (refer to Table 8.2).

A different question that could be generated from the same starting point might be: "How might we minimize intentional complete plagiarism in American Universities?" The process used was the same, but a different question resulted. In addition, this question led to a larger number of solutions and required an independent analysis and comparative analysis.

#	Potential Solutions	Description
	TABLE 8.4 Summary List of Potential Solutions	
1	Awareness in High School	Make students aware about plagiarism in high school level
2	Emphasizing Awareness to Students in Freshman Year	Make students aware about plagiarism in freshman year
3	Professors and Faculty Members Awareness	Make professors and faculty members aware about plagiarism
4	Increase Punishment	Increase the punishment level for submitting plagiarized work
5	Limit Resources	Limit resources for writing papers
6	Law on Selling Papers	Start strict law for selling papers
7	Change Internet Features	Disable copy and paste features
8	Eliminating Papers, Projects, Homework	No outside class assignment, everything will be in class
9	Plagiarism Software	Invent software that is able to find any papers that contain material from the Internet or any previous work

Table 8.4 shows the list of potential solutions and their short descriptions.

	Name	Description	Weight
	TABLE 8.5 List of Evaluation Criteria		
A	Effectiveness	Most effective to minimize intentional complete plagiarism	3
B	Directness	Most directly minimizes intentional complete plagiarism	3
C	Implementation	Least time needed to implement and start the solution	2
D	Social Acceptance	Most people who are involved accept the solution	2
E	Cost	Least amount of cost needed to make the solution effective	1

Table 8.5 shows the list of Evaluation Criteria and their description.

TABLE 8.6	Independent Analysis					
	A(3)	B(3)	C(2)	D(2)	E(1)	Total
1	2	2	3	3	3	13
2	3	3	4	4	4	18
3	1	1	2	2	2	8
4	4	4	5	5	5	23
5	4	3	5	4	4	20
6	5	5	5	5	5	25
7	3	3	4	4	5	19
8	6	5	5	5	6	27
9	5	4	5	5	5	24

Table 8.6 shows the independent analysis for this problem.

TABLE 8.7	Comparative Analysis					
	A(3)	B(3)	C(2)	D(2)	E(1)	Total
4	2*3 = 6	1.5*3 = 8.5	1*2 = 2	1.5*2 = 3	1.5*1 = 1.5	17
6	1*3 = 3	1.5*3 = 8.5	2*2 = 4	1.5*2 = 3	1.5*1 = 1.5	15
8	4*3 = 12	3.5*3 = 7	3*2 = 6	3*2 = 6	4*1 = 4	35
9	3*3 = 9	3.5*3 = 7	4*2 = 8	4*2 = 8	3*1 = 3	34

Table 8.7 shows the comparative analysis for this problem.

Though both started at the same point, these two problem-solving processes worked on different aspects of the problem. Moreover, though the tables are helpful to understand the material presented, without the arguments and full descriptions of the process, it is difficult to know what led to the process, why the decisions were made, and how the arguments were developed.

Once all the solutions are ranked for all criteria and the weighting is applied appropriately, the scores for each solution are totaled. The highest score is then the best solution. If two solutions are close in score, then there may be two solutions that are equally as good but differ in their strong points.

It is important to remember that the criteria that are used are reflective of the decisions being made. Each criterion is a ruler used to judge the solutions to the problem to attain the desired outcome. Different rulers will yield different results so be sure to choose the appropriate rulers as well as use each one as it was intended. In order to arrive at the correct best solution, it is essential for the problem solver to understand how to apply the criteria selected effectively and accurately.

Develop an Action Plan to Implement the Solution

After determining the best solution, it is necessary to give some thought to the way in which it might be implemented since not all solutions can be put into effect. Unforeseen problems may arise as solutions are tested and put to work. Many times, unexpected resistance to solutions can be encountered. Other times, unacceptable results can require that another solution be used. In some circumstances the problem may have been originally identified incorrectly, have been misunderstood, or have changed as a result of research or altered circumstances. The action plan helps the problem solver be prepared for such eventualities.

The action plan can be used to make others aware of potential problems that might be faced when putting the best solution into affect or that will be caused once it becomes active. These problems can then become the first step of another problem-solving process. When solving a current problem, this process will assist the problem solver in thinking of potential problems and thus assist in avoiding unwanted outcomes. Whatever the outcome, it is vital to understand that the choices made during this entire process rely upon research.

Sample Problem-Solving Process

To show a way to use the process and present an argument for an idea, a sample paper is given at the end of the chapter. Though it does not give the exact steps as they are written out, the paper makes an argument based upon the information provided by the process. All of the steps can be seen within the paper without needing to have them listed specifically.

SUMMARY

This chapter presents the steps of a general problem-solving process. Each step helps you to work through the thinking used as you work to achieve a task or overcome an obstacle. It begins with becoming aware of the problem and then moves to defining the problem by clarifying terms, identifying parameters, and deciding upon assumptions. Next and vital to all process is to choose the particular problem to be solved by creating the problem statement that you will use to focus your creative effort. Once this is done, you can identify potential solutions to the problem along with the evaluation criteria used to arrive at the best solution. Once you have a list of potential solutions and criteria, it is important to clearly explain each valid potential solution so that you are clear how they solve the stated problem and relate to each criteria. Having done this, you need to evaluate the solutions to arrive at the best solution. Finally, explain what the best solution is and how it can be put into effect.

Questions and Exercises

1. What are the steps you use to solve problems? What are some assumptions that you have when you approach a problem and create solutions?
2. Why is awareness so important to the process of problem solving? How can you work to become more aware of your own limitations when identifying problems and solutions?
3. Identify a problem in your own life. Phrase it in the form of a question so that you can attack it creatively. Generate a list of solutions and a set of criteria to judge them. Assess these solutions to generate the best solution.

4. What do you feel are the most important factors to consider when judging solutions generally in your everyday life? Why are these most important to you? Will these always work when deciding upon the best solution?

5. Look at the sample paper in Example 8.6 that gives a sample problem-solving process for the power crisis in New Jersey. First identify the steps of the problem-solving process used to create the paper. Critique the thinking and reasoning used in each step. Then see if you agree with the choices made during the process or if you would have made different decisions as you worked through the process. Finally, examine the potential solutions and the criteria. See if you can generate other solutions (Hint: alternate energy generation sources) and chose different criteria. How does this change the outcome of the process? Can you apply this process to the current condition in your own part of the country?

6. Examine the problem statement listed in Example 8.6. Change the problem statement and then see how that changes the choice of criteria and evaluation of the best solution. Do all solutions even qualify if the problem statement is changed even by just one word?

Other Reading

Additional examples and explanations are provided on Dr. Lipuma's web page at
http://njit.mrooms.net/course/view.php?id=14403

EXAMPLE 8.6
Energy Shortage in New Jersey

1. Introduction

Energy consumption has been a major topic in the news, on the Internet, and in our daily conversations. "Since taking the office in January, [2001] President Bush has repeatedly said the United States is in the midst of an 'energy crisis'" (Dizikes, 2001). The fears of a nationwide energy crisis, started in California, have brought concern to the whole nation. The anxiety over energy increased when Energy Secretary Spencer Abraham stated, "The failure to meet this challenge will threaten our nation's economic prosperity, compromise our national security. and literally alter the way we live" (Dizikes, 2001).

In this paper, I will give a brief review of California's energy crisis, provide my definitions, and explain my parameters and assumptions. I will also concentrate on the current condition of the State of New Jersey at the time this paper is being written, discuss the similarity and differences between New Jersey and California, and bring about a definite question related to the possible energy problem in New Jersey. Finally, I will conclude the paper with a variety of possible solutions to the problem statement as well as an evaluation of each solution to eventually arrive at the best solution for the stated problem in the stated situation.

2. Background

2.1 California

The whole misfortune of California started in May 2000, and has lasted ever since. Unpredictable price increases in electricity followed the extreme heat of the summer. "The average price of electricity on the now-defunct Power Exchange soared to $120 per megawatt hour in June, five times higher than the same month during the previous year, and remained roughly at that level until skyrocketing to $377 in December" (Mendel, 2001).

Three main reasons were said to cause California's problem: power supply, transmission lines, and long-term contracts. California has not had a new electric power generation plant in 10 years. In addition, the demand for electricity in California has increased over three times more than predicted. The unexpected power demand comes from the sudden increase in population, which is a result of California's fast-developing information technology industry. Since California is importing up to 25% of its electricity from its neighbors, it needs a larger quantity and more efficient transmission lines to do the delivery. California also initiated bans against long-term contracts, which, as a result, worsen the situation and led to a higher increase in the price of electricity (NCEMC).

2.2 New Jersey

New Jersey is the nation's most densely populated state and has a utility rate that is higher than the national average. Of the four New Jersey utility providers—Conectiv, GPU, Public Service Electric & Gas (PSE&G), and Rockland Utilities—currently, only PSE&G is in the generation business (McNamara, 2001). New Jersey has a wide variety of energy sources, which include coal, nuclear, and oil along with hydro-electric and natural gas. New Jersey, like California, also imports power from its neighbors. Part of New Jersey's electricity is provided by the PJM (Pennsylvania, Jersey, Maryland) Interconnection.

There are fewer unpredictable factors in New Jersey's power supply. "Power producers here (in New Jersey) are required (by the state regulations) to keep a fair amount of energy in reserve" (Dizikes, 2001). Utility suppliers are also allowed to have long-term contracts with industries. In addition, the price of electricity has been limited by state regulations. However, the deregulation phase-in period ended on July 31, 2003. With the end of regulation, the price of electricity is in accordance with the market supply and demand equilibrium.

3. Terms Used in the Paper
In this paper, the words *energy* and *power* both mean electricity or electrical energy. Thus, energy providers are corporations that own the power generating plants and/or are working to deliver power to consumers.

An energy shortage is when there is a greater demand than supply in the power market. Within a free market, the result of an energy shortage is usually a raise in price. The main difference between an energy crisis and an energy shortage is the accessibility of energy at any price. Therefore, an energy crisis is a situation where, even though the consumers are willing to pay as much as necessary, there is not enough power to satisfy the demand of the power market at any price.

In this paper, when I refer to the State of New Jersey, New Jersey, or simply "we," I mean all people, who live in, represent, or work for New Jersey. Thus, it does not only include New Jersey residents, the State Government, and its representatives, but also incorporated companies that provide power to be used inside New Jersey and their employees. Similar definition may also apply to California.

Finally, when speaking of the verb "to prevent" it means to stop the progress. It does not imply to reverse what had happened in the past, but indicates working on the present circumstances to stop the situation leading toward an unwelcome future.

4. Factors Limiting the Problem
The main parameter for determining an energy shortage was the price and availability of electricity. Despite the rare occasions when an energy crisis is compelled by outside influence, such as political force, an energy crisis is often a result of an improperly handled energy shortage.

In California's case, the market was in a shortage; therefore, without proper and fast reactions, the situation slipped towards chaos. Although California's electricity price has risen, it is not always available to every consumer who is willing to pay the price. For instance, there have been blackouts since May 2000. Therefore, consumers are no longer able to purchase the power they are prepared to pay for. Hence, the situation in California can be called an energy crisis.

TABLE 1 Summary on Definitions	
Term	*Definition*
Energy	Electricity or electrical energy.
Power	Electricity or electrical energy.
Power Generators	Corporations that own the power generating plants and/or are working to deliver power to consumers.
Power Shortage	When there is a greater demand than supply in the power market.
Power Crisis	A situation where, even though the consumers are willing to pay as much as necessary, there is not enough power to satisfy the demand of the power market at any price.
Prevent	To stop the progress.
State of New Jersey	All people, who live in, represent, or work for New Jersey.

Table 1 summarizes the definitions used for this paper.

In the case of New Jersey, the regulations were removed at the end of July 2003, and the market was opened for competition. The rate of change in price, demand, and quantity supplied are now the main parameters of whether there is an energy shortage or an energy crisis.

5. Assumptions

The first assumption I made in this paper was that an energy shortage would be a problem for New Jersey. We have always wanted a more comfortable life, which means more consumption of energy. Sooner or later, we will be facing an energy shortage because of the increasing demand for electricity.

Another assumption is that the energy shortage is predictable. The increase in electricity price is an inexorable trend, but when and how much increase is detectable with necessary information. Last but not least, if handled carelessly, an energy shortage could get worse and eventually turn into an energy crisis.

6. Discussion

New Jersey's power supply system has several advantages compared to that of California. For instance, although New Jersey also depends on imported energy, it is smaller and closer to its energy suppliers; therefore, it does not need long distance transmission lines, which lose more energy as the length increases.

However, importing energy implies that our demand is already greater than the supply within the boundary of New Jersey. The high expenses of producing electricity in New Jersey—including its strong commitment to the environment, social benefit programs, long-term contracts, and the nation's highest tax on energy—force New Jersey power providers to import from other states to keep the price under the state's limitation (PSE&G).

The demand for electricity in New Jersey is increasing as the population increases. New Jersey, which is already the nation's most densely populated state—with its excellent living environment and short distance to two large cities, New York and Philadelphia—keeps attracting new population. The demand for energy has risen through the years while the price is forced to stay within a regulated range. Once the deregulation acts are terminated, the price might rise quickly in a short period of time. As the price increases, energy providers are likely to sell as much power as they can generate, which means they would lower the reserve amount of electricity in order to achieve a greater profit. Once there is a sudden demand for energy, an energy shortage or even an energy crisis is possible in the state.

Importing electricity from other states might still help keep the price low once the market is widely opened, but the dependence makes the supply less reliable and more variable. Furthermore, New Jersey is not the only state on the East Coast that is facing a possible energy shortage. No matter how strong the bond is between consumers and their power providers, accessible energy is limited. When a sudden demand for a great amount of energy happens to this area, for instance, an unexpected heat wave in the summer, New Jersey is more likely to lose its energy supply than other states because our out-of-state energy providers are expected to handle their states' energy shortage in higher priority.

7. Upcoming Problem

The United States may not really be in the midst of an energy crisis, as President Bush said. Most parts of the nation still have enough power to provide individuals and industry at a higher price. However, it is undeniable that the energy shortage has hit the West Coast hard. This trend is said to be heading to the East Coast with higher electricity bills and possible blackouts in the upcoming years.

New Jersey faces the challenge of an open market for energy. The demand for power will keep rising causing the price of power to rise causing the amount of reserve to be decreased. All these contribute to the possibility of an energy shortage and even an energy crisis in New Jersey. Therefore, we need to be prepared to face the most important energy problem: how might the state of New Jersey prevent an energy shortage from becoming an energy crisis?

8. Potential Solutions

In order to solve the problem, I generated six possible solutions: building new power plants in New Jersey, purchasing power plants out of state, private power plant/cogeneration, limited power consumption, new transmission line system, and efficiency plans. Following are the detailed descriptions of each solution along with their advantages and disadvantages. At the end of this section, these potential solutions and their short descriptions are given in a summary chart.

8.1 Building New Power Plants in New Jersey

In order to increase the supply of power, it is reasonable to consider building new nuclear and fossil-fuel-burning power plants in New Jersey. This solution will both increase the total supplied power as well as help New Jersey to secure a more independent energy source. It can also help minimize power loss by transmission since the distance between the generation point and consumers will be reduced.

However, the high population density limits possible plant locations. In addition, both fossil fuel and nuclear power plants create air and/or water pollution problems to the environment. In addition, New Jersey's strong commitment to the environment makes building the plant inside Jersey expensive.

8.2 Purchasing Power Plants outside New Jersey

Purchasing power plants or building power plants outside New Jersey can secure our energy supply. PSEG (Public Service Enterprise Group, part of PSE&G Corporation) already owns two fossil fuel power plants in Shelocta and Florence, Pennsylvania (PSEG Fossil), and has 50% ownership of Peach Bottom Atomic Power Station in Delta, Pennsylvania (PSEG Nuclear).

Building new power plants in other states may be less expensive than inside New Jersey because of fewer environmental regulations. However, it is still costly because it needs not only new generators but also new long-distance transmission lines. Buying ownership of existing plants can cost less, but not many plants are willing to sell 100% ownership.

Generating power outside New Jersey can prevent direct environmental damages to our state. Yet, it still affects our environment, though indirectly. "For New Jersey residents, this (purchasing power generated outside New Jersey) is especially harmful: over 33% of our (air) pollution blows in from out of state, largely from coal burning power plants in the Midwest" (Gregory, 2001).

8.3 Private Power Plant/Cogeneration

Another possible solution is to encourage industries who consume high quantities of energy to build private power plants and use industrial by-products to co-generate electricity. The power generated can be used for both private use and for sale. This can ensure power supplies for that industry as well as others in the grid. It also decreases the possibility of a large shortage.

Nevertheless, the high cost of building new power plants may lessen the interest of industry. Cogeneration will not be a steady supply of electricity because of its dependence on the production of the main product. Both private power plants and cogeneration affect our environment with pollution.

8.4 Limited Power Consumption

Regulations on electricity consumption can be placed upon industries by the state government. For instance, the temperature of air conditioning in public and/or private buildings can be limited within a certain range.

By forcing regulations on the industry, the government can limit power consumption and predict future demand. However, passing laws or regulations takes time and the resulting restrictions may not be acceptable to all residents.

8.5 New Transmission Line System

New transmission line systems using high temperature super conductors can be used to upgrade the present system. The four-inch superconductor lines could be used to transfer power from generating plants to substations, and regular copper lines would remain in their role in distribution to users. A similar system was implemented by Detroit Edison in May 2001, for low-loss power delivery. "Swapping copper cables for superconductor ones within existing conduits could allow utilities to triple their power capacity without disruptive digging" (Chang, 2001, p. F1).

As New Jersey is an energy importer, a more efficient power-delivery system can save energy while transmitting from other states. However, this is a new system that has not been tested in practical use. Detroit Edison will report accurate results after 1 year of testing. Although the Detroit system has a lower construction cost, the variable cost of operating a superconductor transmission line system, mainly because of the use of liquid nitrogen, is higher than regular power transmission line systems.

8.6 Efficiency Plans

Efficiency plans are used to increase efficiency both at power generating plants and user side facilities. The Board of Public Utilities recently ordered a 3-year, $358 million energy efficiency development program. This program will get its funding from utility users and use it to help consumers purchase more efficient lighting and heating devices as well as develop renewable energy sources (DeMarrais, 2001). Other plans can be encouraging the use of energy efficient devices with tax discounts and rewards for researching and developing energy efficient designs.

Efficiency plans help lessen a power plant's damage to the environment and are not as costly as other solutions. However, it takes time to attract attention to the possibility of energy shortage and to popularize the idea of energy efficiency. The renewal of certain devices, such as heating systems, also cannot be done in a short time.

TABLE 2	Summary on Potential Solutions	
#	*Name*	*Description*
1	New plants in NJ	Build new power plants inside the State of New Jersey.
2	Plants outside NJ	Build or acquire power plants outside New Jersey.
3	Private plants and/or cogeneration	Encourage industries to build private power plants and cogeneration sites both for private use and for sale.
4	Regulate consumption	Utilize laws to limit energy consumption.
5	New transmission lines	Use new superconductor transmission line to reduce power loss.
6	Efficiency plans	Promote energy plans to increase the efficiency at both power generating plants and user-end devices.

Table 2 summarizes the potential solutions to prevent an energy shortage in New Jersey.

9. Evaluating the Solutions

Rather than just picking a solution from those listed in Table 1, it is important to compare them based upon a series of criteria so the difference between the various solutions can be highlighted and the best solution can be chosen. The criteria to be used for assessing this problem are: time, cost, social impact and acceptance, and environmental impact. Once the various criteria are determined, it is also important to weight each criterion, as some are more important than others for assessing this problem. In the following paragraphs, the descriptions and weight of the evaluating criteria are explained. At the end of the section, a summary chart of the criteria is provided. Each potential solution was assessed with the criteria provided and given points according to the evaluations. At the end of this section is a table that combines the potential solutions with their weighted evaluation. From the table, I was able to generate my choice of the best solution for preventing a possible energy shortage in New Jersey from turning into an energy crisis.

9.1 Time

California's deregulation finished in 1996 and its energy crisis happened in 2000. It was assumed that New Jersey would follow the California model in falling victim to an energy shortage. This means New Jersey would have 4 years after the deregulation act to prepare for this problem. To be conservative, the time limit was set at 5 years from the end of the deregulation process for solutions to be implemented.

All six potential solutions can be completed within the time limit. However, to avoid unpredictable factors, we need to finish the prevention actions as soon as possible. Hence, the shorter time it takes, the better the solution will be. Therefore, time is given a weight value of two.

9.2 Cost

Cost, here, will be the total monetary charge to apply the solution. Since this is a statewide utility problem, no matter who pays the bill for the action plan, the cost will be transferred to the consumers. Thus, it will be easier to look at the total cost of the solution.

Cost is also weighted two because how much it costs to implement the plan determines the possibility of putting the solution into practice. The lower the cost is, the better the solution will be.

9.3 Social Impact and Acceptance

No matter how good the solution is, if it cannot be accepted by the society, it is not practical. In addition, less social impact is required.

Social impact and acceptance is weighted one. Lower social impact and higher acceptance enhance the value of the solution.

9.4 Environmental Impact

Environmental impact is considered not only because it is an important principle of New Jersey but also because damages to the natural environment are not always reversible. Environmental impact is given a weight value of one. Whichever solution has less impact is preferred.

TABLE 3	Summary of Evaluating Criteria		
#	Name	Description	Weight
A	Time	Amount of time to accomplish the plan	2
B	Cost	Total amount of money needed to implement the plan	2
C	Social impact/acceptance	Affect on society and how well the plan is accepted	1
D	Environmental impact	Affect on New Jersey's environment	1

Table 3 summarizes and weights the criteria to be used to evaluate the potential solutions listed in Table 2.

Having identified solutions to the problem and criteria, it is now important to evaluate the possible solutions to determine which one is the best. The chart in Table 4 was constructed by comparing each of the potential solutions with the criteria.

TABLE 4	Evaluating Potential Solutions				
	A(2)	B(2)	C(1)	D(1)	TOTAL
1	2 * (2) = 4	1.5 * (2) = 3	2 * (1) = 2	1 * (1) = 1	10
2	2 * (2) = 4	1.5 * (2) = 3	6 * (1) = 6	3 * (1) = 3	16
3	2 * (2) = 4	3.5 * (2) = 7	3 * (1) = 3	2 * (1) = 2	16
4	5.5 * (2) = 11	5.5 * (2) = 11	1 * (1) = 1	5 * (1) = 5	28
5	4 * (2) = 8	3.5 * (2) = 7	4 * (1) = 4	5 * (1) = 5	24
6	**5.5 * (2) = 11**	**5.5 * (2) = 11**	**5 * (1) = 5**	**5 * (1) = 5**	**32**

Table 4 is the evaluation of the potential solutions listed in Table 2 using the criteria listed in Table 2 to arrive at the best solution.

10. Explanation and Implementation of the Best Solution

From the summary chart in Table 4 , the best solution to prevent an energy crisis in New Jersey was shown to be solution six, efficiency plans. It satisfies each criterion in the evaluation section and was chosen as the most satisfactory solution. The plan takes a shorter time to implement relative to the others, as the state government has already started to implement it. It costs much less than building new or changing current power supply systems, is more acceptable to the society, and is more environmentally friendly.

Although regulating energy consumption come in a close second place, it is not likely to be accepted by society. Thus it is not a very suitable solution. Even if everyone could reduce energy consumption, the need would continue to grow due to added population and new technology that increases the use of electricity even if each individual consumer's usage was minimized.

11. Conclusion

To implement energy efficiency plans, assistance from everyone in New Jersey is needed. The government should promote this policy and have regulations to promote the adoption of the plans. Individuals and companies in New Jersey should be aware of the problem and follow the plans to increase efficiency of their private utility use. Utility companies should invest more money in developing more efficient devices and renewable energy sources. Future electrical engineers should do their best in designing new energy-efficient devices as well as better and more environmentally conscious power generating methods.

Beyond this, a practical problem arises as energy companies and consumers weigh the cost of shifting to new equipment with the savings. Though energy savings may be greater with a new technology, a device that is only a few years old still has a long usable life. Many people and especially large companies may find it difficult to justify implementing very expensive equipment when existing appliances and technology still are serviceable.

Another problem faced when implementing this solution centers on regulatory and competition problems related to different levels of government. Other states may not have the same concerns; therefore, the interconnected grid of electricity may cause the problem to be shifted to other parts of the country or generate environmental problems elsewhere, even though locally the problem is solved. This will have to be considered as the efficiency is achieved.

Energy shortage and possible crisis is a problem that we are all facing. It will take the support of everyone to best solve the problem.

References

Chang, K. (2001, May 29). They're a puzzle, but they work. *New York Times, Science Times*, p. F1-2.

DeMarrais, K. G. (2001, March 2). *BPU orders program for energy efficiency*. Retrieved on August 20, 2002, from: *https://www.highbeam.com/reg/reg1.aspx?origurl=http%3a%2f%2fwww .highbeam.com%2fdoc%2f1P1-42566066.html&docid=1P1%3a42566066.*

Dizikes, P. (2001, April 23). *Is there an energy crisis?* Retrieved on June 10, 2002, from: *http://www.nci.org/0new/energypolicy-abc42401.htm.*

Energy Land. (N.D.). *NJ energy outlook.* Retrieved on June 20, 2002, from: *http://www.energyland.com/?dl=1.*

Gregory, D. D. (1999, May 2). *New Jersey's Energy Deregulation.* Retrieved on June 20, 2002, from: *http://www.gpnj.org/pol_energy.htm.*

McNamara, W, and B. Bellemare. *Success of New Jersey deregulation brought into question.* Retrieved on June 20, 2002, from: *http://www.researchreportsintl.com/*

Mendel, E. (2001, April 30). *A year later, energy crisis shows no signs of cooling off.* Retrieved on June 10, 2001, from: *http://www3.signonsandiego.com/uniontrib/news/*

NCEMC – North Carolina Electric Membership Corporation. (2001, May 24). *Can California happen here?* Retrieved on June 7, 2002, from: *http://www.ncemcs.com/*

PSEG Fossil. (N.D.). *Fossil generating stations.* Retrieved on June 20, 2001, from: *http://www.pseg.com/companies/fossil/*

PSEG Nuclear. (N.D.). *About our plants.* Retrieved on August 18, 2002, from: *http://www.pseg.com/companies/nuclear/*

PSE&G. (N.D.). *Energy costs and New Jersey businesses* Retrieved on August 8, 2002, from: *http://www.locationnj.com/news/v04/loc2000v4d.html.*

CHAPTER 9

Leadership

Key Ideas of This Chapter

- What is a leader?
- What is the distinction between individuals, groups, and teams?
- Who are the people involved in the process of leadership?
- What makes a "good" leader?
- What are the levels of task leadership?
- How do leaders interact with followers to accomplish tasks?
- What are different methods for managing interactions and maintaining power?
- How do you identify a "good" leader?
- What leadership skills and qualities should the best leaders possess?
- What are the dualities of leadership?
- What are the intangibles of leadership?

Introduction

Much of what has been presented in the previous chapters can be used by anyone to improve his or her intellectual and interpersonal performance. This chapter may, at first, seem to be focused on only a small segment of the society—leaders. However, upon closer inspection, it will become evident that everyone can benefit from the information presented whether or not they feel that they are themselves a leader, follower, or completely uninvolved.

The following material describes the principles necessary for leadership. The concepts associated with good leadership and effective leaders are described in this chapter but build on everything that has been discussed earlier in the book. The qualities and skills of leaders are complex and interrelated but will be presented in categories that allow them to be understood and taught more easily to students. Knowing the categories and concepts presented here cannot guarantee that anyone will be a good leader. Instead, these ideas are intended to help each person identify areas of strength and limitation that can be improved, compensated for or complimented by others in a group. Not everyone can have all of these areas and few if any will be excellent in all areas. However, knowing what to look for and strive for as a good leader can assist everyone to improve his or her own ability to achieve goals and accomplish tasks.

What Is a Leader?

Many people feel a leader is the person who is in charge, has attained the highest level of some characteristic, has the power, or the one who is at the front of the pack. However, all of these definitions of a leader are not what is being considered here. The leader presented in this chapter focuses on the idea of leadership and what is necessary to improve the ability to be the person who can utilize those skills associated with achieving success in a task for themselves and for those that are following the leader. This more specific concept of leadership is an important part of what is to be taught in the educational system.

For our discussion, a leader is one who selects and defines a goal and takes responsibility for accomplishing it successfully; while at the same time, a leader accepts the responsibility to be accountable for, motivate, educate, and guide those who are following him or her in the endeavor to be successful. There are many skills and qualities that allow a leader to be effective and be viewed as a good leader by others.

Individuals, Groups, and Teams

To begin it is necessary to distinguish between a group and a team. This starts with what an individual is and how each individual views the interaction with other individuals. In general, we think of an individual as a single thing or one person when discussing leadership. But what is meant by one? An individual is any unit that is treated and viewed as the same. As long as all the characteristics of a thing are seen as part of that thing, it is all part of an individual. If a person loses an arm, they are not now two individuals because the test for personhood is usually related to the whole being. Each person is able to think about things and make choices about their own actions as a whole rather than each system having a say in what happened to the overall body. Just being in the same place does not mean that you have agreed to work on tasks or participate in activities. Many times, people are just collections of individuals rather than a group of people or a team for a leader to work with.

So then, what makes a collection of individuals different from groups and teams? The test for this is the idea of common task and choice or buy-in by the individuals. A group is any collection of individuals that have a common purpose, goal, or circumstance. In no way do these people have to work together or even interact to be considered a group. Everyone in a classroom may have the same assignment and, therefore, the same goal, yet this does not mean that they are working together. In many cases, they might actually be working against one another. Even when assembled into groups, these people may be a collection of individuals sharing the same space and not really coming together as a team. A team then is a group that is brought together for some specialized purpose. More so, a team shares common ways of behaving, interacting, and communicating with one another, as well as sharing common visions, purposes, and rules of conduct in order to achieve a common goal.

Though often the words *team* and *group* are used interchangeably, a leader can benefit by seeing that there is a continuum that exists from individuals to groups to teams. If a group of individuals work well together and are so coherent, it may appear that they are once again an individual unit. Leaders should strive to move groups that are just collections of people towards teams that are striving to become collaborative working systems enhancing each other's performance. More on groups and teams can be found at *http://www.srds.co.uk/cedtraining/bast/bast09.htm*

Roles and Norms

When participating in a group or team, each person has responsibility for completing tasks and ways of dealing with others involved in attaining the goal. Those things that move the process forward towards the goal are considered task processes. These include things like producing products, performing tests, creating designs, and meeting deadlines. Beyond these activities, each group engages in activities that help the process move forward by allowing the members of the group to interact more smoothly. These are the transactional processes such as communicating responsibilities, relating ideas, and exchanging necessary data and information. During the process of goal attainment, each person can have many roles. Moreover, in the same way that an actor plays a role, many people play roles based upon the situation that occurs while he or she is performing the task and transaction process to achieve the goal. These roles are often designated expectations of responsibilities of others. At the same time, many people play other roles that satisfy personal interests and goals but do not contribute to the overall team goal. Both types of roles can be seen in most groups and often mean the difference between success and failure for the endeavor.

At first, the group must forge transactional processes while performing task processes required to achieve success. As time passes, the group moves toward being a team and creates a unique culture. This culture is termed a *norm* or the set of unspoken rules that all the members follow. Rarely are norms written into codes of conduct but rather are the methods the group adopts to deal with daily interactions, meetings, and conflicts. Often it is difficult to join established teams due to the norms that exist because new members are not aware of the norms and face a lag time as these norms are learned.

Whether in a group or a team, it is important to understand that each situation provides the potential for problems. New norms can be established and new roles adopted. Often, the transactional and task-oriented roles come into conflict as the goals sought become more difficult or the stakes become higher. Exercise 9.1 highlights some of the roles that individuals, groups, and teams need to assign or that are adopted by members. Many are needed for success; however, some lead to disharmony and potentially failure for the group.

EXERCISE 9.1

Roles in Groups and Teams

As people come together to work on a task or solve a problem, each one can assume one or more roles within that group. Some roles relate to the task aspect of the group, while others promote social interaction. A third set of roles is self-centered and may be disruptive to the process of accomplishing the task. Read about the roles group members play and try to identify roles that you assume as well as what roles others are playing.

http://www.mindtools.com/pages/article/newTMM_85.htm
http://www.stanford.edu/group/resed/resed/staffresources/RM/training/grouproles.html
http://www.srds.co.uk/cedtraining/handouts/hand37.htm

Now consider whether a leader can assign these roles to people or keep people from acting in these ways. How can you identify the roles others are playing and use this knowledge to your advantage to increase the likelihood of success?

Who Are the People Involved in the Process of Leadership?

As a leader works to attain a goal, he or she must know how to identify and distinguish among many different components in order to more effectively attain the goal. First, there are five categories of people that relate to the process of goal attainment: leaders, followers, bystanders, competitors, and others.

A leader has been defined, but it is important to explain the distinction between groups and teams as it relates to the leader. A group is a collection of individuals that has the same goal and interacts in some way, usually through interconnected influences or shared location. On the other hand, a team is a group in which the members rely upon one another and work together to achieve the goal. Moreover, the accomplishments of each team member are added together as the goal is achieved because each member works together for the mutual benefit of the team. A leader must keep this distinction in mind and often work to build a team from a group.

Followers are those that have, for whatever reason, agreed to give some or all of their own responsibility and decision-making authority to the leader. The degree to which a follower abdicates his or her own power of choice can vary, but some degree of personal choice must be given over to the leader or the follower is not following. Though a follower may not give the leader any power to choose, sometimes the leader is still responsible for that person, which means that person is still be considered a follower. Unfortunately, some followers see the leader as having all the responsibility and choose to take no personal responsibility at all. These followers become free-riders and try to benefit from the work of a group without contributing anything toward the achievement of the goal. This is a major problem that leaders must be aware of and a strong reason for team-building.

By-standers can take many forms. They may be followers that have withheld all power to choose from the leader, those that do not have the same goal as the leader, or are not involved in the process at all. In all cases, the leader has no influence over their actions and bears no responsibility for these people. In many situations, some outside authority assigns the goal to the leader but does little more than measure the success of the outcome against the goal. The leader might be able to convince bystanders to become followers. In other cases the designated leader must report to a bystander, thus sharing leadership with these people. Leaders must identify and classify these different types of bystanders to assist with the attainment of goals.

Next are those persons that are competing with the leader. These people may be trying to attain the same goal with another team, simply by vying with the leader for control of the team itself, or disagreeing with the goal being sought and so trying to work against the team so that it fails. In all cases, a leader must be able to identify and classify those involved in the process. This will allow the leader to create better teams as well as attain goals more effectively.

Lastly, are those that might be called "others." Often there are people involved in the group but not participating as any of the roles given in Exercise 9.1. Since, many times, it is difficult to assign people to specific labels, it is more important for the leader to see the tendencies of those he or she is working with in the group. A problem can arise if the leader classifies someone as a follower, but he or she is really something else, such as a judge, rule enforcer, observer, etc. It is the leader's responsibility to clearly delineate the types of people in the group and not confuse these roles.

So why is this important? If you are the leader or a follower, knowing the stance of those involved and surrounding you during a task is helpful. This is even more so when the leader is not familiar with those he or she is leading or who has just been assigned the task. We've all been part of groups, and it can be easy to see someone who is not participating. However, it's as important to see someone who might, at first, act as a follower but is really a competitor or trying to be a bystander and get the free ride. Whether you are the leader or just a follower, as a participant in a group, the more you know about good leadership and how to identify characteristics, the more you will help to accomplish the task. One of the first areas that most people can see is the level of the leader in the group.

What Are the Levels of Task Leadership?

There are four general levels of involvement between leaders and followers when completing tasks: directional, transitional, interactional, and transformational. The directional leader is one that points to goals and tells the team members to go towards them. This can be seen in the classical lecture method. By telling students what to learn and how others have been able to accomplish goals, a lecturer helps the student learn the specified material. Though at times it is necessary to lead through giving direction, using this as the sole method of leading is not the most effective way of leading in a classroom situation.

If the follower is clearly qualified, or the task is simple enough not to require additional instruction or oversight, directing is appropriate. However, most interactions between the leader and followers require more than just direction.

A transitional leader takes this one step further by actually moving through the process with the follower. Rather than just pointing the way, a transitional leader actually works through the task with the team members or students and helps them to understand the thinking involved.

An interactional leader works more closely with the followers by communicating with and engaging the followers while moving towards the goal of the task. By interacting with the followers, this leader helps smooth out problems and open lines of communication to help the followers work better together and with the leader.

Finally, there is the transformational leader. This style of leadership not only moves the followers from one point to another but also tries to change the followers during the journey. Not only is the teacher trying to dispense knowledge and show how things apply, but he or she also works to create new ways of thinking. As followers are made more mature, responsible, and better equipped to solve problems, the transformational leader continually assesses the progress of students and taps into the skills of the other two leadership styles to help attain a goal. It is vital to note that this goal is more than a fixed point in space or quantity of knowledge. The goal of a transitional leader is a change in the follower. By effecting this change, the transformational leader can internally motivate while, at the same time, provide the tools necessary to learn on his or her own.

No one way of leading is best. Each situation calls for the leader to use a blend of these to accomplish the task. You have to see that at any time the followers will need different levels of control, direction, and freedom to move independently. Usually, it is the followers that label the leader. Often, these general terms are coupled with the leadership styles that are presented in the next paragraphs.

How Do Leaders Interact with Followers to Accomplish Tasks?

There are many different ways each of us is accustomed to interacting with leaders. Research has identified six different ways a leader can interact with followers to accomplish goals. Some leaders adopt a single style and use it exclusively, while others shift among many different styles depending on the situation and those involved. For different circumstances, the leader may utilize these different styles. Depending on the specific circumstances, each style used by each leader has a varying level of effectiveness. However, knowing the characteristics of each can help you as both a leader and a follower when each is brought into use.

The first is the coercive leader that employs power and threats to accomplish missions in the way that he or she chooses. The leader seeks to influence followers by providing strong incentives of reward or strong disincentives through punishments for failure and often relies upon force. This style can have short-term success and lead to quick, immediate results but often does not prove effective in the long run due to the creation of resentment and resistance. Moreover, followers will often stop working once the leader is not present or the rewards are removed and will often seek to be counterproductive, thus thwarting progress by putting up obstacles to success.

Similar to coercive activities is the authoritative style, which seeks to be firm about the rules and relies upon his or her position. The authoritative leader can still meet with resistance due to the follower's lack of respect for the source of power or the ability of the leader. Since a leader must maintain authority in order to maintain control and focus, power struggles and fights about responsibility and assessment of progress can often result in the authoritative system.

Opposed to the authoritative style is the affirmative/affiliative style that puts people ahead of the task. This can be very effective but requires time to develop relationships. It can also lead to a slower and less focused response to tasks and problems that might arise. Since the leader does not stress power and punishment but instead emphasizes personal development and responsibility, followers may decide not to work. While the group works through interpersonal issues, the task is left undone or compromised by too many visions of what is correct. The key to this leadership style is the connections between the leader and the members of the group as well as the positive reinforcement or affirmation the leader provides to increase morale and the spirit of the team.

Next is the democratic style that seeks everyone's participation in leading and works to reach a consensus on issues. Though this is often extremely effective in groups of experts devoted to a task, if the skills and focus of the team are not fully committed, democratic leadership can bog down in debate and never actually accomplish anything. Though democratic leaders can be the most integrated into a group, if the group does not agree about a common cause or has other interpersonal problems not related to the task, the need for participation could lead to dilemmas that will prevent the task from being accomplished. This type of leadership is very complex and can be very difficult to handle in a setting that requires swift and decisive action.

Very different from all those listed thus far is pace-setting. This style has the leader perform an example to be followed and expects everyone to just follow. There is no intellectual meeting-of-the-minds or input from followers so the others involved in the process often can be left behind due to disagreement of thought or lack of ability to follow. In addition, a pace setter must be competent and energetic in order to set a good example and maintain output at a high level. This works best with a group of committed experts that only need to see the direction to move and the goal to be reached. Unfortunately, these types of groups rarely exist.

Lastly is the coaching style that seeks to make a change in the followers so that each can eventually lead them in the task. As the name implies, the coaching leader attempts to teach the followers giving motivation, reasoning, and skill development while directing them towards the goals. This is very effective when new skills or tasks need to be learned and there is sufficient time to accomplish the development. As with the pace setter, the coach must be competent and enthusiastic as well as be able to teach others. This is one of the most demanding leadership styles because so much rests upon the coach and his or her ability to interface with the followers in order to make the desired change. Beyond that, the coach will slowly relinquish control and power to the follower as he or she becomes more skilled and able to work without supervision.

What Are Different Methods for Managing Interactions and Maintaining Power?

When thinking about how decisions are made in organizations and the way leaders manage followers and situations, consider four distinct types: dictatorial, democratic, bureaucratic, and free range.

The dictatorial leader seeks to maintain the power and control by having all decision flow from him or her. The locus of control and all tasks are controlled and directed by the leader. This type of leadership is usually more effective at quick decision making and allows followers to work more closely with leaders. However, many times the dictatorial leader is also more directional and assumes that followers will fall in line and follow the leader as he or she moves towards the goal or gives directions to be followed.

Democratic leaders seek to make decisions by consulting with all those involved in the task so that a consensus can be obtained. Though final decisions may still be made by the leader, followers are made to feel part of the process of decision making and task completion. This type of leadership is usually more effective in groups and teams that work together over long times and for decisions that do not have immediate deadlines. Also, democratic leadership works best if there are open lines of communication and the amount of uncertainty is low. Many times, a democratic leader shares leadership with followers and may feel that he or she is not as responsible for the outcomes of the task because the group participated in the decision.

The bureaucratic leader uses the system of information control, departmental protocols, as well as knowledge of paperwork and processes to maintain control and enact decisions. Leaders and followers in a bureaucratic system rely on the systems and structures that are manipulated when making decisions to handle problems. Both followers and leaders can avoid consequences of decisions by relying on a set of rules and guidelines that are mutually accepted and clearly specified. This type of leadership is mostly used in large organizations that are diverse and widely separated geographically or that have many levels of administrative structure. Many times in a bureaucracy the leader may not have full access to power because of the inability to navigate the structures and systems that are in place. Large systems often have inertia, and this is magnified by the separation and dissipation of influence that can occur in a bureaucratic system. If a leader consults a manual or set of codes on conduct to make decisions, he or she is using the bureaucratic style of leading.

Lastly, there is the free-range leader. This type of leadership allows each person to act on his or her own ideas of what is correct. If all the participants are experts, the leader can allow each to act on his or her own and the task can be completed. Unfortunately, if each person is not internally motivated and is not able to accomplish the task without additional leadership, free range does not provide power to the leader over the followers and often leads to inactivity. In some cases, each follower acts only for his or her own ends and the task is not completed because followers become self-serving. Free range often leads to little resistance from followers until the leader must obtain results and impose some type of method to gain compliance from inactive or competitive followers.

All of these styles may be used, but there are many other specific skills that are employed when taking the lead in a group or team. The following sections detail the major categories of leadership skills along with some more specific skills under each of these categories.

All of the terms in Figure 9.1 are means to label leaders as they try to accomplish a task. These terms can help you judge the quality of leadership and name the behaviors of yourself or others that are in the leadership role. The next sections are more focused on the characteristics, attributes, abilities, and behaviors of "good" leaders. However, before discussing these, it is necessary to talk about what makes a "good" leader.

FIGURE 9.1
Summary of Leadership Terms

Leader and Group in Task	*Styles of Leading*	*Handling Decisions*
Directional	Coercive	Dictatorial
Transitional	Authoritative	Democratic
Interactional	Affirmative/Affiliative	Bureaucratic
Transformational	Democratic	Free Range
	Pace-setting	
	Coaching	

Figure 9.1 shows terms typically used to describe a leader by followers and others.

How Do You Identify a "Good" Leader?

In order to identify a good leader, it is first assumed you can identify the person who is acting as the leader, using the definitions provided. Too often, however, the person that is called the leader or who has that position may not be the one that is actually leading or being looked to for leadership. In addition, though at one point in time a person is the leader for a task it does not mean that the person will always be a leader or show good leadership. The first step to identify a good leader is to focus on three separate things that come together to highlight leadership. These three things are the situation that a person is faced with, the decisions or actions taken in that situation, and finally, the outcome of those decisions or actions. Leadership is dependent on the circumstances and the reaction to those circumstances. As a result, any person at any time can be a good leader and then at some other time, be a poor leader.

Once these aspects are known, you can begin to judge if the person was good. One of the most common assessments of good leadership is success. If a task was assigned and the goal reached successfully, then the leader is usually seen as a good leader. However, things are rarely this simple. In a society, few tasks are so simple that success alone is the only goal. Moreover, though you can isolate a single situation theoretically, in the real world, actions and decision impact one another. As a result, it is necessary to consider other things beyond just success. Many of these other things deal with the abilities of a person to help others accomplish the task, become leaders themselves, form teams that work well, and meet challenges that are not yet known. All of these types of skills and abilities will be discussed later in this chapter. Having more of these skills at higher levels of attainment will make a person a better leader and also have them judged as a good leader by others.

There is another aspect beyond just being successful and possessing skills needed to lead others and be responsible for them. The greatest leaders are able to lead in the most serious of situations (often life-and-death), lead large numbers in diverse areas, and many times can lead consistently over many years in many situations. Just being a leader is a good first step; however, if you are able to improve your leadership skills and abilities as well as become more aware of what makes great leaders, you will be more effective throughout your academic career and your life. In addition, leadership is always something that is highly sought by others looking to work with you.

Many times someone is a great leader of business and industry, of a political movement, in a field of study such as science, or in an athletic competition. Some of this is due to natural abilities or gifts of birth and upbringing that are instilled without conscious thought and learning. Other times, experience is able to teach what is needed without the person thinking critically about what is happening and what is being learned. However, if you apply your mind to the problems that might be faced and prepare yourself to recognize good leaders as well as situations that call for leadership, you will be prepared to step up and demonstrate your leadership. Moreover, since you can encounter a situation that demands you to respond without thought or contemplation, learning to lead and be prepared for these situations is a vital part of the educational process.

What Leadership Skills and Qualities Should the Best Leaders Possess?

Good leaders possess a wide range of abilities that contribute to the success of their leadership. At the same time, each leader is unique and often responds to the particular situation at hand. Nonetheless, some general categories can be identified to assist those seeking to improve leadership skills and learn the principles of good leadership. Though the attributes can

FIGURE 9.2
Leadership Attributes and Characteristics

Self-mastery (leading to credibility)
  Competence—KEES of learning
  Self-discipline
  Positive attitude
  Objectivity
  Trustworthiness
  Global view

Goal Attainment
  Vision
  Mission statement
  Problem-solving
  Cleverness
  Adaptability
  Knowledge transfer

Accurate and Honest Assessment (AHA)
  Decision-making
  Critical thinking
  Research
  Judgment
  Candor
  Fairness

Interpersonal Dynamics
  Connectedness
  Coorientation
  Dynamism
  Creating coherences
  Motivation
  Inspiration
  Empowerment

Situational Command
  Understanding the processes of change
  Manage complexity
      Plan—Organize—Delegate—Control—
      Coordinate—Innovate
  Maintain flexibility

Professionalism
  Moral purpose
  Ethical conduct
  Preparation
  Respect

Figure 9.2 shows the characteristics, attributes, and abilities a leader should try to cultivate and maximize in order to be a better more effective leader.

be rearranged and grouped in many different ways and given alternate labels, the following encapsulates the essentials of what a leader needs in order to be successful.

At the broadest level, there are two distinct types of leadership training that should be addressed: individual and team. Individual training focuses on the qualities and abilities that allow the leader to gain confidence and assist in self-determination and self-improvement, as well as improving decision-making, critical thinking and problem solving. Those qualities and abilities associated with the team increase the leader's ability to communicate, motivate, guide, and educate the members of their team more effectively as well as with those outside the team as the goals are sought.

However, these two types of training should not occur separately from one another. While leaders work on the concepts that improve themselves, they must also work on the interface with those that they encounter while leading or while they are following another leader as part of a team.

There are many different concepts related to leadership. To make it easier to identify and work on improving leadership, these abilities have been separated into six major categories related to the various parts of the process of leadership: self-mastery, goal attainment, accurate and honest assessment, interpersonal dynamics, situational command, and professionalism. Self-mastery deals with the aspects of leadership that can be improved by examining and controlling oneself in any situation. Goal attainment refers to the many different skills necessary for a leader to identify, select, and accomplish the task as well as deal with and solve problems that arise as the task is being completed. Along with this is accurate and honest assessment that deals with a leader's ability to judge and make decisions for themselves and the team. These two are particularly important when selecting goals and assigning tasks. Interpersonal dynamics deals with the ways a leader must communicate and interact with others. Situational command concerns all the qualities and abilities a leader needs to deal with the process of handling a task. Finally, professionalism is the overarching characteristics that the leader brings to the team to ensure the goal is attained and the outcome is judged as a success by all involved.

Many other concepts are found in each of these large categories and will be described in more detail. As students work on each of these smaller concepts, they improve as leaders.

Self-Mastery

Fundamental to leadership and almost all education is the abilities of the individual person engaged in the process. Many times the competence of the leader is what convinces followers to listen to a leader at first. Though knowledge and the accompanying understanding are often what students feel they are receiving from the educational process, there is more than just that being gained. As mentioned earlier, the four major aspects of learning that are provided are knowledge, experience, expertise, and skills (KEES). It is important to distinguish these terms at the start of the educational process. Knowledge contains both the ideas of factual knowledge and process knowledge (understanding) working together as the body of learning that a person has acquired. Factual knowledge can be defined generally as the list of facts a person has gathered and can access through thoughtful reflection. Process knowledge or understanding refers to the set of processes related to the gathering and use of facts. With the learned knowledge and understanding comes the idea of experience. Each time something new is lived through it is added to the list of experiences that a student has at their disposal. When a new situation is encountered, past exposure to that type of information or situation allows better judgments to be made and a clearer course of action to be taken. This leads to development of expertise. With knowing and experience to draw upon, a person can have a feel for the outcome of an undertaking or effect of a decision. As a result, an expert, one with expertise, can make choices that lead to success more often. Lastly is the idea of skill. Having a skill means having mastery of a set of processes and knowledge so that they can be applied in the appropriate situation to obtain the desired result. Leaders must know the skills that he or she has mastered as well as the skills of the followers that can be relied upon to be brought to bear during the process of completing the task successfully. All four of these aspects must be utilized together during learning to build better individuals and more complete leaders.

Beyond basic KEES other individual aspects are also important for leaders to develop as part of the principles of good leadership. The KEES demonstrate an individual's competence, which helps leaders establish credibility. However, this is only part of what the literature identifies as important to a leader's ability to establish credibility. Individuals must also be aware of the need for objectivity and trustworthiness.

Objectivity is the ability to look at all sides of an issue, to suspend any personal biases, to be reasonable and dispassionate, and to examine evidence, reasoning, and value questions before taking sides or making final decisions. In Western societies, where issues are decided by discussion and debate, the ability to be an objective judge is particularly crucial. Trustworthiness is how consistent and honest a member's behavior is understood to be. It is the confidence other people have in your sincerity and your ability to behave ethically even under pressure.

In addition to being objective and instilling trust, leaders must have two other attributes—self-discipline and a positive attitude. Self-discipline in this sense means both maintaining control of one's emotions as well as not leaping to a conclusion or acting rashly. An even temperament and calm demeanor is important for good leadership. Though emotion can be a useful tool to motivate followers, not being able to control oneself in situations can undermine the leader's control and negatively impact the ability to complete tasks. Along with self-discipline is the idea of a positive attitude. This means both optimism and creating a feeling of success for oneself and the group. Leaders must promote the possibility that through work, any challenge can be overcome and success is always possible. If this feeling is not internalized and held by the leader, followers will not believe. The leader's positive attitude promoting the idea that a goal is attainable allows many teams to overcome what might at first seem to be a daunting task.

Lastly, global awareness or viewpoint deals with a leader's far-reaching awareness of events occurring outside the specific task the leader and his or her team is charged with. Having a narrow focus without connection to the outside world and the bigger picture can lead to many problems for the leader and the team. A leader's global awareness allows for responsiveness to outside events that affect the endeavor.

Goal Attainment

For many people, the main measure of a good leader is success or victory. As the saying goes, "Winning isn't the best thing; it's the only thing." Though that may not be completely true, goal attainment is a vital part of leadership. It is the responsibility of the leader to achieve the goal and make the task successful. In order to do this, several different skills are needed, such as choosing a goal to seek, clearly specifying what that goal is and how it is to be attained, and handling problems that arise when the goal is being sought. Having the necessary skills to do these three things is essential to effectively and efficiently achieve a goal.

The first thing a good leader needs is vision. This means the leader can see the current situation and decide upon a course that will lead to successful completion of the goal. Having vision is more than just being able to see a path in the forest, it deals with the intuition a leader has for the correct path to take as well as the expertise he or she shows when choosing a less- traveled path or following an alternate route to an obscure or far-off end. Many times the followers do not or cannot know all the things the leader does and so must trust the leader's vision of where to go and how to arrive there.

Along with vision is the ability of the leader to translate the vision into a mission statement. Clearly stating the goals, values, and aspirations of the leader, the followers, and the organization are essential to cohesiveness and success. Though the leader may know in his or her own mind the goal, a clear mission statement allows for the vision to be clarified, shared, and refined. Also, having a written mission statement allows those inside and outside the organization to see the direction everyone should be moving and the ultimate goal towards which everyone is working.

Once a vision is defined in the mission statement, the leader moves towards the goal. As this happens, obstacles and challenges may arise and must be overcome. Problem solving can be defined as the ability to follow a systematic method for examining a situation, determining a course of action to reach a desired outcome, and justifying that decision. Whenever a challenge arises, the leader must be able to solve problems and know the various aspects of the processes needed to overcome these challenges. A leader may not be able to solve all problems, but knowing the process will allow the leader to use the abilities of followers to assist in problem solving and thus more effectively attain the goal.

Along with problem solving is the idea of being clever. This is a difficult concept to master or for some to even develop. Cleverness is being able to apply a novel solution to a problem or make a decision that is correct for the situation and leads to success. More than just making a decision and thinking about it afterwards, cleverness asks the leader to see an answer that is new and others cannot see in that situation. Clever solutions often solve a problem with less effort, last longer, or utilize less time, effort, or other resources. Some say these are shortcuts to the goal, while others think of these as creative answers to the question. In any case, being able to attain the goal through clever means often helps followers to feel the leader is doing well and is a good leader in other situations.

Whenever problems arise, changes might need to be made so the leader must have adaptability. Adaptability relates to the flexible nature of all leadership activities. A professional must remain calm under pressure, draw upon resources to innovate, and utilize all the principles of leadership to make decisions and adjustments to the objectives as the goal is pursued and the outcomes produced. As the leader works to solve problems and adapt to the situation, it is necessary for knowledge to be transferred to and from followers.

Though the leader may know what is happening and where he or she is headed, it is important for this to be shared with the followers. A leader must be able to create and share knowledge in order to attain goals successfully. By sharing what the leader knows with the followers, the bonds of a team are strengthened and the networks of the leader with others can be developed. True leaders commit themselves to continually generating and increasing knowledge inside and outside the organization. Turning information into knowledge is a social process; for that, you need good relationships. Once the team can develop and share knowledge, they can work more effectively to accomplish the goals of the team as set by the leader.

Accurate and Honest Assessment (AHA)

Another important ability that needs to be developed by leaders is the assessment of various aspects of a task and the members involved in its accomplishment. Each leader will be faced with a daunting number of tasks and choices. Being able to honestly and accurately determine the ability to accomplish a given task, in a given time period, to a desired level of achievement is essential to attaining goals. Too often, inexperienced leaders take on too much or make promises that cannot be kept. Moreover, leaders and others in the leadership dynamic are not aware of the various steps involved in problem solving and cannot make good judgments when faced with this lack of knowledge. Without a good feel for the AHA of themselves, those that are following the leader, and the parameters of the task, the success of the entire endeavor can be compromised.

Evaluations must be made while leading, especially when decision-making, which rests upon critical thinking and research. There are many associated skills to these listed here that have been presented earlier throughout the text. As a reminder, critical thinking is the ability to objectively examine a problem and the motivations behind decisions as well as to rationally evaluate different facets of a problem or issue. Decision making is the process by which informed choices are made in order to evaluate, narrow, refine, or choose between alternatives. Research is investigation either through review of other published work (literature search) or direct/indirect observation (surveying and experimentation) to gather information, test hypotheses, and assist in the evaluation of choices.

Underlying the problem-solving process, as mentioned previously, is a series of learned, interconnected skills that serve as a foundation. These are part of self-mastery but also are closely connected to the assessment of oneself and others. In order to think critically and make good decisions, it is vital to be well informed. Thus, research is needed to inform the decision makers, and good research skills are necessary to find answers to questions and help support the decisions made.

A large part of AHA is the judgment that the leader shows when setting and attaining goals as well as meeting challenges. Risk assessment, setting priorities, and having good intuition all come together as the leader assesses a situation. When making a decision, the leader must assess the amount of resources to invest as compared to the risks and rewards involved. Whether the leader decides to take risks while pursuing a goal can have a tremendous impact on the success of the leader. Along with assessing risk, the leader must use judgment to prioritize tasks and delegate resources. Poor judgment of risk and squandering resources in a situation may lead to disaster. The leader's judgments are often questioned when a task fails. and if these judgments were seen as two risky or focused on the wrong priorities, the leader may never recover and may not lead again. Unfortunately, it is difficult to always have good judgment or have a set of rules to follow when judging.

Though there are rules of thumb to follow and advice that can be gained through education and experience, many times intuition is what the leader relies upon when making judgments. This is a blend of KEES and comes from the self-mastery and goal attainment skills that the leader has attained. The more intimately a leader knows what is happening in the situation, the more that judgments or intuition can be made effectively. In the end, there is not one exclusive way to come to a proper judgment, and even if you do everything correctly, you may still choose incorrectly and so fail.

There are many methods used to evaluate and determine truth. Accurate decisions reflect the ability of the leader to determine the true outcome or desired goal. However, equally as important is a sense of honesty with oneself and others. It is not that the leader is intentionally being dishonest or lacks trust but rather may suffer from selective memory or allow personal feelings to cloud judgment by withholding the truth to spare someone's feelings.

Selective memory is the idea that a person can remember only certain facts and events rather than an accurate picture of what really has happened in the past. This can be intentional or unintentional. What a person notices has much to do with the environment, situation, and background. If you are asked to find a blue minivan, you are more likely to begin to notice how many more minivans and blue cars are on the road. Though to you this may be a sudden realization, it is more likely due to the fact that you just ignored these facts earlier. When assessing others, a leader can overlook many small things or hold every action up to scrutiny. Selective memory can be seen when the leader only sees the good things that have been done and glosses over the disappointments or shortfalls on his or her part. It is important to have clear recollection of things and be honest about what is happening.

Another part of honesty is candor. This means how honest the leader is about what is happening and how transparent the process of leading and attaining goals can be. Candor is important because if a leader keeps too many secrets from his or her followers, distrust can arise and the judgment of the leader can come into question.

Along with candor is the idea of fairness. This deals with the leader making a good decision for one member of the group compared to the others. If everyone is treated the same, then there is equality. If each person is given what he or she deserves, then there is equity. One way to think about fairness is how to pay someone for work that is done. If you treat someone equally, you give everyone the same amount for the same job no matter what is accomplished or how long it takes. If you treat them equitably, you pay for the products. The more one produces the more one gets. To be fair, a balance must be met, and more importantly, the rules for how the rewards will be distributed should be established beforehand. The difficult part is determining how to be both equal and equitable when dispensing the benefits and burdens as a task is completed. The leader is usually the one who distributes the rewards when there is success and the consequences when there is failure.

Interpersonal Dynamics

Leaders need to interact with many different individuals and groups as they create teams and engage in tasks to achieve success. Most important is relationship-building, but many other principles are also concerned with this central principle of leadership. Building relationships is central to the discussion of leadership and teamwork. Simply put, this is networking. Building relationships concerns developing the necessary abilities to establish connections with and communicate messages to others. To help accomplish this, many other skills are needed.

As stated, the competence of a leader is important and deals with the interconnection between the leader and others related to the process. Competence is an essential component of teamwork, in which each member must contribute some expertise, information, analysis, and creativity to the problem-solving process.

Connectedness deals with the leader's ability to establish and develop a tie with the followers and all others related to the attainment of the goal. These connections and interrelated networks of personal ties assist in fostering good relationships. Knowing how to identify areas of commonality and maintaining lines of communication and connection are essential to good interpersonal dynamics.

Co-orientation and dynamism are also important to the interpersonal relations of a leader with others. Co-orientation is other people's sense that you are similar to them, that you are concerned for their well-being, and that you share their interests, values, objectives, and needs. They can identify with you because you can identify with them. Credible communicators care about how their actions might affect others, not just about their own personal objectives. Someone who wants a team to excel so that he or she will look good is perceived by members as having far less credibility than someone who wants all members to succeed.

Dynamism, or being dynamic, combines the leader's activeness, interaction with group members, and energy used to foster team spirit to give the impression of enthusiasm to inspire interest. Though often seen as positive, it can have negative consequences, which leads a group to perceive a dynamic individual as maintaining influence by being pushy, which reduces consensus and group satisfaction.

Once a relationship is established and built, other concepts must be developed. Another important responsibility that a leader must assist with is that of creating coherence within the team. All of the complexity of personal interactions can make people feel uneasy or at times overwhelmed. A chaotic situation that creates stress as people interact can put everyone on edge.

It is important to be sharp and allow people to have some freedom because that allows for creativity. However, too much freedom can lead to anarchy. Therefore, effective leaders tolerate enough ambiguity to keep the creative juices flowing, but along the way (once they and the group know enough), they seek coherence.

All of the aspects can lead to confusion and apathy in the group as the goal seems far off. A vital ability of all leaders is to generate enthusiasm in themselves and others for the goal that is being sought. This is one of the most difficult and most essential skills of leaders. Knowing how to best energize the members of the group so that they work most effectively without too much laxity or pressure is difficult but essential to the optimum working state for all the members in the team. Balancing personal requirements to remain motivated with the needs of all the other members of the team is difficult but essential to success.

This leads to the idea of inspiration that is closely tied to motivation and eventually empowerment. A leader needs to reach out to the followers in order to find out what will make them work, which is motivation, but this may not be effective for everyone at all times. If the leader can inspire the followers, a stronger deeper bond can be formed. Inspiration happens when the vision of the leader can be translated into the followers so that he or she can internalize the messages and mission statement. Eventually, if the leader can motivate and inspire the followers as well as trust them, he or she can give some of the power to the followers. Empowerment occurs when the leader shifts the responsibility for part of or the entire task to the followers. By shifting the power, the leader is creating more leaders and strengthening the bonds of the team. Many leaders find it difficult to relinquish power and control so empowerment is difficult. In other cases, leaders shift responsibility without empowering the followers, which leads to dissension and often failure. However, if the leader has good interpersonal dynamics, empowerment can lead to greater success for all.

Situational Command

A leader will face different challenges as a variety of endeavors are undertaken. Though difficult to generalize, being prepared for these challenges is a vital principle of leadership. It is a cliché to say "expect the unexpected," but that is the most appropriate way to put what leaders need to expect. To do this, leaders must start by understanding the processes of change. There is a very complex set of situations that may be confronted as a goal is sought, and the leader must take command and maintain control. To understand change it is important to know the goal is not to just make changes for the sake of change or to have the best ideas. Change is never set or easily reduced to easily predictable choices between simple alternatives.

More important than just knowing change is complex is having the ability to manage the complexity and those skills involved in dealing with it to accomplish the overall goal. Being able to manage an endeavor is important to the successful attainment of goals. The vast research into effective management styles can be applied to improve the effectiveness of leaders. A manager should endeavor to do the following tasks in order to be a good manager: planning, organizing, delegating, controlling, coordinating, and innovating.

Planning is defining the short-range and long-range goals the leader has for the team in order to achieve the goal. Organizing is the method by which the leader brings together teams to address these goals. Delegating relates to the assigning nature of leading that includes choosing teams, overseeing teamwork, and keeping the work on track towards the goal. In addition, this is concerned with finding the right person for the right job on the team, which involves interviewing, promoting, rewarding, and removing team members. Controlling is concerned with the power and position of the leader. The leader must remain calm and composed when making decisions and be prepared to make those decisions. Coordinating refers to the inherent interlacing and interpersonal structuring that the leader must do to keep the team working effectively and the goals in focus. Finally, innovating simply means being creative and always trying to develop new things and cultivating new ideas.

Lastly, the ability for a leader to maintain flexibility is necessary to his or her situational command. Flexibility is important because of the uncertainty that any situation can present. The leader must be able to perform many different tasks and fill in for the other members of the team if they are unable or unwilling to do what is necessary to accomplish the task. In addition, many times, the leader must be willing to allow the followers to work through a problem or complete a task at their own pace. The flexibility to allow others to take the lead for part of the project as well as the ability to teach the followers so that they might eventually lead for themselves is an important part of the situational command and flexibility of the leader.

Professionalism

In general, all of the principles listed previously aim to create professionals that can lead themselves and others. The concept of professionalism is overarching and incorporates all of the principles to varying degrees. It deals with the things necessary to assure the goal is reached and the outcome meets external standards and represents the team to others. Ideas such as moral purpose, ethical conduct, preparation, respect, and completeness are the important concepts that lead to professionalism.

Michael Fullan (2001) put forth that moral purpose means acting with the intention of making a positive difference in the lives of team members and others involved in the process as well as society in general. The leader has a belief in the goal being sought and those being led see it as right.

Ethical conduct deals with the standards of conduct for practice in society. Following rules of conduct, having principles and acting ethically correct in dealings with team members and others is vital to being seen as professional.

Preparation relates to the ability of the leader to be ready for the task at hand, challenges that arise, and questions that team members may raise. In addition, the idea of preparation means being able to draw upon past knowledge when appropriate but also identifying when a gap exists that must be addressed. Often, a follower must be given more power because he or she is more knowledgeable in a specific area of expertise. Being prepared for such eventualities is a vital skill of the leader and calls upon many of the other skills discussed.

Respect is the idea that the leader gives value and thought to others in the process. Valuing the ideas of others is one part. In addition, realizing the backgrounds, customs, and traditions of others as well as individual needs are a vital part of leadership. Finally, having an awareness of and appreciation for other people's limited time, effort, and other valuable resources is necessary to being professional. These resources must be valued correctly, treated carefully, and not squandered.

Finally, completeness deals with the power of the leader to decide when a task is finished. The leader is responsible for achieving the goal, but because there are always limitations on time, effort, and other resources, the leader must determine when the goal has been attained to a sufficient level to be considered complete. Many times, a leader must sacrifice quality of the product to have it delivered on time. Other times, the product is delivered late so that it can be finished. These decisions are complex and often rely upon many of the other skills previously identified.

Other subcategories and delineations can be used when describing leadership principles. In any endeavor, success is achieved when the team is able to efficiently produce high-quality outcomes in a timely fashion that meet the standards established without compromising and sacrificing personal integrity. All of these abilities come together to assist the leaders as he or she leads and strives for success.

Dualities of Leadership

In addition to the skills and abilities listed in the key concepts, many other aspects of leadership can be discussed. In particular, there are attributes of a leader that must be considered along a continuum rather than as something to simply master and improve. Figure 9.3 lists leadership attributes that should be considered. As a leader demonstrates each of these while leading, its counterpart must also be present or problems can arise. These traits are tied together so that a balance is sought in order to be the best leader. These dualities are not two separate things that work together, but rather simultaneous attributes that balance one another like the riders of a seesaw.

FIGURE 9.3
Dualities of Leadership

Power—Responsibility   Courage—Wisdom
Action—Reflection   Decisiveness—Participation
Drive (Persistence)—Responsiveness   Vision—Realism
Pride—Respect   Passion—Reason

Figure 9.3 shows the dualities of leadership that must be thought of together and balanced so that the leader can be more effective.

Power—Responsibility: Many see the person with the power as being a leader because they are in charge and thus must be listened to or face the consequences. On the other hand, in some situations, the person that is responsible is seen as the one to look to for instructions since they have been given the responsibility for success. These concepts deal with the ability of a leader to handle the task given to him or her while shouldering the burden of being in charge of others. As a goal is sought, the leader takes responsibility for others and gathers power, but in return is then beholden to the followers. Success is not the only measure of a good leader. The interaction among the group and external members contributes to the measure of a successful leader. Just getting results or exerting power is not sufficient to be a good leader. Success for all involved to varying degrees, of course, is also an important criterion to consider. Using power appropriately and to achieve the desired end without being arbitrary is showing responsibility.

Action—Reflection: A leader is often seen as the one to act or direct action. Taking the lead means moving a process forward. However, just acting is not enough. Throughout the process a good leader reflects on every aspect of the endeavor. Continual reassessment and reflection is necessary to achieve the highest levels of success. Action without reflection can lead to missteps, faulty decisions, and group-think. Taken too far, unthinking action by a leader can lead to alienation of others and ultimately cause the leader to defend poor decisions that will result in failure. However, constant and overwhelming reflection without action leads to hesitation and paralysis. Thinking too much can cause as many problems as not thinking at all.

Drive (Persistence)—Responsiveness: Once an action is decided upon, the drive of the leader becomes a vital aspect of the endeavor. Similar to action, drive reflects the push, persistence, and continued effort put forth by the leader in pursuit of the goal. However, as with action and reflection, the drive must be balanced with responsiveness. Simply choosing a course and plowing ahead until completion may not always result in a successful outcome. It is vital to understand what is happening so that adjustments and changes can be made. Drive without responsiveness leads to headstrong blind pursuit of a goal. Though this type of persistence is sometimes necessary if the goal is difficult to reach, if the goal is not selected correctly, this type of drive leads to a runaway train on a track leading to a devastating end. The ability to work diligently and continually move towards a goal while being mindful of the potential need for continual adjustments is what good leaders need.

Pride—Respect: The last set of concepts is often the most difficult balance to reach. Taking pride in one's work without praising oneself and being overly proud is difficult. Many say, "Self-praise stinks," while others say, "Delight in a job well done." Leaders must have pride in themselves as well as work to instill a sense of pride in those that are being led. At the same time, it is necessary to balance this sense of pride with awareness that too much of a good thing can lead to hubris, or false pride. Respecting others, both those that are following and others not in the group, is necessary for good leadership. Pride without respect can lead to dissension and provincialism as one group competes with others for pride rather than to achieve the ultimate goal. A sense of pride is vital for quality work, as well as a sense of competition. However, pride without respect can foster hostility.

Courage—Wisdom: Courage has many different ways to be identified and defined, but a good way to think of it is choosing to act despite the fear of the consequences of taking that action or doing the right thing even though it is easier to follow another course. Courage is that aspect of character that a leader displays when faced with a difficulty and must choose between options. However, courage is not enough. Forging ahead in the face of fear and uncertainty may be courageous, but it does not lead to success in all cases. Each decision and action must be tempered with wisdom despite the fear that might arise. Understanding a situation and weighing all options helps a leader gain wisdom. This understanding is often gained through experience but simply being experienced does not guarantee wisdom. Making the same mistake hundreds of times gives experience, but if one does not learn from these experiences wisdom is not gained. Some say, "discretion is the better part of valor" while others say "nothing ventured, nothing gained." Courage without wisdom leads to recklessness, and wisdom without courage leads to inaction.

Decisiveness—Participation: Making decisions is vital to leadership, and the ability to be decisive is often seen as a key attribute of a good leader. It is important, however, to include followers so that the leader is connected to the followers. Compromise through negotiation tempers the decisive leader of a team in which all members share the process. A decisive leader that does not foster participation can devolve into a dictatorship leading to resentment and counterproductive situations.

Vision—Realism: For many people, leaders are those that have a grand vision of a goal that must be achieved. Vision relates to the many characteristics a leader possesses and uses to understand the overall situation as well as plan for the future of the group. Without vision, a leader is just working for someone else or missing a part of the big picture. However, too often vision comes at the price of everyday concerns. It is vital for leaders to maintain a sense of realism. A balance must be struck between the overarching, far-reaching concerns of a leader and the everyday necessities of leading others. Without a sense of reality, a leader may seek a fantasy world that can never be reached. Without vision, the leader may never be able to inspire followers, foster a sense of purpose, or realize a grand plan. Those with vision but not realism are dreamers and those with only realism and no vision are often seen as unimaginative. Good leadership conveys the vision while keeping in mind the reality of the situation.

Passion—Reason: Some of the most recognizable characteristics of a leader relate to passion or enthusiasm. Passion is exhibited by the strength of belief the leader demonstrates as well as the fervor shown when executing actions. However, passion alone is not sufficient.

Reason is the counterpoint to passion. Leaders that are passionate but fail to see the logical means for making the passion a reality do not succeed. The energy of passion fuels the fire of the leader, but reason uses that fire to forge the tools needed for success. On the other hand, having only reason without passion can lead to cold and unenthusiastic leaders that cannot inspire followers to achieve the desired goal.

In the end, all of these dualities exist. A leader needs to be aware of how the different aspects of humans and their interactions affect his or her ability to lead.

Intangibles of Leadership

One difficult thing to discuss that must be mentioned in this text about leadership, and about learning in general, is that sometimes there is not one answer that can be arrived at or a definite end to seek. When dealing with other people, often times every situation requires different things from different people depending on the feel of the situation. These are the intangibles of leadership. One person can interpret a leader's actions as perfectly on target, while from another person's perspective it is completely wrong. Though there may be many intangibles, some major interconnected concepts that affect leadership are listed in Figure 9.4.

FIGURE 9.4
Intangibles

Charisma	Composure	Consideration
Charm	Confidence	Commitment
Chemistry	Cool	Consistency

Figure 9.4 presents the intangibles of leadership, which are dependant upon the situation, the people involved, and many other factors at the time and place being judged. Leaders must know and prepare for the intangibles of leadership.

We will start with the idea of charisma. Many people feel that charisma is something that is difficult to describe and a person is born with. It is the characteristic of a person that attracts others to them and instills a feeling of devotion in others to the charismatic person. This is very useful to a leader that wishes to have devoted followers. However, it is impossible to know who will find you charismatic and if charisma will always work. Associated with charisma is the idea of charm or the ability to sway people to your point of view. Though charm may be an innate ability like charisma, it is often something that is consciously used to sway others. As with charisma, not everyone will react to charm in the same way. While one person might feel that a person is charming and thus be swayed to believe him or her, another person might feel the charm is sickly sweet or a cover for devious and alternative motivations. The exact same behavior can be interpreted differently by different people and thus is an intangible. The difference between these two things can be seen as the active role of the person. Charisma exists as an attribute of a person drawing you in and making you more likely to follow him or her. On the other hand, someone hoping to convince you to follow actively uses charm as a means to achieve his or her ends.

In any event, neither of these has a set rule or means of attaining the skill in every situation and thus are said to be intangible. Along with the two concepts is the idea of chemistry.

Chemistry is applied to a group rather than an individual. In any situation, the way the members of the group interact is the chemistry of that group. There are so many factors related to this intangible it cannot be planned for or anticipated. It is entirely dependent on the situation and the people that face it together. The social, physical, and mental conditions of the people involved along with the conditions that these people face and the problems that arise all add to form the chemistry of the group. A leader must be prepared to deal with the problems of chemistry by utilizing his or her leadership skills. However, sometimes people just do not hit-it-off and the chemistry of the group does not gel. This can happen more often if the leader depends on charm and charisma to create chemistry. In cases such as this, the leader must work to keep people on task while negotiating the interpersonal dynamics of the situation and solve problems as they arise.

Next we will examine the idea of confidence or the sureness you have. A leader that is confident in his or her abilities, decisions, or actions is often seen as a good leader and may gather followers due to that confidence. However, too much confidence can lead to mistakes or be seen as arrogance. In another connotation of the word, maintaining confidence can mean keeping private matters of followers private. This can also be interpreted as being secretive and showing favoritism. Each situation demands that the leader have the appropriate level of confidence without exuding too much or this. This can lead to the next intangible, composure, or the relative poise that someone shows. Being composed can instill confidence in those around you and can come from the feeling of confidence you have in yourself. However, some followers need the leader to show emotion or be energetic because being composed can make the leader appear to be rigid, inflexible, or just not care. Once again, it is not just something to maximize since it depends on the situation and those who face it.

This leads to the idea of being cool. A cool leader can be one that remains calm in the heat of battle, seems to have some quality that makes him or her attractive and desirable to others, or one that does not show emotion in situations and thus is removed, objective, or standoffish. Rather than something internal to the leader, coolness is judged by those around you. If you work to gain confidence and remain composed, you can be thought of as cool, but it is not really something you can work on and cultivate. This is an intangible because just saying that someone is cool does not clearly explain what is happening. As with composure, being too calm in a heated situation can lead to inaction; therefore, coolness is not necessarily desirable. Furthermore, trying to remain composed can give the impression of coolness to others. When listening to followers and evaluating ideas, simply remaining composed might convey the idea you do not like it and that your coolness conveys disinterest or dislike. Cool is not an easy thing to handle and pull off.

Finally, we look at the last three terms together since they are all related and similar to the dualities except exist as a trio. Consistency, consideration, and commitment need to be examined together. Being consistent might, at first, seem to be an excellent trait that should be maximized. However, treating everyone the same all the time or always returning the same result with the same effort is not always good. Being consistent means you do not consider what is involved in each situation and may not deliver more when needed. This may be thought of as rigidity. On the other hand, if you are considerate, you are responsive to the needs of others, you think about the situation, and you realize that things happen in the lives of the followers. You can put yourself in the shoes of others, but this can lead to you being taken advantage of or being seen as someone that plays favorites. Thus a balance is sought between consistency and consideration. But these are not a duality because there is a third aspect that makes these intangibles—commitment. If you stick to a decision, you might be said to be committed, but at the same time, if you care for your followers this may also be commitment. Some say that if the leader does not show both consistency and consideration, he or she should be committed to an insane asylum. Commitment means devotion to the cause or the decision but without consideration and consistency, commitment leads to problems of inflexibility, lack of adaptability, and a sense that the leader is too focused. Without commitment, the leader is seen to waffle and change things too often. All three of these terms must be brought together to navigate the troubles faced in any situation and, thus, are intangibles.

The most significant factor related to the intangibles is that they are heavily dependent on many factors when judging them of a leader. Your perspective, the situation itself, the other members of the group involved, the view and number of followers, and many other factors contribute to whether or not the intangibles exist in the leader. As a result, relying upon them is a risky thing since not everyone will respond in the same way in every situation. Also, generally, you cannot plan ahead and learn these. Nonetheless, knowing that these are highly variable and dependent on many factors can help you as you look at other leaders or see these characteristics in yourself. It may be the best idea to always rely on an intangible as your major means of obtaining success as a leader.

Sharing Leadership

Having become more aware of the many aspects of leadership, it is important to discuss one last idea—sharing leadership. When working in a group or team, the leader and the followers will need to work together. Sharing leadership means sharing the responsibility for achieving the goal as well as for developing all members of the group. Whether you are the leader or a follower, sharing leadership can move the group towards becoming a team and make accomplishing the goal more likely. Sharing leadership is not easy and requires a negotiation of both task and transactional processes. Beyond this, individual concerns must be given less weight as the welfare of the entire group or team is considered. This can lead to fear by those who are asked to relinquish control and for those that are given new and greater responsibility. However, without risk, gains cannot be made.

In any situation, working to become a better follower and knowing your own strengths and limitations will help the process of goal attainment. If the leader knows when to assign leadership responsibility to other team members that are more equipped to handle that facet of the situation, he or she is sharing the role of leader. In turn, followers must be able to honestly and accurately assess the situation and his or her own abilities to know when to step forward and take that leadership role. By working with the leader to share leadership, groups become more effective as followers learn to lead themselves and others for the benefit of the group; it becomes more of a team. Good leaders can foster strong teamwork, promote the development of followers, and allow each individual to grow as a leader. Slowly the leader shares leadership and eventually is no longer needed in that situation. As this happens, the leader can move on to other tasks and be confident that the followers can lead themselves successfully.

By successfully sharing leadership, the leader magnifies his or her effectiveness so that more can be tackled more easily and more efficiently while promoting the goals of everyone involved. Leaders that make leaders of the followers, through sharing leadership and transforming the followers, have attained greater success. The best leaders lead other leaders in order to do greater things themselves. In the end, leadership is a process of learning and growth in which each situation is an opportunity. The things discussed throughout this text have tried to make you aware of what may help in these situations and how to be more prepared for when the situation arises. Only you can improve yourself and achieve the goals you have set for yourself.

SUMMARY

The chapter presents an introduction to leadership to help provide understanding of how it is handled and how to improve as a leader and follower. It begins with a definition of a leader and leadership. It then moves to a discussion of individuals, groups, and teams along with the idea of how each is related and functions. The remainder of the chapter presents various means of describing leadership: the roles people play, how leadership is accomplished, and the abilities and skills associated with good leadership.

Questions and Exercises

1. What types of leaders do you respond to most favorably? Is there a leadership style that does not work for you?
2. What actions, behaviors, and abilities do you think make a good leader? How can you recognize these in others and yourself?
3. Think about leaders you feel are good at leading. What attributes do they possess? Do they have the intangibles in leadership situations? Do you feel that the leader has the dualities or is missing part of them as they lead?
4. Think about your own decisions in situations. How can you improve your outcomes by knowing what makes a good leader?
5. Think about a group or team in which you participate. How can you help the leader by being a better follower? What ways can you share leadership by assuming some of the roles a leader has to perform?

References and Other Readings

Additional examples and explanations are provided on Dr. Lipuma's web page at
  http://njit.mrooms.net/course/view.php?id=14403

Some texts that were consulted in order to develop this leadership information are listed here.

Fullan, M. G. (2001). *Leading in a Culture of Change*. San Francisco: Jossey-Bass.
Lumsden, G., & Lumsden, D. (2003). *Communicating in Groups and Teams With Infotrac: Sharing Leadership* (4th ed.). Belmont, CA: Wadsworth Publishing.
Mazwell, J. C. (1999). *The 21 Irrefutable Laws of Leadership*. Nashville, TN: Thomas Nelson Publishing.

Group Roles

This exercise asks you to observe a group that you are part of or one that you can watch live or on video. Use the chart below to analyze the group members and the roles each is playing as the meeting unfolds. Start by listing the group members along the top, then fill in some details about each at the bottom. As you observe the group, mark each time one of these members demonstrates one of the traits. You can list other comments at the bottom, such as interruptions, other activities, major issues raised, or the progress of the meeting.

Role\Person						
Task-Oriented Roles						
Initiator-contributor						
Information-seeker						
Opinion-seeker						
Information-giver						
Opinion-giver						
Elaborator						
Coordinator						
Orienter						
Evaluator-critic						
Energizer						
Procedural-technician						
Recorder						
Social (Transactional) Roles						
Encourager						
Harmonizer						
Compromiser						
Gatekeeper/expediter						
Standard Setter						
Observer						
Follower						
Individualistic Roles						
Aggressor						
Blocker						
Recognition seeker						
Self-confessor						
Dominator						
Help seeker						
Special interest pleader						

Persons:

Other Comments

Personal Skill Assessment for Leadership Attributes

Use the chart below to rate your own skills as a leader and comment on how you demonstrate this or can improve those skills you feel are not yet fully developed.

Attribute	Score	Comments: Complete master (10)→ Average (5)→ no skill (0)
Self-mastery (leading to credibility)		
Competence—KEES of learning		
Self-discipline		
Positive attitude		
Objectivity		
Trustworthiness		
Global view		
Goal Attainment		
Vision		
Mission statement		
Problem-solving		
Cleverness		
Adaptability		
Knowledge transfer		
Accurate and Honest Assessment (AHA)		
Decision making		
Critical thinking		
Research		
Judgment		
Candor		
Fairness		
Interpersonal Dynamics		
Connectedness		
Co-orientation		
Dynamism		
Creating coherences		
Motivation		
Inspiration		
Empowerment		
Situational Command		
Understanding the processes of change		
Manage complexity:		
Plan		
Organize		
Delegate		
Control		
Coordinate		
Innovate		
Maintain flexibility		
Professionalism		
Moral purpose		
Ethical conduct		
Preparation		
Respect		

INDEX